MANSON

THE UNHOLY TRAIL OF CHARLIE AND THE FAMILY

Cover Design: Kevin Hanley

Photo Sources: Los Angeles Public Library, Nick Bougas, James Mason

Amok Books are available to bookstores through our primary distributor: The Subterranean Company, Box 160, 265 South 5th Street, Monroe, Oregon 97456. Phone: (800) 274-7826. FAX: (541) 847-6018.

UK Distributors: Turnaround Distribution, Unit 3 Olympia Trading Estate, Coburg Road, Wood Green, London N22 6TZ. Phone: (0181) 829-3000. FAX: (0181) 881-5088.

Non-Bookstore Distributors: Last Gasp Distribution, 777 Florida Street, San Francisco, California 94110. Phone: (415) 824-6636. FAX: (415) 824-1836.

To view the complete Amok Books catalog, please go to the Amok Books web site at www.amokbooks.com. For personal orders, please contact Book Clearing House, 46 Purdy Street, Harrison, New York 10528. Phone: (800) 431-1579. FAX: (914) 835-0398. Email: bookch@aol.com.

Amok Books is located at 1764 North Vermont Avenue, Los Angeles, California 90027. Phone: (323) 663-8618. FAX: (323) 550-8833. Email: publisher@amokbooks.com.

MANSON
The Unholy Trail of Charlie and the Family

by

John Gilmore
and
Ron Kenner

LOS ANGELES

Publisher's Foreword to the Revised Edition

This edition of *The Garbage People* arrives over twenty-five years after the celebrated series of Southern California murders which came to be known as Tate-LaBianca. *The Garbage People* has been until now a spectral "third" Manson title — a sought-after "true crime collectible," listed as "missing" from nearly every library in America. Now it is available again with important additional text and photo material. New vectors into the kaleidoscopic tale which spins inexorably out of the slayings emerge with the new material on Bobby Beausoleil (convicted killer of Gary Hinman), and on Beausoleil's occult alliance with experimental filmmaker Kenneth Anger. This revised edition of *The Garbage People* includes previously unpublished and very graphic crime scene and post-mortem documentation which depicts the aftermath of the Manson Family's frenzied brutality. Also included are rarely-seen images of life in the Family prior to the murders and through to the present, important locations and personalities, and the radiant beauty of slain actress Sharon Tate.

The originality of *The Garbage People* is largely due to the brief but voluble encounters between the personalities of Charles Manson and John Gilmore (author of *Severed — The True Story of the Black Dahlia Murder*). Gilmore's biography up to the point of meeting Manson provided him with a sympathetic yet hard-boiled take on Charlie's magnetic persona. Literally born and raised in Hollywood, offspring of an LAPD officer dad and a former starlet mom, ex-child actor Gilmore had already seen plenty of action on the seamy side of Hollywood before reinventing himself as a true crime writer. This accounts for his jaded perspective on Charlie's frustrated ambitions to stardom and desperate hustling for a record deal which are an integral part of this sordid tale.

Both Gilmore and Manson came of age in the '50s under the shadow of the Rebel Gods of the Big Screen, Brando and Dean. Both had been on the fringes of the Beat scene, Manson in Venice and Gilmore in San Francisco's North Beach, and were a few years older-and-savvier than the giddy tie-dye and moccasin set. As a method acting buddy of James Dean, Gilmore shared in Dean's attempts to push the bounds of sexual experimentation and in his legendary deep-seated fascination with violence and death. Soon after writing *The Garbage People*, Gilmore was also instrumental in the marketing of the hippie love affair with The Road, having pitched the original treatment for *Easy Rider* to his "rebel" Hollywood pals Dennis Hopper and Jack Nicholson.

While it is now conventional to either revile Charlie as "monster" or to hail him as "misunderstood prophet," Gilmore's own experiences have accorded him a kind of empathy with Manson's desire to go beyond conventional morality and his will to manipulate women to obtain his ends. The author recalls, "I think there was a strong sense of recognition if not identification between Manson and myself in some odd way, the leather-jacketed guy — outcast, rebel, dreamer; impelled to 'go where no one has gone before.' *Impelled.*"

Ed Sanders, author of *The Family*, swooped into L.A. from his Woodstock-area home with a mission. By valiantly wading into the "sleaze" around the deadly fringes of Hollywood, he would attempt to restore the good name of peace-loving flower children around the world from the stain of guilt by association. Gilmore, however, saw those times in a less floral hue. "The hippies by the time of the book were on the skids; drugged-out, syphilitic slumps of forgotten kids huddled in rags in piss-stained doorways — lost, lost, lost. Whatever they'd started had been sucked right into the commercial machinery and the skeletal remains of intent was left fit only for starving dogs. In the wake, or field of wreckage, of the hippie movement the Manson Family only kicked to death a few of the things still standing — a kind of *coup de grace* to the social pillars." Meanwhile, grandstanding prosecutor Vincent Bugliosi (author of *Helter Skelter*) was Mr. Straight, ready to cash in on all the gore and take his righteous "drugs-and-free love" indignation all the way to the bank and hopefully the Governor's Mansion in Sacramento.

When he first encountered Manson, Gilmore was already somewhat comfortable in the vibe-laden company of celebrated killers. In writing his previous book he had become a trusted confidant of the "Pied Piper of Tucson" Charles ("Smitty") Schmid, a much-hyped "lothario" and killer of at least three. (Access to Smitty also required extensive dealings with Schmid's then-leaner but equally ruthless defense attorney, F. Lee Bailey.) Gilmore's reputation from *The Tucson Murders* apparently preceded him to the remote reaches of Death Valley. He recalls that when he arrived in Independence, California, where Manson had just been booked on property damage charges, "Charlie knew who Smitty was, and he knew who I was and said to me regarding Smitty, 'I love the guy.'"

While quick to dismiss Charlie as "nuts" for the record, when pressed Gilmore will cop to a grudging respect for Manson's eerie ability to tap into the Irrational. "He was a very imaginative and energetic and charismatic man, and Polanski is right in a sense, that he *was* an artist, and he *was* spurned, as was Smitty, and Starkweather — all would-be artists, thwarted or spurned, and getting even by their murderous rages. They've settled old scores. To me, having repeatedly supped with the Devil, you might say, it is very understandable."

The Garbage People is noteworthy for its view of Manson's sadly truncated childhood and coming-of-age behind bars as being actually *significant* to all the events which followed. What emerges in the course of *The Garbage People* is that Manson wasn't just marking time in the string of reform schools, jails, and penitentiaries where he has spent the vast preponderance of his existence. He was also picking up an interest in psychic phenomena from his early mentor and mysterious boyhood pal Toby, and learning to play guitar from Barker Gang hoodlum "Creepy" Karpis at Terminal Island. A powerful and otherworldly mind was being shaped by Charlie's travels through the American Gulag and brief, frenzied forays into the wonderland "outside." The harsh realities of that oppressive upbringing forged a man whose psyche was "at war" with American Society in a way that hippie "dropouts" could scarcely imagine. Manson's case study in penology becomes well worth reexamining in our furiously myopic era of "three strikes, you're out" and prison-construction mania.

Reporter Ron Kenner's bifurcated situation at the time of the writing of *The Garbage People* was certainly a factor in its view of Manson as a *symptom* of American society rather than simply its nemesis. Kenner had been on the *L.A. Times'* blood-and-guts *Metro* section staff during the Watts Riots while at the same time a committed left-wing activist. At the time of Manson's first arrest, Kenner was a police beat reporter who was also involved in an organization called "The Committee" made up of ex-cons, families, community members, and professionals who would take up complaints from prisoners with the corrections authorities. A well-timed intervention by "The Committee" was actually credited by both sides of the bars for heading off a prison riot in Chino.

This updated edition of *The Garbage People* derives additional narrative power from the inclusion of a new voice from the "inside." It is the voice of the uncontainably virile warrior spirit of the "Lone Eagle," convicted murderer Bobby Beausoleil, looking back on the events unrepentently from his vantage point on San Quentin's Death Row. Psychedelic musician, underground film cult figure, warlock, and finally catalyst to Helter Skelter — his outlaw tale is now told in its entirety for the first time and largely in his own words. Bobby Beausoleil's epic saga from El Monte grease monkey to seminal noise-music pioneer to camp Occult Messiah to Topanga teepee-dweller doesn't actually end at Death Row, as he has also been involved in the founding of the infamous white prison gang, the Aryan Brotherhood.

While the media-demonization of Charlie at the time of the killings was nearly instantaneous, the '80s and '90s have seen Manson transformed through the relentless permutations of marketing forces into an inchoate icon of rebellion. This latter-day Charlie-mania has extended to such absurd heights as Axl Rose sporting a Manson T-Shirt in his arena rock appearances and recording the Manson composition "Look at Your Game, Girl" as a CD bonus track, and Nine Inch Nails' Trent Reznor moving into the now-demolished Cielo Drive mansion to allow its ambience to infuse the recording of his *Downward Spiral* album.

As Gilmore sees it, "these killers are not so special as killers of humans. They just became famous from it. Others have killed but the chemical ingredients to make them *stars* just wasn't on the menu. We're in a 'star system,' and being a star is what it's all about. Jimmy Dean and Janis Joplin and Lenny Bruce became stars in other ways. Manson is a star. It's no wonder to me his face is on T-Shirts. They are sociological stars — trailblazers of perhaps a new vision of reality where we have finally learned to love the bomb and we've mutated to the point where 12-year-old junkies and mass-killers grinning from headlines is just our American way of life now. We are mutants perhaps — and these sociological stars are our knights

iv

who ride ahead, lowering the lance of annihilation. Charlie doesn't even see himself as real anymore. He sees himself as a spirit — *the* guru of annihilation."

The persona of Charles Manson and his bizarre sway over the Family remain undeniably riveting to the public a quarter century down the line. *The Garbage People* is a gripping account of one of the most multifaceted and chilling sagas of our time, containing elements of random murder, cursed glamour, mind control, hallucinogenic drugs, psychic phenomena, Satanism and witchcraft, rebellious sexuality, Haight-Ashbury, rock'n'roll, and biker gangs, not to mention dune buggies tearing across the desert floor in search of the "hole in the Earth." I am pleased to announce the publication of this new revised and updated edition of *The Garbage People*, which is both a greatly overdue re-publication and, with the additional text and photos, a fascinating new work in its own right.

Stuart Swezey
Publisher
Amok Books

Preface to the Revised Edition

They'd all been sentenced to die in California's gas chamber, mass-murderer Charles Manson and his handful of hippie renegade killers — Tex, Susan, Bobby, Leslie, Patricia . . . But they would live on, death sentence erased by the moratorium on capital punishment. They would live to marry, bear children, "find God," and as some claim, to be *born again*; the once-pending deaths by lethal gas commuted to life imprisonment with eligibility for parole.

"But we cannot be killed by *you*," says Charles Manson from behind the bars separating him from the society that asked for his death. "I cannot die," he says, "because I live eternally, the reflection of the soul that is you, you see — that you hate, as you hate yourselves . . ."

Facing Charles Manson is like watching a caged inmate in a nut house. *Watching*, because you can't really have an *exchange* with Charlie. You are the target, appreciative or otherwise, for a gamut of histrionics and double entendres that could've dumbfounded Sigmund Freud.

Charlie *looks* nuts. Most of what he says *sounds* nuts. I'd seen the scam before, and for a guy like Charlie who's spent most of his sixty years locked up in any number of cages — a lot of the punishment unwarranted and without real provocation on Charlie's part for the amount of time he'd be behind bars — he had the shuck down to a first-rate act. Basically seeming like a Damon Runyon kind of "dese'n'dem" guy off an East Coast street, lizard-like Charlie could pop into another role — Hollywood Boulevard con man or leathery hillbilly, guitar-twanging drifter. He gave all his roles a new twist by turning hippie at an opportune time. His freshly paroled sexual appetites hit at a run the free love shenanigans — the air-head teenies and doped girls jumping like pogo sticks through the Swing-

ing Sixties of the Great Society. That was a challenge Charlie was ripe for
— *the line of least resistance*. As a short, homely little ex-con, Charlie was-
n't keen on resistance. He was the kind of guy that went in through the
back doors, always ready for a hand-out, and what he couldn't get, he'd
steal. His instincts, as hot as a dog's, could lead him to the hidden stuff —
usually, no matter whose house it was.

For those that would offer resistance, there'd be trouble — though
not necessarily with an apparent, *direct* connection.

Charlie talked and talked during our Los Angeles County Jail
meetings, and to give his ricocheting mental aberrations a little religious
zing, he'd mouth half of what he said in what appeared to those around him
as cryptic parables — a seer whispering through his beard. But to an eye
trained to the cages, it was philosophical mumbo jumbo; the old vacuum
salesman's heart-hunting line, gibberish intended to be elevated to wisdom
in the listener's ear. Basically it did nothing more than clog like wax.

You had to be susceptible. You had to have shed your *self* — that
skin of who you are, via tripping on chemicals or by having had it flogged
off your hide in the "corrective institutions." "You must be empty," Charlie'd say in the goosing spiel of a sideshow barker. Empty yourself to be
filled with Charlie; worn as a glove, as it were, and if you could be filled
with Charlie, you could do his bidding. That was what he was after. It was
no accident.

What did Charlie want . . . ? What was his bidding?

To be king on a personal mountain — somewhere locked down
in the center of Charlie, to be viewed as a kind of god-figure filtered out
of Charlie's jailhouse thinking like you'd siphon gas from a rusty can. He
wanted to wreak some small havoc on a traitorous society by letting slip his
ragtag dogs of war — geese, throat-stuffed with Charlie's kaleidoscopic
philosophy of hate which they pranced about calling "love." Havoc — on
a small scale like Charlie, but sufficient to set the world on its ear for a
spell. And Charlie's name would be in the history books as one to be reck-
oned with.

There was no other meaning or message. For a person beaten,
tormented, raped, warped and abused throughout life, it was simply time
to swing back a little of the medicine. There was nothing in our "society"
(as we call it and know it), for Charlie — a dog whipped and chained,
learning only the whip and the chain. "There is *never* freedom," Charlie

would say. "There is only the whip and the chain."

Ejected from prison as he'd been spit out of society, Charlie faced a fate he'd fought against in a world desperate with its errors. Knowing only the whip and the chain, this vagabond-alien went in search of some hole he could climb into but found a social order he could kick around for a change — *subtly*, for unlike the "garbage people" he found to do his bidding and labeled a kind of "family," he would make caution and patience his hand maidens.

Charlie knew how to "read" pain in a soul shredded and whipped, and beneath the flowering facade of the new *counterculture* he encountered (the hippies and light shows and dope and the Beatles), he saw the "Age of Aquarius" and the "hippie movement" as a joke. "Existence was a simple joke —" the Great Society convulsed in heaves, regurgitating what it could not absorb. It was, Charlie believed, the breaking up of the world.

Revolution festers in such a state, and a dictator could shoot up like a spring stalk, unfooled by the self-excusing liberalism and the "freedom" rhetoric babbled by Timothy Leary, Ken Kesey or Alan Ginsberg, or the clot of literary and scholarly fringe-kickers looking for late-night T.V. notoriety. "Wads of phlegm in the throat of life," Charlie called them. He saw with socially untarnished eyes, *new* eyes accustomed to walls and basins and uniforms. What he faced in the *out*side world was nothing more than a jailhouse joke.

"What this society needs is a *Hitler*," Charlie told some hippies in San Francisco. "A goddamn Hitler to set this system straight."

Not many men could be a Hitler, but seeing himself as standing knee-deep in puke, Charlie says, "I could *see* these people on the street — see them with clean eyes, you know. These people on the street were like me," he says. "Thrown out of life like your paper coffee cups and hamburger sacks and rags and stinking Kotex pads and dirty rubbers. They were the garbage floating around and shit sticking to the sides of your toilet and your drain holes . . . That's what they were doing as hippies," Charlie reasoned, "floating around like orange peelings and sinking to the bottom like rotten garbage — food for the sharks and for the barracudas . . ."

Charlie realized he could bunch together this garbage, and he could "gather your old tires and tin cans, and I can go out in your deserts and make use of all the junkyard," he says. "So I took these people that were your garbage, that'd been thrown away by society, and I put them to use. I made them put water in cans and make things work in order to keep living on the outside. Because that was *me* — the *out*side, and the biggest joke is I never wanted to *be* on the outside. *You* put me on the outside and whatever's gone down is what *you* created — that is *your* reality, not mine."

Following the murders of Hollywood actress Sharon Tate, coffee heiress Abigail Folger and several others savagely slain in a bloodbath reign, Charlie and several "garbage people" would be tried, convicted, and sentenced to death. While in prison, he had put together a book, supposedly in his own words, but written by another inmate, in which Charlie is portrayed as allegedly having killed a black drug dealer. But one of Manson's ex-followers says, "Charlie never killed anybody. When it came down to letting blood, the most he could do was cut an ear or someone's hand. He couldn't personally cut off a head or stab a knife or point-blank lay someone out . . .

"But he *knew*, man, he knew who *could* do it. He could smell it like a disease that was stinking on you. It was like he knew what you were capable of, even though *you* didn't know it. He put the guns and the knives and rope in our hands and said, 'Over there, you go over there and do it,' and we all went over there and did it. He didn't even *watch* it going down, but stayed home rocking and daydreaming like some old Aunt Jemima or someone's grandmother waiting for the chil'ren to come home and get washed for supper . . ."

There was the real Charlie Manson: the shrunken Svengali as ultimate garbage collector, grooming his found-art to revere him as a "Jesus superstar," or the Hitler he dreamed of — the one and only to deliver redemption. Others under his spell saw him as the Devil — "here to do the Devil's work . . ."

Whether Charlie's powers as super refuse man on the outside reeked of the amazing or of the *numero uno* jailhouse con, the bearded little man who would carve a swastika onto his forehead carries in his marrow the same sort of hatred for his "followers" (and humanity in general) as did Nazi propagandist Joseph Goebbels, another shriveled, crippled man, whose personal disgust for *menchheit* reached to murdering millions — even his own wife and children, and finally himself.

Armed with a Goebbels view of mankind, and out of his of twisted past, Charlie Manson piecemealed together a personal *Armageddon*. Marshalling a league of troopers — a band of garbage people — he unleashed an attack at a world that had not only caged him in a shrunken body, but deposited him like a used bottle in some dark corner while gifted others of physique, of beauty and of talent, basked in the limelight. And it was these others taking the bows that Charlie sentenced to death.

He wanted to kill those that claimed the fame and fortune and the good life that had been denied him since before he knew there the difference between right and wrong — before he knew there was life beyond the whip and the chain.

"Charlie picked out people to be put to death," the ex-follower says, "the same as you figure out a Christmas list. He picked people everyone knew as heroes — like Steve McQueen and Frank Sinatra — Tom *Jones*, for god's sake, and Elizabeth Taylor, and people that everybody *adores* and wants to be like. That's how you put the fear into people, Charlie told us, you butcher what they dream of being. You kill off these gilded replicas of fame and happiness, and when you smash these you can go right into the heart of the dark . . ."

It is there — "into the heart of the dark," that this revised Amok Books edition attempts to escort the reader. Quotations in this book are from extensive personal interviews with Charles Manson in Los Angeles County Jail, and in later penal institutions. Other statements by Manson were obtained from intermediaries, from court appearances and from convicted Family members now spread in numbers and vehemence through several states and institutions, with a steadily increasing allegiance to the notions espoused by Manson.

Material herein not derived from official records, police files, transcripts and documents is the result of interviews with principals whose names appear throughout the text.

Convicted murderer Robert "Bobby" Beausoleil, charged with the first of the so-called "Manson murders," invited the author to San Quentin to "set the record straight."

Bobby Beausoleil had not been "told what to do" by Manson, he claimed in 1972 while awaiting excecution on Death Row. Beausoleil said he did what "needed to be done," as the culmination of his personal "philosophy" which he calls "the swinging of the pendulum of death." He had his own band of followers, Bobby says, a "philosophy" that paralleled Charlie's, and together, as he would assert, they "brought society to its knees." Everything they did, he says, "was *right*."

Similar exchanges with other Manson Family members — Sandra Good, the now-high priestess of the "Manson Movement," and Lynette "Squeaky" Fromme, serving a life sentence for the attempted assassination of then-President Gerald Ford — has made necessary this revised publication, now under the Amok imprint.

Some names of those still wishing to remain anonymous have been left fictitious, fearing retaliation by any number of Manson activists: the Aryan Brotherhood factions co-originated by Beausoleil on Death Row, numerous Satanic cults and cells associated with Sandra Good and others, and several neo-Nazi skinhead "action committees" interviewed by the author. This horror story was invented by Charles Manson, and is now rooted in the American consciousness as indelibly as the Kennedy assassinations, the Vietnam War, Richard Nixon, the murder of Martin Luther King, Jr., the surfing sounds of California's Beach Boys, and the Beatles — their own leader, John Lennon, "brought to his knees" by another American murderer.

John Gilmore
Los Angeles, 1995

Prologue

Caught in a Toxic Culture

About thirty years ago I suddenly could see the change. It's one of the reasons I wrote *The Garbage People*. Like I was witnessing from one side of a hill the burning of a town; everything that it had been was funneling up in black smoke. I'd been visiting Mansonites Lynette "Squeaky" Fromme, the most direct link to Charlie, Sandra Goode, a kind of high priestess of the weirdoes, and Bobby Beausoleil, then on Death Row for murder, awaiting his seat in the gas chamber.

I was heading back to L.A., where, though everything would seem familiar, it was only props because of the smoke and the fire. "The breaking up of the world" was a phrase that came to mind. I'd touched the breaking up of the world the same as if I'd hoteled on a fault line, floated naked in a poison river.

Everything that had been laid out as gospel for as long as I could remember had been torched and was turning to ash. What would follow wouldn't quite be the anarchy that was going on at the time, but a clear caving-in from within. A quiet implosion, and Charlie Manson had grabbed up the banner.

Nobody was going to volunteer for Vietnam, and if anyone did he'd come back a schlemiel or a schizo — for sure somebody's target for rocks and rotten tomatoes. Richard Nixon was an asshole and everybody knew it. His hands were in the cookie jar and crumbs were falling from his kisser.

Cops weren't giving a shit if you shot the geek next door instead of loaning him the mower, or so it seemed. Everything we knew or had held in our hands was turning to jello and running between our fingers.

Politicians were the real scum and what we'd been fed as truth was lies and illusion.

We've come to discover there's nothing on the other planets — dirt, rock, gaseous or frozen wastes. We're apparently whirling around alone in the universe, and the fact we're facing is that in time there'll be nothing. We'll have ceased to exist and what's left will be dirt — broken rock, nothing else.

From the beginning of human history there has been a so-called generation gap between parent and child. Ancient Egyptians complained, "What are we gonna do with these damn kids? What's becoming of this generation?" Ancient Chinese said the same thing: "What're we gonna do with these damn kids?" Everyone's family (except maybe Pat Boone's!) felt the same way until the Sixties when a cavernous breach split in the earth. The world of rules, standards and regulations structured back in Biblical times rocked violently under the spreading quake. The foundation failed and the old standbys of respectability and morality could not bridge the Grand Canyon of distance.

The youth of today stand before us as aliens, heirs to a garage sale of platitudes and standards that are worthless to them. The children are now on the Internet with instant access to a world of information and experience that didn't exist a few years back and an aptitude to function in that world that few elders understand. They are the future, but they are caught between two worlds — a failing past and an uncertain destiny. We are the past and there's nothing left to learn from the past. Most modes of public education are obsolete. Franz Kafka had it right when he said "Probably all education is but two things: first, parrying of the ignorant children's impetuous assault on the truth and, second, gentle, imperceptible, step-by-step initiation of the humiliated children into the lie."

Our culture has turned to poison — our world a hazardous-waste dump site. Youth has evolved to the point where it knows it's been lied to. We've created a Frankenstein society. We've made our children prisoners to the monster. There's nothing to learn from the past. If the child survives our blunders, wars, neutron bombs and diseases, she will be miraculously washed up on the shores of a new world. The rule that only from the past comes the truth of the future is but one of the platitudes winding up on the rubbish heap. The child faces a world of unexplored territory — it's the Amazon jungle, the Sahara desert. It's walking on the moon. A great wave is breaking and laying bare a new, exciting, promise-and-potential filled world, a virgin world of experience that most present-day adults have no access to. We'll be dead and buried, and good riddance.

The Colorado shootings and the mounting teen suicides, drug use and apathy are only symptoms of our failure. Charles Manson holds the banner. The "breaking up of the world" really began mid-century. What we've created and handed to youth is a disposable world of throw-away values and empty standards, of clay-feet heroes and expediency, with profit as the only attainable glory. We created the automatic weapons now in the hands turning against us. They attack us not as a deliberate affront to ourstandards, but to fulfill their evolutionary role. A quarter-century back we lost the "war on drugs" as a result of political expediency, and we've emerged in this time and space as relics to our mutant youth. In clinging to our warehouse of standards we've forfeited real communication. We are burying ourselves with our artifacts; our hands struggling out of the sand as we suffocate.

John Gilmore
Los Angeles, 2000

One

He is standing behind bulletproof glass in the Los Angeles County Jail, a windowless concrete complex bordered by a cement wash and old freight yards. He puts one palm flat against the glass. An odd gesturing. Strange. His bones themselves appear to bend. He contorts his body with the control of a fakir — into a shape not human. His skeleton seems rubbery, unbreakable; mystifying. The small hands, the thin lengthy fingers with long squared-off nails, mash together suddenly. They move protectively across the body, knotting at the chest. Hunching down, his habit for effect, he makes the ugliest face possible: the cheekbones themselves bend up, wrenching as the brows gnarl down in creases and the whole face folds into itself. In a moment the skin has a gum rubberiness, drawing tight, stretching tense as a drumskin. The eyeballs seem sucked inward and the insistent outline of his skull is right there. You are shocked. He is a monster.

This is Charles Manson.

Just as quickly he beams, laughing again with broad expansive gestures. The face has changed from a mask of death to a glassy mirror now while he reveals himself as a self-proclaimed prophet, a seer of souls: his eyes are glistening with an intense shine that makes you wonder if he is sane, or even human.

"I live in my world, and I am my own king in my world, whether it be in a garbage dump or if it be in the desert or wherever it be, I am my own human being," Manson says. And those who traveled with him in the garbage dumps and shadows of the "Establishment" made up the force of the "Infinite Soul" — an "all-seeing, all-knowing" strength believed tapped by Manson and responsible for the murders of actress Sharon Tate and seven others in one spontaneous act that struck society like an avalanche.

He is talking rapidly now, the words strung together with grunts, animal sounds — more grimaces, the Joker behind a gruesome "Helter-Skelter" murder spree. Any victim could have served as well. The murderers didn't know the victims. The crimes violated all sense of order. He has to be a "madman, a Devil," they say — perhaps even more guilty for the slayings than those "followers" of Manson named as the actual murderers.

"When you talk about me," Manson laughs, "make me a tough guy, the meanest man in the world — make me the Devil."

He shrugs at the legalities. "I'm dead!" he declares.

"I have a race to run and I am the race horse. It doesn't matter what they do with my body. They can move it here and move it there, but they can't get me!"

If one could believe it — the Manson Philosophy — perhaps this small bearded man has a head start toward dematerializing into pure nothingness where the physical world with its physical pain and its physical bodies means nothing. In the new immaterial dimension Manson foresees, who cares how physical bodies are treated? In such a mind trip, everything is reduced to a sequence of meaningless disconnected events as cause or effect, consequence or action, all but the "now" fades to oblivion — no past to hang onto, no future to fear, nothing solid to get in the way. A devil's trick, such "freedom" from the physical body? A new dimension? Or a convenient, programmed response to a lifetime of deprivation, brutality and pain?

Most of Manson's life had been spent behind bars. An unwanted child, he was shipped to foster homes or confined in juvenile centers. No ballgames, fishing trips, brothers or even friends attended his adolescence. Only delinquency courts, reformatories and city jail. He was educated and became an adult largely in prisons or penitentiaries spread across the country, arrested or charged under aliases on forty or more occasions, the crimes filling six pages in the Bureau of Criminal Identification.

His hair straggly and unkempt, Manson strokes his beard carefully, describing a philosophy of "peace" he claims to have found in confinement.

"I've been handcuffed all my life," he says. "There was a picture of me in the paper the other day with my hands crossed and they thought it was a special pose. But it's like instinct, when you see a camera, you cover your handcuffs. That's been my life — a cot, a basin, a wall. In reform school I had a cot, a basin, a wall. I was on the outside. I had a cot, a basin, a wall. I'm not sure how much time I've spent in solitary confinement, you could say that's where I'm from. There and from the line of people nobody wants. What happens is you spend most of your life in reform school, in prisons, in institutions, and you forget what the world is all about. You are the stranger and you don't know how the free world works anymore. Your body, your physical body is locked up, and it's been that way most of your life. But then you understand that your mind is free. I realized I was better off in the penitentiary because I was free!"

Earlier, in the pawning off between foster homes and reform schools, Manson gained a "secret" confidence in what he alone could do, as though he had been singled out by some quirk in the structure of things and left with an awareness he believed to be his alone. It was not something he could willingly discuss, as it were, in words and theories. He wasn't even sure what it was, but he knew its existence as a part of him, no less real than an arm or a leg.

One of Manson's institutions "for correction" was the Federal Reformatory in Chillicothe, Ohio. There, in late October, 1951, he befriended a boy named Toby who spent most of his time in solitary confinement.

Manson later told an acquaintance, "Toby had one of the best voices I'd ever heard that wasn't strictly professional, and he played blues guitar. He could hypnotize with his voice. And he could hypnotize by suggestion. He could have you turn into stone, your hands; you could hold them together in front of you and you could have four people, even six others, divided at each side of you and pulling on each arm and they couldn't separate, couldn't break your hands apart."

Manson learned from the inmate, though for some time, he admits, he feared the man with this strange power.

"He had a power, a real power that was in his eyes, coming from inside him. He had things going that I hadn't even heard about."

Toby, the teacher, was "definitely satanic," but perhaps it was only "natural" that Manson, the pupil, should soon overcome his fear of strange "satanic ways" and find a new appreciation and hunger for power. Just sixteen years old, already long "pushed around" from place to place — insecurely footed, with nothing backing him up and nowhere to turn but to himself — Manson had for some time already been developing a con man's eye for survival, storing up tricks to give a small man the edge. It was a habit he would keep. And in those early days with Toby the excitement

3

grew as he began to comprehend the power and the possibilities of the mind.

"The powers of the brain are so, so vast, it's beyond understanding, beyond thinking, beyond comprehension," Manson says. "People reflect themselves into things they want to believe . . . It is reflection and illusion," and Manson's trick.

No one knew where his new trick would lead, but it was a beginning. Manson's own mind was quick, with his IQ estimated at 114. Though during his reformatory years he gained only the equivalent of a seventh grade education, more and more he began turning to the "mind" for survival. Perhaps remembering from Toby, and developing his own powers of persuasion, Manson adapted in a special way to the "ins and outs" of prison life. The ease with which he could control and manipulate inmates aroused authorities. They expressed concern yet believed nothing could divert his will. Manson had discovered the power of the mind. And while using his mind to influence, he also used it to escape. He had "inclinations" and "feelings" that basically he was not the body they kept locked behind bars — he was something "other" than what they could beat on and cage.

Before being transferred to Chillicothe, Manson had been sentenced for auto theft in March, 1950 to the National Training School in Washington, D.C., "the *hard* joint," where beatings became a part of his normal environment.

"Any new guy that came in there, was right away they'd come up to him. The prisoners and the bulls, they tried to put fear in you. That was their thing, to make you afraid, to put fear in you. And if they got their fear into you, and you showed that you were afraid of them — eight or ten would jump on him and fuck him and make him suck them off. And when he was in his cell, the big guy will come over to him, he will say, 'gimme those cigarettes,' and the little guy will say, 'but these are all the cigarettes I got, man,' and the big guy just grabs them from the little one, and says, 'I said gimme those cigarettes,' taking them like that. And if you're scared at all, and show it, and let them take what you've got, the others are there, beating on you, and the more fear you show the more they beat. You had to be a tough guy. They had to know how tough you were.

"At the other reform schools," Manson recalls, "the Christian Brothers had whacked us around a lot, slapping us here and there, and I ran away, so they put me in tougher places and I kept running away. I'd managed to escape from one reformatory twenty-seven times. None of us ever had any fathers there, there was no one to look up to. My father is the jail house. My father is 'the system.' The cops and the counselors in the reform schools, they were on their own ego trips. All they'd do was try to get everyone to squeal on each other. We'd get in fights over it, over squealers. The counselors got their kicks that way. They liked that, the cops. We'd fight and they got their kicks . . . Where I am from if you snitch you leave yourself open to be killed. I could never snitch because I wouldn't want someone to kill me. So I have always abided by that law. It is the only law that I know of . . .

"There was a guard there who liked to push me around a lot and beat on me whenever he got the chance. Once I knocked over a piece of machinery by accident and he hit me about fifty times with this big wooden paddle, like a big stick. He was a sissy, like that, and really got a kick out of beating me. And that night I had to go to the associate warden and let him beat on me with a leather strap. So that was what I knew, that's what had been home for me . . . I'd been in a lot of bad violence and I showed them how tough I was by putting on a bad face. You couldn't treat them with any sort of feelings of love. If you did, or if you ever expressed that you were not a bad one, they'd think you're really afraid of them, and that's what they wanted."

Manson put on his mask. It seemed the "real" Manson was never to appear again. After awhile he learned to push aside fear, to be as "tough" as they come. He was, after all something "other" than what they could beat on and cage, and more and more he believed that his mind could not be imprisoned. "In jail there is a whole new attitude, a whole different way of thinking," Manson says. He admits he doesn't think like people in the "outside world," people who put importance on their lives.

"My life has never been important to anyone, not even in the understanding of the way you fear the things you fear and the things you do . . .

"Now," he says, "I'm dead, but so what? I have no fear of dying, because I'm free." And he doubles his fist and places it against his chest. "These others are not free. I am, and when I get tired of this little game I'm going to pick the time to die, pick my own time out of it. I'll know when and I'll know when it is my time," he smiles. "I'm going to lie down, put a little white tag on my toe with the name Charles Manson on it and then I'm going to lay back and die."

5

Two

He was born out of wedlock on November 12, 1934, in Cincinnati, Ohio, to a teenage alcoholic prostitute. Charles Manson was unwanted. He was not born a devil, though a friend was later to rumor that he had been baptized in hell. His sixteen-year-old mother, Katherine Maddox, later married an older man to give the child a name. But the man disappeared soon after the wedding and the boy was never to see his father. He would remember him only as "Scotty," though he might not have been the real father. "So from birth," Manson would say, "I'm a five-and-dime bastard . . ." There was no proof that Scotty was his father, and in the future it would make little or no difference when Manson himself was to become the "father image" in his relationships with others. Particularly young girls. But for Manson the "universe" became the father, a substitute father with deeper roots yet, supplanting the more personal guidance he never found. And, Manson asserts, when the universe is father, God and the Devil and all become one, all is as it must be and all is perfect and nothing matters.

"There is no good and no bad," he says. "There is no difference between you and I. There is only one thing and that thing is everything. I am the father. You are the father. And I understand the universe through me. The truth is, and that's all. It doesn't matter what words you use, millions of words. The truth is what it is — that's the truth, what's here and now. I go there and I'm not here anymore. And now I come back and I'm not there anymore. Deductive logic says *this*, comparative logic says *that*," he continues. "Just what's here and now is what counts. It's infinite and it's nothing. It's all there is and it doesn't matter what you do — it's all perfect and the way it is supposed to be."

Telling a story, he elaborates: "There were these two kids — everybody thought I was cruel because one day the youngest boy fell in a three-foot ditch. There was a lot of bushes, the slope was three or four feet above the ditch. Down there it was muddy and he was crying. Others standing around said, 'Help him out,' but I didn't. I said, 'Watch.' About twenty minutes passed or so and he stopped crying and started to climb out on his own. And the second time he tried to climb out he fell back down, but kept on climbing out more. Finally when he made it, climbed out, he was really tired, and stood in front of me and smiled. I pushed him back in the ditch again."

Manson says he showed his followers "the best I could what I would do as a father, as a human being to be responsible for themselves, not to be weak and not to lean on me. And I have told them many times, 'I don't want no weak people around me. If you are not strong enough to stand on your own, don't come and ask me what to do. You know what to do.' I said, 'Let the child go down. If he falls that is how he learns, that is how you become strong, by falling . . .' And when the boy came out the second time I told him, 'I am not your father. The universe is your father. It's the universe.'"

So the universe is the father and everything is perfect. But with Manson the universe is never the mother. His own mother, long since but a shadow in Manson's memory, was arrested and sent to prison when he was four years old. Along with a brother, she was convicted of assaulting and beating men she hustled along the riverfront, and the problem of Manson's custody was transferred to reluctant grandparents in McMechen, West Virginia. Then the elderly woman became ill and the boy was sent to live with an aunt and uncle in Illinois, in a declining neighborhood of frame and stucco houses with untended yards. The household was one of constant tension, and while his mother served her sentence the boy found little affection or guidance. At times his aunt was harsh, and as if to "soften the blows" his uncle would give him pocket money for movies or ice cream, sometimes even taking him on trips around the countryside. For Manson, though, it was a cold, unreal place where grown-ups spent their lives. He was a stranger to his immediate surroundings within that larger, "perfect universe" he was later to praise.

A neighbor remembers the child as being "very quiet, keeping to himself most of the time and giving the impression of being scared. At other times he'd be as peaceful as you could imagine. They didn't have no trouble from the boy."

By the time Manson's mother was released from prison, his uncle had developed respiratory trouble and it was decided the boy should be returned. His mother complained, however — he was a responsibility she couldn't handle. There was no money, she said, and soon found ways to relieve herself of his custody. There were foster homes — there was always an orphanage. Whenever the boy returned as his mother's "responsibility," she would disappear for days at a time in the heavy-drinking, fast-moving crowd she followed. One bartender recalls her as "in and out of the place. She had a drinking problem," he said, "but as long as she's got the money she's entitled to live as she likes." Manson vaguely recalls a climate of remorse that would often follow these sprees. The young woman would make stern promises to "be a good mother," but each vow would be broken by subsequent binges of liquor and men. She constantly moved. Manson's childhood spanned "what seemed like a hundred" dingy apartments and rooming houses. "I was always waiting in a room somewhere for someone to return." He found momentary playmates on the streets, passing strangers or straggly neighborhood children. "There was nothing but emptiness and violence . . ."

If he wasn't being beaten at home, he was being beaten on the street or seeing others being beaten. "I don't know how big I was," Manson says, "I wasn't *big*, I know that, and I stopped on the sidewalk and watched these guys beating on this other guy. I didn't do anything except watch this *big* guy that was doing most of the serious beating, and I was worried he'd go after me with that stick or club and I'd run or get busted up. He whacked the guy across the face with it and the guy's teeth came out. They just popped out like you'd flip a coin in your fingers, popped and hit the sidewalk right in front of me. I wanted to tell someone about it but there wasn't nobody to tell it to."

His mother was as much a stranger as the different foster parents, administrators, streetwalkers, policemen and sleeping tramps in all-night movie houses. In most of the rooms where his mother took him to live, the boy was the brunt of aggravations, and an eyesore to his mother's visitors — "the johns and tramps she'd drag in off the street," he says.

He kept to himself. Though friendless, his young mind bypassed

8

the loneliness of his surroundings. He watched, listened, pretended his imaginative resources knew no limit. And he began to steal, as if to hold onto something that continually flew away. There was a consistency and permanency to the habit of stealing and it became easier. With everything transient, the thefts and goods he carried with him offered a sense of stability, a kind of reward. An object owned gave identity to an owner, an identity that had yet to be acknowledged.

He finally accompanied his mother on a trip to Indianapolis with a traveling salesman. The man made promises, but instead of security his mother found herself stranded. Again she turned to foster homes or distant relatives. "I'll be back for him in a couple of days," she'd say, but weeks would pass. The scenery continued to change but the boy played little part in the decisions made.

"He just didn't fit anywhere," a relative says. "Going back and forth like that he didn't have any practical sense of where he belonged. I suppose soon enough he didn't care."

Manson continued to steal, was finally caught, and was sent to reform school. "When I was nine years old I was sent there. One of the kids that nobody wanted, that society didn't want, so that's where I was sent . . . What they gave me there was a room — a wall — a wash basin."

He was caught stealing again three years later, declared delinquent and sent to the Gibault School for Boys in Terre Haute, Indiana.

"They show the front of a reform school, show some old lady smiling that is supposed to be helping the kids. All the old rich bitches. Then they take little Joey and Skinny Frank who ass-kiss all the guards, and put them out front 'Look how happy these kids are!' But they don't show the kids in the back. No, they don't show the ones that're in the back of the place, the ones that don't ass-kiss with what's going on out in front. They're the ones that aren't going to be used up front for the programming and whitewashing, for the old ladies that want to see how good it is there and how happy the boys are. But what about the ones in the back? Nobody wants them, nobody's got any use for them."

Manson was in the back, an outcast. At home now with the incorrigibles, the "tough guys," they became his "own kind," and branded by his own needs and by his surroundings he was to remain an outcast for the rest of his life.

"The first time I'd been in reform school it was for a year, the second time it seemed like a hundred. And when I got out, I hit the street by myself like that with nothing happening, no breathing down my back. I hadn't ever dialed a telephone in my life. I'd never gotten on a bus and rode one. I wasn't ready for the world of society — I didn't know anything. All I knew was that in reform school I'd had a basin, a cot, and a wall, and I'd learned that whatever hand you're dealt, that's the one you got to play."

He tried to live life on his own terms, not returning to his mother or other relatives. He found a messenger job and rented a small room in a downtown flophouse. Those who knew Charles Manson then reached similar opinions: "There was nothing discernibly bad about him but there wasn't anything especially good in him, either. He was a personable young boy, but there just didn't seem to be anything backing him up."

Too young and ill-equipped to assume the adult role in the "outside world," Manson sought to impress his will on whatever situation he was faced with, to use reality as a tool he'd learned to handle effectively only in confinement. Secretly, he preferred the life in reform school and already regarded himself as a "stranger" to society. He began to live on the outside as though he were still in jail. "At times I'd wake up somewhere," he says, "not knowing where I was. Am I locked up? Am I on the outside? I didn't know whether I was in or out. And then I'd find I was outside — and I'd open the door. I used to get a kick out of the door handle. I could feel it and put my hand around it and open and close the door. People thought I was nuts and they'd say 'hey, you dummy kid, quit opening and closing the door,' and then I'd think — shit, I hear them saying that and I wish I was on the inside and not here to listen to their bullshit . . ."

At fourteen, fired from various odd jobs when they'd discover he'd lied about his record, he further developed a painful sense of hostility against the "free world." The third time he was arrested for theft, his mother acted quickly, fearing a parental neglect complaint. She now believed she could permanently unburden herself of the boy. By declaring him "errant" he'd be sent away, and the authorities would have full charge over him. In her desperation to turn the boy over — to get rid of him — however, she was forced to reveal her own background as well as her son's and was charged with adultery. She fled the county to avoid prosecution, but her plan had not backfired. Manson was made a ward of the Marion County Juvenile Center.

What was this *Center* life? More beatings, more fear — more overcoming pain and trying on the tough-guy role.

A reverend who served as a chaplain for the Catholic boys and visited the juvenile center almost daily recalls making a "wholehearted attempt to get to know and understand the boy . . . He attracted my attention because he didn't have anyone who ever came to see him or cared much about him, so I kind of took over and tried to be sort of a daddy, I guess. And he certainly had a great need for people in his life. So I'd take him over to my mother's — she remembers him very well as a kid that sort of followed her around the house and when she was fixing supper he'd be standing right there, wanting to help her. He was a very dependent type kid who craved attention and affection, and never got it, except in anti-social ways." So the priest saw Manson as "a lovable young boy who needed lots of attention — a very genuine lost little boy." He continued to visit Manson at the Center, hoping to break through "the callus" the boy was gathering between himself and adult authority. The priest then made an effort to generate community support to send Manson to Boys Town in Nebraska. The priest regarded the effort as "a very good way to bring to the attention of the people in Indiana what was going on, how boys like him get stranded in centers and cannot get out of them."

The reverend's attempts were successful in 1949. He personally accompanied the boy to the bus for Boys Town, U.S.A. An Indianapolis newspaper carried a photograph of Manson in a suit and tie, with a story captioned, "Boy leaves 'sinful' home for new life in Boys Town."

But Manson had long since formed ways of his own. He wasn't "fresh fuel," as he recalls it, for propaganda. He stayed only three short days in Boys Town. On the first day he met another recent arrival who shared his distrust for team efforts and for the absence of hatred and fear. Two days later both boys ran away, stealing a car, then a motorcycle, on their way through Illinois. There, after a day of "nothing to do" and ready to show the "world" how tough they were, they pulled a robbery of a super-market for more than two thousand dollars.

In April, Manson was committed to the Indiana Boys School in Plainfield, but during the next six months he escaped several times. His "runs" soon reached a sleight-of-hand perfection. He thought, "Could it be possible to make myself unseen? Could I be invisible by some kind of power? To be there but not to be there . . ."

In the years to follow, it would become almost second nature to

Manson to believe in secret passageways, hatches, trap doors, exits that all others were blind to. Years later, charged with the toughest of all crimes — murder — he would lay claim to being the only one knowing the whereabouts of a "secret river that runs beneath Death Valley, right under the ground."

Though records at Plainfield indicate "frequent escape attempts," Manson was paroled to live with relatives in West Virginia. "I'd rather spend another six months here," Manson told an inmate on the day of his parole. He reached the home of his uncle in July, convinced that his relatives resented his parole and that by now *he* was a "different breed" of man. "They wouldn't look me in the face while they were talking to me," Manson recalls. "They were afraid."

A shopkeeper near the residence remembers Manson as "a very ingratiating youngster who'd walk right up and shake your hand . . . Talking about how you felt and if you were fine or not. Never did it dawn on me that he might pull a gun or something of that kind."

But beneath Manson's façade, "the kind of nice young man" he resented at Boys Town, he was generating a "dynamo" full throttle. He could barely sleep — barely stand still until he was on the run again. It came a month later. He left his uncle's home, having stolen $90 and a pistol, and the fact that he fled broke his probation. Charged with parole violation, he was returned to the boys school in Plainfield. Greeted back by "fellow delinquents," Manson felt more comfortable there and entered the grounds almost with a sigh of relief.

"Charlie believed," a boy recalls, "that what was on the outside was getting greyer, and meaner, and colder than anything we had in Plainfield." But unknown to Manson, the more time he spent behind bars the more the "outside world" shifted in perspective.

Manson's ability at making quick friends revealed more than a personable nature. Officials observed that he possessed an unusual gift for taking command as a leader, and was beginning to be consulted daily by younger boys for advice. He impressed many with a trick he'd developed — "feeling no pain." He'd burn himself with cigarettes or thread needles into his skin, claiming he felt nothing. Not that he was "insensitive" or had no nerve endings, but that he could "will it away" — as though nothing could get to him.

About seven months after his return to Plainfield, Manson

escaped again, this time with two other boys. They stole a car and made their way to Utah where their capture was accidental — a roadblock set up to intercept two bank robbers ended the journey. The boys were held in Beaver County Jail to await federal officers for having driven the stolen car across the state line.

"Boy," a law officer said to him. "You're too hot for us — you're a federal case now, you know that."

Manson, a true stranger to the "outside world," was to spend so much of his life behind bars, in institutions and prisons, that eventually he neither knew nor wanted any other way of life.

Many years and many shadows of bars later, in jail for multiple murder, Manson doodled in a note pad propped against an edition of the Constitution. The designs were circular, round doodles, certain parts of which he had colored solid with radiating sunbeams symbolizing "rising signs."

"Hey, somebody said, 'What sign are you?' I said, 'Are you kidding? Everyday's my rising sign. Everyday there's a new rising sign.'"

The "rising sign," astrologers explain, is determined by the position of the sun at the time of one's birth. Yet even if there was a "rising sign" daily it would matter little — for Manson admits having rarely seen the sun. From earliest memories he recalls being fascinated by shadows playing mysteriously through dirty window panes, then the shadows of iron gratings over orphanage windows, the slats of steel bars in city jails, prisons; the shadows changing as the bars multiply in numbers and thickness, more and more until the light of day is hidden, until even in his doodles he shadows the sun.

"And they want to know what my philosophy is," Manson said. "You know, I don't have any philosophy except that I don't think. I don't have hardly any thoughts. I just am."

Another lesson he learned in the penitentiary, he'd remember, was, "You don't tell nobody nothing. I have learned not to tell people something they don't agree with . . . I just listened. I never made opinions. I never learned how to do that, to make opinions. I never learned how to make decisions."

In prison he knew "the score," he found out who he was. "All my life I used to believe that the good guys were on the outside and the bad guys were on the inside, in where I've always been," he said, facetiously. "Because everybody knows that inside all you have are convicts, thieves and liars. And you know they are the bad guys. And when they talk to you, you don't believe them. That is how I learned to 'put-on,'" Manson explained. "By looking wide-eyed and nodding and saying 'yes' and nodding some more. 'Yes, yes, is that so?' and 'Yes, I believe it, yes.' Because when they talked to me, I'd always say, 'Yes, sure, yes, sure.' But you don't believe people like that. I didn't disbelieve them, either," Manson said. It was, actually, too dangerous to think. So he learned to play it safe, to "put-on."

For a long time now he'd believed his mind could not be imprisoned. "It had nothing to do with anything *they* knew. So in a way, just by being locked up, I knew everything I had to . . . On the outside, all the people walking back and forth and going in and out of everything, you see that their bodies are free, going this way and that; they are free to move, but their minds are locked up the same as in prisons and institutions — I realized I was better off in the penitentiary."

One high-ranking prison official observed, "The worst that can happen to a person is that he loses the ability to make an independent decision — the man under a strict prison routine where every single minute of the day is planned by others has simply no possibility for taking a position of any kind. I have known cases where the personal insecurity has made people anxious about leaving the prison grounds. They prefer to live under a regimen and cling to an existence where all is arranged for them." Manson never learned to make decisions, and no effective "rehabilitation" ever reached him. Some believed the wall between Manson and society had become so impenetrable that even he was not yet aware of its density. His agile mind still sorted through muddy rationalizations, excuses he erected as to why it was all so difficult, why he was so innately a stranger — and was this condition as irrevocable as it seemed?

A reformatory official recalls, "By the time Manson was twenty-one, when we had to parole him, it was as though *he'd* gained something and we'd lost. Just talking to him for a time, if you were on the other side, you could see he thought it was a contest — we'd had our war and he was coming out on top. But he didn't want to get *out* especially, and I knew he'd be back behind bars. The outside world was a different world and it wasn't Manson's world."

Manson says, "When I got out then, I said where can I go from here? I was from the street, from the alley, I had no father, no mother. I'd been in and out of orphanages and reformatories. I'd never had much schooling and I said to myself, 'Where to?' Here we are. That's what there was and that's all that there was and I had no more thoughts about it . . . Someone asked me, 'Aren't you thinking about it?' I said, 'No.' They said, 'Aren't you worried about it?' I said, 'No,' and I said 'no' when they asked me if I was even thinking about what I was going to do. I had no thoughts about what I was doing. There had never been any thought. I was twenty-one years old then. I hit the streets and I'd never had a drink of beer in my life. I'd never been with a woman — never made love to one in my life. 'Women' had always been so far away from me. I mean *distant* that I was actually frightened of them. In back of myself I kept saying 'no,' and 'no, I wouldn't be able to adjust to what they were all doing . . .'"

Three

With little direction, Manson returned to West Virginia and drifted from one menial job to another, dissatisfied with each. For a short time he worked as a waiter in a cafe where he met Bertha, a movie usherette. She had an old Ford convertible and allowed Manson to drive her around the city. She was the first girl he had sexual relations with.

Another was a young waitress in a hospital dining room. She became pregnant with his child and they were married in January, 1955.

He worked in a gas station, a parking lot, was employed as a box boy in a market. Prior to his marriage, a relative Manson stayed with remembers, "Charlie slept a lot and would wander around. It was plain he wasn't doing anything in particular to help himself, but like he was waiting around for something to happen. I personally couldn't see that he had anything to wait for . . ."

Even after marriage, Manson says, "I met a few girls and they all had something I liked. I could see how much of a stranger I'd been to people living in the free world. After awhile I met this one girl and she wrapped her pussy around me. She wanted to go to California, so I stole a car and we drove to California . . ."

After reaching Los Angeles, he was arrested and charged with car theft. Convicted, he was sentenced to Terminal Island Prison at Los Angeles. The judge who sentenced him later told an attorney: "I asked Manson if he had anything to say, if he was willing to present some extenuating circumstances, but he said nothing and showed no concern about returning to prison."

Manson was to return repeatedly, and with each trip back to the "joint," the gulf widened between the "tough guy" and the man who might

16

exist in an organized society.

Back in West Virginia, his wife put together her belongings and brought Manson's baby to California. She took a small apartment in Los Angeles near San Pedro to make regular visits to the prison. The visits continued for almost two years. "During that time," says a friend, "she must have aged ten years. She began to feel she was wasting her life — her time. She was pretty confused. She'd say, 'I sit there and look him in the face and I can't get the feeling that he cares or gives a damn about me or the baby. I don't understand him . . . I don't think I even know him. He doesn't make any sense.' She said she couldn't get into Charlie's way of thinking and so she stopped visiting him. There were too many problems."

Manson then made an unsuccessful attempt to escape from Terminal Island. An inmate says, "He just had to do it, had to try, he said. Something about his wife. Ninety-nine times out of one hundred it can't be done. Charlie figured he had that one percent on his side." Another excuse to keep his inner "dynamo" going, on the run.

He was still doing time when his wife served him with divorce papers. Her life with Charlie had ended.

Released on five years probation, Manson drifted to Venice, California. Those who knew him then knew a man of many faces. One musician, Bob Shell, remembers: "In that short time I'd known Charlie I felt one could get to know him many times over, even in the turn of a day. I had no knowledge of what he was up to but we talked and talked around the beach. I could see he was hitting on some pretty negative factors, that he was calling on them, and I tried to show, you know, that those factors couldn't be taken apart from the others, but he thought they could be. He had an answer for everything, and he didn't believe that he had any particular limits. You have to understand that Charlie wasn't on the same bag he's onto now. He had a lot of the 'punk' going for him, like a young hood. You know, the Elvis hairdo, and he'd worn this leather jacket around the beach. In the time I got to be around him a little I don't think he had much use for other people."

Another who knew Manson in Venice was Jeanie Morse. "He was a 'straight' person as far as I was concerned. There was this time in Venice and when we'd gone into town there was a place on La Brea and Sunset Boulevard, and he knew some of the other people there. You could say he was hanging around with some pretty heavy people. Not like the hippies are now. I mean they were a rough bunch of people. And they had conflicts with the law. It is my opinion, that being what I felt from Charlie, was that he wasn't anything like, you know, dudes on the street, in the cars, in the restaurants, and in all the big buildings with all the straight lives going on. He didn't even trust me or get close to me and I was a goddamn hooker then. He wasn't the same as the others. What he had to do, he had to go down there where he'd find some of the people that he was like, and that were like him. The same kind of, I believe most were in or out of prisons, that's the only people he had."

The more Manson became the "tough guy" through the many "faces," the less he could emerge as the one person who might have really cared, who might have developed a strong enough identity to hang on and live instead of "putting on" another face. But he ran, failing to recognize the limits of human personality. For awhile he fancied himself a "movie producer" and sought to enlist young girls as starlets. He wandered through Hollywood, drifted around beach towns, through odd jobs. At times he gave the impression of being a "businessman," but none of the schemes he dreamed up materialized. And "bad trouble," his lifelong companion, dogged a little bit nearer every day .

He wrote a bum check for $37.

Soon after, he was arrested again for forgery. The problems mounted. Three days later he was released to the U.S. Treasury Department and held on mail theft and forgery of treasury checks. He was also charged with parole violation and was sentenced to ten years imprisonment.

From Los Angeles he was sent to the Federal Penitentiary at McNeil Island, Washington. "I was given a name and a number and I was put in a cell," Manson says, "and I lived in a cell with a name and a number . . ." He remembers mainly "just sitting in jail, thinking nothing . . . Nothing to think about . . . Everybody used to come in and tell me about their past and their lives and what they did. But I could never tell anybody about my past or what my life was or what I did because I have always been sitting in that room — I had a cot, a basin, a wall. So, then it moves on to awareness, to how many cracks can you count in the wall? It moves to where the mice live and what the mice are thinking, and you see how clever mice are.

"I am only a reflection," he would claim. "I have done everything I have always been told. I have mopped the floor when I was supposed to mop the floor, and I swept when I was supposed to sweep . . . As you put two people in a cell, so would they reflect and flow on each other like as if water would seek a level. I have been in a cell with a guy eighty years old, and I listened to everything he said. 'What did you do then?' And he explains to me his whole life, and I sat there and I listened and I experienced vicariously his whole being, his whole life, and I look at him and he is one of my fathers. But he is also another one of society's rejects." With the other "rejects," Manson knew he belonged. One ex-convict friend of Manson's at McNeil says, "Some guys like Charlie are institutionalized . . . He was at home in prison."

Another McNeil friendship bloomed between Charlie and a man almost twice his age. Alvin "Creepy" Karpis arrived at McNeil after spending a total of twenty-six years on "The Rock" — Alcatraz. One ex-McNeil inmate says, "Creepy — who nobody called that to his face, had been the FBI's most wanted man — Public Enemy Number One in the thirties until he'd been busted in New Orleans by J. Edgar Hoover himself. Like a lot of guys who'd wind up on The Rock after being bad ass in the other joints, Karpis was sent straight to Alcatraz. So Karpis was there with Floyd Hamilton — who'd been with Bonnie and Clyde, and Machine Gun Kelley, and Doc Barker — the youngest son of Ma Barker's gang. What the law nailed Karpis with was kidnapping, and they had him tucked away on The Rock longer than anybody else ever did time there, and he wasn't going nowhere until they sent him to McNeil.

"It didn't make no difference to a lot of people that he'd done all that time in Alcatraz. He was still *Karpis*, you know, and he wasn't even sixty years old . . . A lot of people tended to shy away from him, even though you're in the joint and nobody's supposed to be nothing. They didn't shy away because of him being any threat to someone's personal safety, but because he was like a *star*, you know — he'd always been that . . . He was A-OK, and what made it easier on people was that Karpis was such a skilled musician. He'd pick up a guitar and play it like a professional . . . Also he could do this with other instruments, but the guitar seemed to come alive when he picked it up. *Blues*, boy, blues, and he could play snappy stuff. Man, it was a real joy listening to that man play, and that's why Charlie Manson went to him, to learn what he could from Karpis about playing the guitar . . ."

Ex-Public Enemy Number One Alvin Karpis, record-holder for

time on The Rock, says, "Charlie came to me a few times at McNeil, at first, proposing some situation in which he could learn more about music and the guitar from me. He said he knew a little and I told him to sit down and play something, and he went ahead and did that. I saw he had a feel for it — he wasn't bad at all, but there was a lot of room for improvement. I was working with the recreation committee at the time and had a pretty free reign. Charlie wanted to write music, compose stuff he had in his head, and learn to play that successfully.

"He wasn't impatient . . . I instructed him and we often played quite a bit together. He had a serious devotion to what he wanted to do . . . musically, and where there is that desire in one, it's not a long ways to actually achieving what it is you want to do. We talked often and there was something unmistakably unusual about Manson. He was a runt of sorts, but found his place as an experienced manipulator of others . . . able to take the run of something and go with it . . .

"He wasn't educated but had a great deal of native ability, though it was in a manner of getting whatever it was he was after. For instance, I wasn't in the business of instructing, but found myself in that position with Manson. So it was like I could be sitting here and it dawned on me that this fellow had gotten me into something I hadn't intended. You see, it was the manipulation — quite skillful, and then at that point we talked about it and he laughed. Oh, friendly enough, though he had a very uneven personality. I don't mean his temperament, but more of his personality. And he told me he had approached me in the 'reverse,' by showing me, as he put it, the qualities of myself that were in line with that he was after . . .

"Until after I'm dead, I'd be unwilling to let it be known I'd been fooled like that, but the fact is that he was right in that I was not resentful or reluctant to teach someone to play an instrument or to be friendly, but I did feel manipulated, and under circumstances where it hadn't been necessary . . . It revealed to me that this fellow, as interesting as he could be at times, undertook his situations as part of a deception. You see, in a devious manner for some personal gain. If you're 'conning' someone, you're 'conning' someone, but if you fail to tell the difference between it being a necessity to get what you're after, then you're not only fooling the other party, but you're pulling the wool over your own eyes as well . . . What you wind up with, is two blind men."

Karpis says Manson had "the run of the place. He joined all the prison groups and got to be on all the committees, especially the recreation committee. He learned how to get his way by conforming to what his case worker wanted. He'd talk, by saying what it was that was right for what he wanted . . ."

But finally, in March, 1967, despite Manson's protests, his "time was up." He was conditionally paroled again.

"They were ready to let me out and I said, 'Oh, no, I can't go outside there. I can't and I'm not able to adjust to their world. I'd be a stranger.' But they said, 'No, it was time. I had to go outside.' But I wanted no part of that world outside. The people there are the ones that smile and shake your hands and pat your backs, and smile some more and pretend that they are good, that they are your friends, but there were none of them there . . . I knew that I couldn't adjust to that world, not after all my life had been spent locked up and where my mind was free. I was content to stay in the penitentiary, just to take my walks around the yard in the sunshine and to play my guitar and sit and play it in my cell, or do all the things that I'd been used to doing in prison . . ."

"After I got out I was frightened. It was being frightened in a funny way. I didn't know where to go. I was thirty-two, on the streets again, and I didn't know anything. I didn't even know anything about dope or LSD. I didn't want to leave jail, but they insisted I go and they gave me — I think it was $35 — and I had a suitcase filled with old used clothes."

Karpis was still serving time the day Charlie left the prison. "I shook Charlie's hand," he says. "And when he'd gone off, I shook my head. Manson was definitely ill-prepared for life. He left McNeil and I saw nothing but a string of penitentiaries before him. Bad, *bad* news all the way down."

Four

Out of prison, Manson knew no one. No one knew him. He had a guitar, and plans about music he could formulate only in close-cornered spurts. And, he said, his mind was portable, that was a fact. He had carried it through jail cells and penitentiaries most of his life. It was a portable Pandora's Box.

The streets of the city and crowds and buses were foreign to him. He was a stranger.

"For several days I just rode the bus around. I slept on the bus and the drivers woke me up when we reached the end of somewhere. 'You're at the end,' they'd say. 'End of the line.' Getting off the bus was the same as getting out of jail. Finally I wound up in Berkeley and I looked up this friend I'd known in prison. They were poor and I stayed there, but I felt I was eating the food right out of their mouths, and also, he had been ordered that he couldn't associate with ex-cons, people like that. I didn't get along at all with his old lady and they fought all night. So I left there and took another bus, and another one and I was in San Francisco . . ."

For some time Manson had followed the news of the "flower children," who they were and where they were. So, with a guitar across his back, fancying himself a sort of wandering minstrel, he drifted around San Francisco, eating where he could, moving whenever he felt like it.

"I never thought about being a hippie. I don't know what a hippie is. A hippie is generally a guy that's pretty nice. He will give you a shirt, and a flower, and he will give you a smile, and he walks down the road. . . I found myself in Haight-Ashbury and I got to know a young kid who carried a sleeping bag he said he lived out of. He didn't work and, in fact, he said nobody he knew worked. I wanted to know how he managed to live

22

that way and he said, 'Come on,' and he'd show me how. He put his arm around me and we went off like that 'There's no sweat,' he said."

The boy introduced Manson to life on Haight. For awhile they slept in parks, went to the Diggers for meals, attended the Sunday Feeds, existed from day to day.

"We just lived on the street. The weather was beautiful and everybody there was living on the street . . . I started playing my music and those on the street, they liked it, and they had smiles that were real, and they would put their arms around me, and anything I needed was there in front of me. The whole thing just grabbed me up and sent me spinning. I couldn't get over that these people were so *real*. Their minds were there, buzzing, everybody was making music, and we grooved on it, and it was as simple as that . . . I didn't know anything and yet I knew everything because I had one thing, and that was an infinite, pulsating thing inside me that was me, and yet it wasn't me in any special sense, it was everybody. Everywhere. It was love because it was all perfect. My hair was growing longer then and all the people around me had beards and were giving out love. It buzzed, it made you tune in with it and once you were in with it you saw it was everything . . . We sat in the park and smoked grass together and just felt living inside of us. We sang and made music and were alive and what we were."

A young girl named Nancy Hart, a would-be folk-rock singer, remembers when Manson settled in San Francisco. She was "hanging paper," forging checks in order to support a drug habit, or "balling for cash" just often enough to pay her keep. She moved with the group through the park and the free-feeds, and "made the Free Clinic scene every week for VD checks, along with everyone else. Most of them had syph and it was something I had no use for at the time . . ."

While sleeping in the park one night Nancy met Manson, who crawled into the bundle of "blankets I'd scored from the Diggers and the Salvation cat." Charlie said he was cold and asked could he warm up with her, "because, he said, I was giving off this tremendous heat . . ."

She had "acid" from Owsley, a well-known basement manufacturer and distributor of LSD, whom she "balled" along with a rock group "when I was still a groupie," and that was when she turned Manson on. It was his first experience, "at least he told me it was," and he claimed to have received a great message under the acid influence which was how powerful he could be if he got his whole thing together and let it groove with what was happening." Nancy says, "Charlie wasn't a great lover, but acted out the role of it, and he was a great con artist, perhaps the best I have ever seen or come across in the business. He went around with me and hung paper around San Francisco and he'd rap on all the con tricks he'd gathered. What he knew could blow minds . . . "

He talked to Nancy about his "mentor," as he called "Creepy" Karpis, "bad man number one," who dug Charlie's music. "We'd ball and he'd get bored with what we were doing, so he screwed me with a broom handle after he got tired and had me do it with a Coke bottle, both sides, and to myself *so*, while he jerked off. And he had me rap it all, like relating to him how I was experiencing and what it was that I felt from him — from his *near*ness, if you can dig it. On the acid it was that especially," she remembers, "that no contact thing and his relating what was happening."

She said she didn't want to do some of the things Charlie'd suggest, but did them anyway, she admits, because he had her sort of hypnotized.

Manson admits that until meeting Nancy he had not been involved with hard drugs. She turned him on to LSD, saying, "You're already there, you don't need it, but it'll help straighten the currents."

Charlie says, "My awareness after acid of what was going on became that much more enlightened. I was with them, part of them. We were all really a part of one another."

He liked that part he was playing, if it was a part he *was* playing, Nancy says. "He was a chameleon. He looks one way and then the other, and it is no longer the other you are seeing, but one that you have not seen before."

In a poem, she wrote of Manson, "Smilingly the face you saw and lost so many minutes before has averted, Ah! shines again."

Nancy says she gave Charlie $150 and lived with him in a room in Berkeley for about "four days and one hundred nights" before she was arrested in downtown San Francisco for possession of narcotics.

When she was in jail, Charlie moved on. "What really made me alive," he says, "was just the kids walking up and down the streets. They'd give you anything they had and wanted nothing for it . . . I just fell in love — it was all that perfect, I loved everything."

The "civilization" of cold concrete and institutions, of indifference and formalities that had smothered Charlie for thirty-three years had somehow changed. It seemed to him that not only was his mind free and self-perpetuating but so were those surrounding him — "these wild flowers that had sprouted up everywhere."

But Charlie was a late-comer. He did not know that he had missed the warmest days on Haight. The "flower children" he met were only the die-hards of a disappearing scene. And then there were those that came to take what was left, like hyenas and jackals. One such person was Joe Brockman. Later, in a small, dingy motel on U.S. 99, a mile south of Madera, California, Joe would recall the events that led to his friendship with Manson and to later becoming a member of Charlie's "family."

Twenty-two-year-old Brockman would sit on a rumpled bed, shoulders hunched as he squinted through dark prescription glasses at the surface of a small table. He'd focus on a razor blade between his fingers, then pressing down through the center of a white tablet coated with a yellowish color.

"You see," Joe would say, "no one that wasn't straight could see what was happening up on the Haight. The whole scene was jammed, no one could even get through the traffic in the night time." Referring to the summer of 1967, he explains, "If you could stand on the roof, and looking down, you were seeing into a kaleidoscope. It all moved the same as colored glass does. Wow, it was beautiful. Being alive was a groove because the same thing in the air was being felt by everybody. They were there from all over too, they'd come in on buses and even old broken-down bicycles."

Looking up from his task of quartering the halves of the pill, Joe remembered he was "one of the first to really turn Charlie on to really good acid. It was Owsley acid the first few trips, the biggest load Owsley'd produced before his major bust. And it was being distributed like water, so I hoarded. I made ten thousand dollars in three months on the Haight . . ."

Joe believed Charlie was an artist, "in the real sense, or like a priest, but then I saw that I couldn't hack his way. I got to be free, on my own terms and not on someone else's bag, no matter who they are. I guess it's that Charlie had started his Jesus thing going and I had dope."

It was in San Jose that Joe first met a girl named Susan Atkins. "And mind you," he says, "this was before Charlie Manson ever knew her. She'd been in jail, I think on a stolen car thing, and had already been in and out of Frisco, and even Los Angeles. I'd never been to L.A., and she rapped on it for me. We all got smashed on hash, and I dropped some pills. I didn't know what they were.

"This friend of mine had been going up there on his bike and seeing her. I really dug her, and I believe I told her, 'If I had enough bread I'd buy you what you want.' And my buddy said, 'She doesn't know what she wants and if she did it wouldn't be you buying it for her.' So I said, 'Cool.' If you really look at her close, she doesn't look like she does from across the room or someplace — like when you meet her. She seemed to be forty years older than the rest, not that she looked it. She was *fine*. She told me she wasn't going to stay in San Jose, that she was heading back to Frisco. I said 'That's where I'm going one of these days,' and she said, 'Well, it's just an out-of-sight place and it's the only place to get your head.'

"Time passed and we went back up to San Jose to see the girls, but by then Susan Atkins was already gone. 'She's working in San Francisco,' her friend said . . .

"And then a year later, when I was in San Francisco, I saw her, but under acid Susan's face was like two feet tall, but really pretty. Some of the others I knew already, and there was this girl named Marge Smith, I guess she was with Susan.

"Marge stopped and looked at someone, her face just going open like this — as open as a window when you open it in the morning, a good morning. Just looked like that at this guy. And then she said to me, without looking at me, 'This is Charlie, like I told you so.' He looked at me, and said, 'Oh, I know you.' I said, 'No,' but he said, sort of shaking his head slow-like, 'Yes,' meaning he knew me. It was a put-on, I said to myself, so all right, and I shook my head, too . . . You'd never forget his face.

"Later we had a mutual respect for one another. We shared ideas. We shared what we had, whatever it was. I laid bread on him . . . other people laid bread on him. We shared and made some kind of trade deals and I never burned Charlie and he never burned me. I don't believe he had it in him to burn anybody."

According to Manson, "This guy up in San Francisco, he said, 'Here is five thousand dollars.' I told him, 'I can't take five thousand dollars, man, what do you own, five thousand dollars' worth of my life, how much is that?' He said, 'No, man, I just want you to have the bread. You just be you, no strings to it.' He laid it on me and I took it and gave it away to kids on the street. I did it with a girl. It took about two days to give it all away. I bought some candy bars, a couple keys of grass, we all got high. One guy, I bought him a truck he wanted, and this other guy was down on me, telling me, 'How could you give it to him — he is a bad one. I'm the good one, give it to me.' And lots of people said that I stole the money and that I wasn't any good . . ."

Joe says he wasn't a joiner, and that neither was Charlie Manson. "Like he went that way, joining nothing but being everywhere, if you know what I mean."

Another young man who met Charlie at this time, Carl Shapiro, kept his distance. "I was going to school — I hadn't dropped out, but I'd turned on, man, but this guy was fooling around with people's heads. He was tricking them like you train a dog by substituting what it needs for something else so it thinks what you're giving it is what it needs . . .

"One night he had this conversation with me about guys getting fucked in the ass. He wanted to know if I'd been fucked in the ass, and he went into a long thing about guys taking it up the ass in prison . . . He meant against their will, like being raped and how it was approved of by the institutions because, he said, it kept a kind of 'governor' on things, it gave control and power to people doing time, and created a world within a world that was not governed by the Establishment."

Joe Brockman says, "I don't remember which night it was, oh, we went down and I saw this guy I knew. The other one was a cop and they were in front of the drugstore. The guy was listening to some dude that Manson said was a 'nark,' and I said, 'No shit,' and turned around, you know, heading the other way. But Charlie took my arm sort of gentle and said, 'No, man, don't let him put any of his fear in you. It's the only way he can go around, by laying his fear on you . . . And then he's got it out of himself and likes to corner you, having put his fear in you. And he reacts to that, your fear which was really his, you dig?' And then Charlie walked up to the 'nark' and he said, 'Man, you don't look so good. You look down. And can I turn you on? Maybe you should be turned on to what's happening — you should smile.'

"The nark looked at Charlie and said, 'Fuck off, willya.'

"I can't say what the living was," Joe says. "It was a motion, going all around and getting into all kinds of things. The groups were all joined by something bigger."

27

He said a few days passed, then he and Charlie drove out in a pickup to where Joe kept a "brick" of marijuana stashed behind a 7-Up billboard. "Then, we were at Charlie's and he was sitting on a beat-up Turkish rug, rapping to these girls," he said. "He looked like a lion as he talked. I could hear his words but the way in which he was saying his thing, or had them put together, was far out."

He recalls laying the "brick" before Manson. "And I felt in the center of the scene, like I'd made an offering to their gods.

"They all grooved. 'Bullshit,' I said. I busted up the brick. They just sat and watched the pile of grass grow bigger and bigger.

"What was sort of freaky was Marge Smith. She was as smashed as anyone, and on a trip I couldn't groove with. I wanted to ball her.

"Charlie said, 'ball her,' and I — the rest were tripping on what he was saying and I suppose I should've been too, but I wasn't — I kept flashing. 'This is some con. Like number one.' What did he have, I asked myself. Even asking myself that while I was balling Marge that Charlie gave me, on the rug there . . . which was a trip, because Charlie reached out his hand and put it over, the palm of it, over the chick's eyes and forehead while I'm balling her. She laughed and came on like someone talking — someone speaking tongues."

It seemed almost as if controlling the act of sex with the palm of his hand, or by mental association as it was earlier with Nancy, was more important to Manson than the physical contact he might have. As Nancy had said, "On the acid" it was "that no contact thing and his relating . . ." It seemed Manson's intent was to get into the girl's mind, to learn to control her.

During this time, Joe managed to obtain several plastic baggies of "Owsley gold" and glimpsed the "freaky power" Charlie possessed.

"There was this picture of Jesus, like the one that's on the book jacket cover of *The Prophet*, hanging on the wall. Charlie was squatting in front of it, his back to it, rapping, and I was going up faster than I'd ever gone up, a tab and a half, probably because I hadn't eaten in a couple days, just dropping a lot of bennies and shit, and there was this merging . . ." Joe brought his fingers together, entwining them.

"The picture of Jesus on the wall and Charlie's face in front of me . . . Both began to sort of melt in a funny way, I guess like plastic or something, Manson and Jesus, merging on this trip and into one and the same. I said, 'Wow, that's how it works,' not really knowing myself what

28

I meant."

Joe realized then that "if you've had enough acid, Charlie could, at will I guess, turn himself into a Jesus." And this caused Joe to grope with thoughts of the Devil and reincarnation. The picture of "Charlie as Jesus was branded into my thoughts, and I was like in a movie, or watching a long movie. Charlie was the hero, and the more I stayed stoned, the more of a hero he was . . . But it was a painful thing, too, because I still had my resistance going and I knew I couldn't just sit in that movie for the rest of my life, and I knew I couldn't submit to whatever it was the idea of Charlie as Jesus expected of me. I only knew the man was playing heavy games. Charlie could plant that in a person's head, or create it, the same way a magician creates a bunch of flowers in the air . . ."

Five

Marge Smith lived in the Haight during its era, and knew many in the Manson crowd, though mainly she knew Susan Atkins and lived with her in San Francisco. Marge says, "I was very hung-up on Susie at one time, we had a girl-chick thing going between us for some time; oh, it was earlier than when she met Charlie. I had known Susie for maybe a year and she had come and gone off a few times. That was her habit to do that, and every time she came back we had a sharing thing, and it was as though she was emptying herself of whatever it was that had bugged her, brought her down so. So we had been involved with one another. I mean there were a couple of times — we had been high together so often . . . like there is a complete blending-in of two people — two persons' bodies into one. So there is an equal balance of the mind, and of the soul. Because, being as high as we were and not just on drugs, but on love as well and the whole physical nature of it, the soul or the soul and mind which is the same would be so locked up together as to be one. This happened especially after Charlie came into our lives and both of us, Susie and myself, had made love with Charlie and then with each other as we had in the past. But Charlie made it much different, made it more real between us whenever it occurred . . . By more real, I mean more locked in with it. That's all.

"Before Susie split the scene we were on I got busted on pills," Marge recalls. "Then I was busted on a really foul bit of bullshit on the part of the cops there. I was picked up for soliciting. Imagine, soliciting. I have no need for money, no need to keep it or save it like they do," she explained. "We were the same, Susie, Charlie and I and those that were grooving with us. The cash, the more it kept flowing the better it was; the more it was worth whatever it was. Nothing had any other meaning except what we gave it."

When Susan met Charlie in San Francisco, she thought she had found what she'd been looking for in life, that there was no need to look any further.

"Before I met Charlie I felt I was lacking somewhere," she admits. "He didn't show me how to become a real woman, he gave me me — in other words, I gave myself up to him and in return for that he gave me back to myself. He gave me the faith in myself to be able to know that I am a woman."

Born in San Gabriel, California, May 7, 1948, Susan and her family moved to San Jose soon after, where she later attended elementary school. She took part in the church choir and Sunday school regularly, although her home life, "with many ups and downs," was not an easy-going one. She had one older brother and another brother younger than herself. When she was in the fifth grade, her family moved again and she entered another school. On the surface her life appeared relatively stable until she reached adolescence. She was fifteen years old and had entered high school when her mother was diagnosed as having terminal cancer. Oddly enough, the dying mother's presence in the home didn't seem to disturb Susan deeply.

A relative recalls, "Susan had an almost indifferent air about it." Although near Christmas, Susan brought her church choir to the house and stood beneath her mother's bedroom window. They sang Christmas carols until late into the night.

When her mother died, Susan's grandparents came to help organize the family. Her father was unemployed. The costly funeral had been a burden, and Susan was constantly fighting with her brothers. The grandparents were rejected by Susan as they exerted supervision, authority coming much too late in the girl's life. To some extent, Susan had had her own way.

In school Susan was an average student, with no disciplinary record or trouble. A friend of the family says, "She had been a good kid, basically, sort of lax at times . . . not really expressing herself, but I think the trouble was that she was left alone a lot of the time. And there was really no place for the girl to turn if she happened to have any kind of problem . . . if she needed help."

Susan's father had been able to get into construction work at the

San Luis Dam, when the girl enrolled in Los Baños High School in 1965. Those who knew the family remember numerous quarrels, often heated arguments, between Susan and her father. Her father seemed unable to provide the guidance Susan began to need, or the discipline that might have stabilized her emotions for the future. A friend of Susan's recalls: "She just didn't seem to care. Like when her mother died, she didn't show any real sadness about it. I don't think Susan cared about anything very much. There was something wrong with her . . ."

The following year Susan broke family ties. She went to San Francisco and involved herself with young men who moved quickly, usually just ahead of the law. Susan bragged to one girl friend that she had taken part in some gas station holdups, in the robbery of a liquor store, and that she was helping a man steal cars.

She was arrested in Oregon, and held on charges of car theft and concealing stolen property. It was not long after her release on probation that she was arrested again.

Her father, remarried by then, pleaded with the courts to keep his daughter "off the streets . . . She needs help," he said. "She should have been out and away where help could be given, not turned back on the streets to go through it all again."

Out on probation, Susan returned to San Jose to live with a relative — then with a girl friend. She was going to "stay put for awhile," she told the friend, but there were parties, there were people with dope, and when the parties were over there was the "boredom of San Jose . . ."

Susan returned to San Francisco. She tried different jobs, but, as her friend recalls, "Susan would go off with some guy if she thought he was treating her okay. She didn't care too much who the guy was if he offered her some square deal. She made a lot of trips back and forth to Los Angeles, and I think she felt for a while she was right on top of it."

She got a job as a cocktail waitress, then as a topless dancer in a small go-go club. The entanglements with men went on.

"One guy was going to marry her, and when this didn't pan out I think she took it more to heart than anything else," the girl friend says. "He'd been a good dude. So she started staying with different guys like she was trying to prove they were all for nothing, and none of it worked out for her. She didn't know what she was after. Just going with the tide."

She wound up on the Haight. There, trying to shake loose of her past, "not giving a damn" about a future, she felt she could drift with no demands.

"I was living in a house that primarily consisted of young people living together," Susan says. "We all shared our means of support, and I was sitting in the living room on the first floor of the house when a man walked in and had a guitar with him. All of a sudden he was surrounded by a group of girls. Well, I sat and watched and he sat down on the couch and I sat down to his right and he started to play music . . . First he just started playing similar songs and went through Spanish — a couple of Spanish songs and sung a few songs, and then the song that caught my attention most was 'The Shadow of Your Smile,' and he sounded like an angel . . . And when he was through singing, I looked up and asked him if I could play his guitar . . . I wanted to get some attention from him. I don't know why, I just felt I wanted some attention from him, and he handed me the guitar and to myself I thought, 'I can't play this,' and then he looked at me and said, 'You can play that if you want to.'

"Now, he had never heard me say 'I can't play this,' I only thought it. So when he told me I could play, a common expression, I blew my mind, because he was inside my head, and I knew at that time that he was something that I had been looking for. But he just represented something to me inside, and I went down and kissed his feet. I don't know why I kissed his feet, I just kissed his feet, and then . . .

"Well then, a day or so later, Charlie came back to the house and I knew it was him and I went running downstairs to meet him at the door, and we walked back upstairs and he asked me if I wanted to go for a walk with him and I said, 'Yes,' and we walked a couple of blocks to another house in Haight-Ashbury and he told me he wanted to make love with me. Well, I acknowledged the fact that I wanted to make love with him and he told me to take off my clothes. So I uninhibitedly took off my clothes, and there happened to be a full-length mirror in the room and he told me to go over and look at myself in the mirror. I didn't want to do it, so he took me by my hand and stood in front of the mirror and I turned away and he says, 'Go ahead and look at yourself, there is nothing wrong with you. You are perfect. You always have been perfect.' He says, 'This is in body form. You were born perfect and everything that has happened to you from the time you were a child all the way up to this moment has happened perfectly. You have made no mistakes. The only mistakes you have made are the mistakes that you thought that you made. They were not mistakes . . .'

"He asked me if I ever made love with my father. I looked at him and kind of giggled and I said, 'No.' And he said, 'Have you ever thought about making love to your father?' I said, 'Yes, I thought I would like to make love with my father.' And he told me, he said, 'All right, when we are making love imagine in your imagination that I am your father and, in other words, picture in your mind that I am your father.' And I did, I did so, and it was a very beautiful experience . . ."

Susan says, "In time, he was to call himself Satan. And the Devil sometimes. He personally never called himself Jesus, but he represented a Jesus Christ-like person to me. He said Jesus Christ was but a man like any other man and with awareness of the world and the universe, and he gave up his life willingly so that we could live in order to become the same, not Jesus Christ, but the same consciousness that Christ was endowed with. We must be willing to experience the same thing Christ did for us."

Was Charlie Manson evil?

"In your standards of evil," Susan says, "looking at him through your eyes, I would say yes. Looking at him through my eyes, he is as good as he is evil, he is as evil as he is good . . . You could not judge the man."

Six

During the summer, "black magic" and "white magic" became a religion for many on Haight. To those who knew him, Manson not only participated, but saw himself as a kind of wizard. Within a short time he had banded together a following, younger than himself, a group that relied on sex and drugs to escape "Establishment pressures." Once released from the "vise-grip," they were open to "mystical experience," and Manson, the wizard, was there to show the way. Yet even to them, Manson would remain a stranger.

A San Francisco priest observed, "They lacked the will to fight the Devil's invasion." What will they had, the priest says, "had been smudged out like a little pencil line you rub over with an eraser." He believed that "evil is not neutral, and the older I get the more I'm convinced of it. It is a force as active as good. No, I no longer believe that evil is a neutral thing."

Those who grouped themselves around Charlie Manson came from scattered families, and in a short time acid and amphetamines altered their personalities.

Joe Brockman says, "Maybe no one's had as much acid as Timothy Leary, but here was a man that knew what he was doing. He had objectives — he had his thing before him. That there's what makes the difference. Now those that were hanging around Charlie that I dealt to, the ones that come in flowers on buses, BANG, they're up — the trip is a groove. They think that's what's happening — I mean, the way it should be, the trip, so they stay up as long as they can. I think out of maybe a hundred people I turned on personally, there were maybe three I heard went on actual bummers. One, this girl Willa, she cut her throat with some scissors, to release her soul. But that's the average law, same as walking across the street or driving your car." Joe claims LSD is softer on life and limb than the family automobile. "You get it or you don't . . . But what happens is not some sudden bummer like Willa, because that's a natural deal to happen. But the trip for those of Charlie's crowd, and the others that hung around, the trip became the thing that was happening, what you'd call reality. And like being down was being down, unreal. They didn't turn their eyeballs around and look themselves in the head and see what's happening in there like Leary did. No, the others looked right out like I did at first, and what they see they think is what's happening. Now, that is not what Leary preached. He never said a groovy trip is where it's at, because a trip like that that goes on and on and can only lead to a giant bummer in a broad sense, like the whole thing is a bummer."

Despite the insight Joe attributes to acid advocates, Timothy Leary, a university professor, writer, and scholar, was reduced through LSD to a criminal on the run, having escaped from jail on drug charges, and seeking refuge in foreign countries.

Charlie, who had been to the "bottom" and claimed to have unlocked his own mind, had a way of controlling those who turned their backs on their pasts. And in part he aided in that amputation. With no pasts, they sought the immediate — a grouping together as a sort of family that could share on their level of "awareness." So they created a family and placed Charlie at the "head of the table."

Marge Smith, nineteen then, says, "I was so wiped out and had to have something to go by. Charlie's thing was spontaneous, he turned me on and I seemed to turn him on, and he rapped love and being together and that's what I wanted. I never had it where I came from, so I said, 'Fuck what's back there.' Like some people believe in the Holy System, the Establishment, I believed in Charlie and where we were at."

As she says, "Nothing had any meaning except what we gave it." Manson "rapped" that there could be no guilt, no shame, no blame; no past to hold onto, no "individual" to be singled out. He claimed to "unlock" their minds and clear away their past.

"There is no good and no bad," he'd tell them. "There is no difference between you and I. There is only one thing and that thing is everything. I am the father. You are the father. I understand the universe through me. The truth is, and that's all. It doesn't matter what words you use, millions of words you use, the truth is what it is. That's the truth. What's here and now. I go there and I'm not here anymore. And now I come back and I'm not there anymore . . . Just what's here and now is what counts. It's infinite and it's nothing. It's all there is and it doesn't matter what you do. It is all perfect and the way it's supposed to be."

One young man soon to become close to Charlie was Robert Beausoleil — "handsome, strong, a leader in his own way, sun in Leo," says Robert Aiken, a Los Angeles astrologer and actor. "Beausoleil — *beautiful sun*. He had a movie star Robinson Crusoe quality, very open in a primitive way, apart from society with no use for its codes, its restrictions. They simply didn't apply. A freedom bound person. But yet he was no young idealist spouting off mystical witticisms, and no soft loving hippie. Not that way at all. The sunny magnetism, but an element of mystery and the dark, a darker cast to his aura that leaned on the sinister. Freedom bound, but one that the freedom binds, and one such as Beausoleil was bound for trouble . . ."

While Charlie was opening to the new environment on Haight like a Venus flytrap, Bobby Beausoleil migrated into the hippie scene from his last stop-over — Los Angeles. On the Sunset Strip they had called him "Bummer Bob," a name that angered him and drove him further into his own silence.

Hazily gazing back into his own life, Bobby says, "Maybe it began with my birth in Santa Barbara, California — November 6, 1947 — another Scorpio, like Charlie Manson.

"I had no desire to wait the full nine months," Bobby says, "I wanted to get going, so I kicked myself out of the woman's womb weeks earlier than I was expected."

He'd eventually say, with a nonchalant air, "They were a nice enough family, I suppose, but I hit the road when I was twelve years old without any interest in looking back over my shoulder . . ."

Perhaps Bobby's dread of backwards glances stems from the abuse he experienced as a small child at the hands of an aunt and uncle. According to Vickie Devin, a girl Bobby would try to marry several years later in Hollywood, "Bobby went through that mill — it was bad," she says, "typical of the worst of the sexual and other abuse brought down on a little kid. But he couldn't tell anyone — he *didn't* tell anyone, and it went on and he kept trying to get away from it . . . He wanted to run. He never told anyone, I don't think, except me — a lot later, and underneath the cool attitude, he was filled with some kind of ugliness — the abuse had twisted him awful."

Bobby's wandering was cut short when he was brought back as a runaway. "It went against my grain," he says, "this rude imposition of being pulled back against my desires . . . There were things I had to do — places to go, things I *sensed* and knew that I had to throw myself into. I knew that life was a big arena and I was ready for anything that could come along."

At age fourteen, Bobby was made a Ward of the Court by a Juvenile Court judge. "That was when my parents washed their hands of me, and inside of myself I said it was good riddance — not *me*, but their having separated themselves from my life by their own desires . . .

"That was after I'd been sent to reform school. When I got out of there, I was sent to live with my grandmother in South Gate, California, which is just part of Los Angeles, just outside of L.A., but a *part* of it. A dump. The house I was in was a dump and then it was condemned. My grandmother was moved out of the house and I just hung around South Gate. It was like hanging around some tin gate to Hell."

Bobby describes himself back then as "a greasy kid in a greasy leather jacket and boots, and with chips on both shoulders like the size of ammunition boxes." His grandmother rented "a flop" in El Monte — "just east of L.A., where all the new Nazis were hanging out . . . Officially I was supposed to be staying with her — the old woman — but I was actually sleeping over in a trailer with a couple of buddies down the block . . .

"I stayed with them most of the time," Bobby says, "sleeping in the trailer, in a part of it, and these guys brought this young girl in and we all had sexual relations with her. She had hair on her pussy and everything. About a week later she came back, wanting more. She wanted to be fucked by all three of us, but the other guys were gone so she stayed with me — hanging on my cock. We screwed around all day until it was time for her to leave and go home because she had to go to Mass at the church."

The girl came back to the trailer, "knocking on a little window over the mattress I was on," and Bobby climbed over one of the other kids that was still asleep and went outside. "I don't even think the sun was up yet — she was supposed to be going to school but wanted me to fuck the

38

shit out of her, so we walked over behind a water tank and I took her in the weeds, kicked some tin cans aside and laid her there. She'd already taken off her underpants and had them in her coat pocket.

"The best one could call me," he says, "was a petty crook . . . a greasy punk, because that's what I was. I swiped things. Got good at it. I could swipe things right under your nose without you even seeing me do it . . .

"The boy's uncle who had the trailer ran a broken-down gas station where I used to hang out, working for this screwy uncle sometimes, goofing off in the grease. I wore Levis that were all greasy, and a black leather jacket." Bobby had the feeling that he wanted to kick ass, but he wasn't sure how tough he was. He was a "pretty boy — a pretty-faced boy," who had the girls coming around all the time.

He knew about cars, "fixing this or that," he says. "I could fix things that I didn't know about by trying to figure them out, taking them apart and then I could put them back together. I built a few carburetors while I was hanging around the gas station — the other boys didn't help much. I guess their uncle figured I liked to do it, so he'd ask me instead of them. Like knowing it was something I could prove myself at, so he'd have me do it for what he called the experience of it. He didn't want to pay me anything — as it was, he figured since I was staying in the trailer I was sort of like a son maybe, and rooming me was enough, I suppose. I couldn't kick because I was getting sexual activities with the girls around there — they weren't anything you'd write home about, anything you'd take to a dance or somewhere nice — it was just sex, and they came around hot and wanting to screw around. I was there to accommodate them. And they'd accommodate me."

But Bobby's mind was always somewhere else. "Like this Martin Luther King, I had a vision, too, only I wasn't sure what it was. When I'd try to think about it, I'd get this distance sort of feeling like I was drifting in a fog — a sort of airplane without any engine and going into a fog over some black forest, and down into it. Gliding, you know. It was somewhere in the forests in ancient Germany . . ."

He saw a cartoon, "way back after I'd booted myself out of the woman," with Bugs Bunny and Hermann Goering, a fat, bumbling cartoon of the Luftwaffe leader and henchman of Hitler. In the middle of "farting around with Bugs Bunny," the rabbit disguises himself as a Nordic maiden in a steel helmet, riding through the woods on a gigantic white horse, muscles rippling in its shanks. "You couldn't even hear its hooves because it was like a dream — that same fog. That's how it came into my mind — not the *cartoon* of it, but the images it made in my mind. She had steel shields over her tits and long blonde braids hanging down to her ass . . ."

Things started coming through to Bobby the following summer. "Pictures and images," he says. "It was like I was an artist and my canvas was my mind. I was stealing things and selling them, there was no kick in stealing, it was like a profession with me, and other things were going on in my head . . .

"It was like I could hear the clanging of the Viking swords, echoing in some great hall. Just a little ways down the line, a little later on, I realized that it was Valhalla — that great hall where Odin eats the souls of heroes slain in battle. Odin's the god of war, the god of the souls and the god of poetry . . . It came to me to write, I wrote very early. It was just coming from me . . ."

Then Bobby was arrested for stealing. "It happened because I was off-balance," he says, "getting arrested. I was disconnected with the act of it, and so consequently I got my ass in a sling. Breaking probation."

Back to reform school, where the notions and images of the Vikings came to him almost nightly. "She'd come to me and I'd ride with her," he says. It was as though with the sinking sun, the clouds would shape into Vikings, rising up over the horizon, "like a lot of rolls of smoke and fog — like they were riding out of the clouds, and I'd lay there and listen to the *clanging* of the swords — that sound of steel on steel . . ."

He fancied himself a collector of *things* and people as well as ideas. "I always had stuff that had to do with war. Like I had a First World War leather helmet and the goggles pushed up on it. I'd wear the goggles around, but it was always the helmet I was after. That came to me after I got out of reform school again, and was just goofing off and then I saw that what I always wanted was the war helmet. Later on in San Francisco I'd wear a top hat, and this was the extension of the helmet — like a war bonnet. I could feel myself in a helmet to be the shining warrior of the North — the great white warrior . . . the bringer of light.

"It wasn't anything that fancy at the time — the fancy stuff came later through Kenneth Anger, the filmmaker. But I can remember as a boy, and I told Kenneth this, that I got a big tin can like an old coffee can and

I shined it up and painted on it, made it intricately into a Viking helmet.

"I knew as a boy that I was a warrior. I would have the power and I would be above other things. I could live as I wanted to and I wouldn't have to account to anyone for my doings — my comings and goings. And everything I'd do would be right. I could do no wrong. It's like having this magic amulet — this magic helmet or wand, or a magic walking stick that would make one more powerful and there'd be no failing, or no doing wrong . . ."

Experimental filmmaker and writer Kenneth Anger, proclaimed a "warlock" by his peers, was presenting a Winter Solstice at a rented theater on Haight. One San Francisco reporter said, "They came from all over to attend. I saw faces from Hollywood and New York. A field day for the avant-garde. The Winter Solstice was offered in the true Aleister Crowley tradition."

Astrologer Robert Aiken recalls, "Kenneth was planning a new film which he was calling *Lucifer Rising*, and in a room that contained close to a thousand people milling around, he went straight through the gathering and stood in front of Bobby Beausoleil. He picked him out 'as though sight by destiny,' Anger would later claim, and stared at Bobby and said very loudly, 'You are *Lucifer!*'"

Seven

Though Bobby Beausoleil became the *Devil* in Kenneth Anger's film, his special notoriety was yet to come through Charlie Manson.

"The writing and the music that was coming out of me," Bobby says, "my thoughts and my energies were like concentric circles — expanding and shifting." He felt that it was as though someone could reach out and grab hold of his energies like you'd clutch at a handrail or a ring on a merry-go-round. His idea of music was not, he says, "governed by the rules of melody and time, handed down by stiff-collared composers of years past." No, for Bobby it had to be something quite different.

"I'd been interested in music from an early age. My ear was sharp," he says, "and I knew music as if by some inner balance. I could make up songs as easily as I'd steal."

Cut loose from reform school, Bobby "went with the wind, earning the name Lone Eagle," and he moved through the "underground movement" as a snake slides through grass.

Passing tourists who viewed the "Magic on Haight" through closed car windows, scoffed at the witches and warlocks in their multicolored robes or black sheaths, adorned with stars, talismans, amulets and "shields of secret seals." One such "spectacle" and soon-to-be friend of Beausoleil's, was a lean young man with sunken cheeks and shoulder-length hair called "Loomis." In a small leather sack that hung from his neck was "the silver ring of a witch burned at Salem."

"Manson and I have much in common," Loomis claimed. "There's no need to say it between us . . ."

Joe Brockman says, "I stayed with Loomis for about a week once and he told me he had things going with Charlie Manson. I said, 'Loomis, it sure don't show on you.' He said, real calm, 'The Devil is with us.' I said, 'I don't think so.' He smiled and said, 'Then it doesn't matter to you, you are the dealer, aren't you?' I said, 'That's right.' But dealing as I was, I got busted on a car theft thing. When they busted me I had no fear. I did have three or four tabs in my hand I was taking somewhere. I dropped them — swallowed — and I didn't start going up then. In jail I was up, up, up and away! I was so stoned that when they took me to court I was a giant sunbeam in there. They were all dead and downers and I was pure sunshine, just beaming. I spent a few days and kept seeing Charlie in my head, like his face saying something but it was a whisper, and I couldn't hear it. Back in court, I was still so stoned I wasn't tuned in to what they were doing with the papers and all that, with me and my case. But they dismissed it and then I was walking back on Haight and here comes Loomis. He saw me and gave a funny salute like he did, but his eyes were really serious. I said, 'Where's Charlie?' He smiled and said, and that was all he said, 'You see, dealer, we've been thinking about you.' And that blew my mind. I just said, 'Wow!'"

Loomis, who claimed to practice black magic, says: "Satan exists the same as God does and Christ. People who believe that Satan cannot exist are denying that God exists — denying that there's a day that follows the night. An atheist is just a materialist, someone that's on a bummer from birth to death. Just nothing. If you have a Ying and no Yang you've got zero, dig. You're isolated from nature. So long as Satan's there, there's the balance. Like Germany, look at the God-produced stuff, the great music and writers, artists . . . But on the other hand, the Nazis and concentration camps, the six million Jews. I mean, it's the same thing, Germans, Mexicans, English . . . You believe in life, you believe in death. You believe God, you believe in Satan, and they're all together, all one, like our bodies and this-here world. It is true that you are me and I am you and all that separates us is individual souls that are locked up inside our skins. There's no fucking difference. It's as plain as the nose on your face, and there is — there cannot be any real death, just getting into something else . . . Death is a figment of man's imagination," Loomis goes on. "It's a fraud perpetrated by the Establishment that's being driven in by greed, and that's what makes him nothing . . . Like acid. It's the real way to free yourself from the system and get in touch with what's happening, with what it means to be alive. Not that you want to escape, that big boogie word, from the system, but that you want to step back and look at it, see its flaws and how it's shot to shit with faults and is slowly killing anyone that's got something going. Now when you're up, if you go on a bummer it's only Satan trying to say something to you, and by denying him you're denying yourself. I mean, that's how Charlie and I'd rap. I say God, the idea of Jesus which is held as sacred by the Catholics is only a put-on. And they have killed his real way of reaching them by the fraud they're trying to sell, man, and because they deny the existence of the other side of the universe, which is Satan. And he lives fully, man, and he digs the whole scene. Just by being a criminal you become an acolyte in the Devil's parish, and I mean Manson," Loomis goes on, with a cryptic grin. "He was baptized in Hell . . . You swing one way or the other, and in plain truth, one is no more holier than the other. I mean, if you're a holy person, you're a holy person, and you do what you feel is right — I mean, it's up to the one on the other side of the fence to say it's wrong . . ."

Contrary to Loomis' theories on Satan, one California minister, George Peters, believes Satanism is a threat to modern society. He traveled through San Francisco, and had opened the doors of his Los Angeles parish as a shelter for hippies. He administered food, warmth and spiritual aid to hundreds who had "dropped out too far." Among these, he said he encountered hippies under hypnotic spells. "But the most alarming thing," the clergyman says, "is the Satanic mind power hypnosis. There are some people who have a fantastic, unbelievable mind power, and they are able to control the thoughts, emotions and motivations of an individual entirely and completely. I've talked with doctors and psychiatrists — to decide what to do with them."

Reverend Peters relates his own experiences with "those in possession of the Satanic power. They can sit down with two or three people, and in a minute they'll be under his control. It is like a total power. They'll do anything he wants. Get fifteen to twenty people together, this one person controlling them. We can't allow this to happen, the controlling of minds. What do we do with them? If you question a person with this power, he gets very angry. 'Isn't this a place of freedom? What am I doing wrong?' he asks. They don't want you to disturb the hold they have over others. So we get in and say, 'we want to talk to you.' But they don't want to be alone, won't meet you alone. They have to have someone with them.

They want to look you in the eye. 'Look me in the eye. If you don't, you're afraid. Look me in the eye . . .' So, they can get control of your eyes. Satanic hypnosis is not the Pat Collins Hypnosis, or any other sort of hypnosis used by doctors or laymen for any benefit. It is a mind communication. Thoughts are being imposed — someone they've never seen. Those who have been heavily on drugs like LSD, STP, mescaline and strongly in that, are the ones that are most receptive. They are ripe for capturing what they call vibes, sensitive to things unseen. It's a spiritual kind of power. These kids on drugs, they're already sensitive to vibes, so those with the Satan mind thing can send vibes into these people and capture their minds. Say, 'He's talking to my head.' They may not talk. Just look at them, maybe thirty minutes to an hour, then when they walk out everyone else walks out with them. I have seen this, one person taking everyone with them like a shepherd."

In time, the Reverend would say that he feared the idea that Robert Beausoleil and Manson could be glamorized into cult status. "The followers," he says, "the true believers — they simply get in line . . ."

Kenneth Anger said that he was working on his "masterpiece," *Lucifer Rising*. Bobby says, "He fancied himself to be skilled and proficient in the black arts — and had this contact with this group called 'The Process.' This was part of the group that swiped the Aleister Crowley materials and occult ropes and supplies . . .

"Everything had to do with homosexual themes," Bobby says. "Kenneth began showering me with gifts. He told me, 'You will become the beloved and through me you will rise to be feared and held in reverence.' He said I'd be remembered for generations. I said it sounded okay to me . . ."

Bobby had written a long narrative poem, his *Wanderings thru Frisco*, about his attempts to put together a rock group — playing with makeshift and spur-of-the-moment combos and "no-talents." He "designed" in his mind what he wanted to do — a group made up with the idea of blending "maybe two — maybe many types of sounds and music to create a new, weird, free-styled music — to hear it as a *clanging*, a clutter of banging noises and weeping and moaning, and all exploding out at the same time . . . I walked around Frisco with the sounds in my head, going around and around — I got so I could pinpoint every second of it."

With several other "junior rock players," Bobby staged a concert at the Glide Memorial Church along with the Sexual Freedom League.

"I'd been living with two guys in a warehouse," Bobby says. "An old abandoned place with two other artists, and we were coming up with some sort of money to keep from getting kicked out. I kept trying to get some action going, form a group of musicians. I'd lettered and plastered posters all over the Haight area, announcements for auditions, for any sort of musicians looking to join up with a group. The idea was to form an orchestra, cut a record and move ahead with it into the commercial business.

"Finally we put together an eighteen piece orchestra. I called it Orkustra — an All Electric Jazz Band, and we opened at a place in Berkeley. Gerald Wilson composed some of the music and arranged it, and worked with the group. I had the idea of making an album for the Pacific label — *The Golden Sword.*

"I had this image in my mind of a sword — like it's pictured on the cover of a book called *Imperium,* by a guy the FBI was hounding and busted into infinity . . . a hated and feared man by the name of Francis Yockey. He wrote that book under the name of Ulick Varange, a pen name. It was a big book and I read it a lot — studied it and tried to make as much of it as I could — but my course was different. There was something about it — some passive idea that kept me put off by it. I finally would come to believe that *I* was a man of action, I had to go *through* things no matter what they were or how dangerous they may have seemed to someone on the outside.

"It was the same with the music . . . We were close, real close, but the orchestra fell apart, and out of this came the Bedrock One, a five-piece group and we screamed impromptu music at the hippie happenings and clubs, and around the Haight area — that's how we were working at the Glide Memorial along with the Sexual Freedom League.

"We played behind a scrim, had about ten girls from around the Haight as belly dancers, if you could call them that — but it was okay, and they wore clothes and stuff and outfits made up for the show — some of the costumes were rented, some swiped, and some I designed and had made up with a couple of local dressmakers who were into doing shit for the hippies. The purpose of the show was for audience participation, to get everyone wild and to take off their clothes and start screwing — right there where they were, screwing in the aisles, on the seats, man, and wherever they could get it in . . .

"One young girl is raped on the altar of the church. I was leading the music, the Bedrock One, but I was more taken in with the idea of raping the altar than the girl being raped on it.

"It was a fiasco — lights blew up, the tape started breaking . . . No sooner was I finished with this disaster than this other young girl has been pregnant, and had a child she says is mine. I said, 'Okay, that's fine — it's fine to have a child, but the Lone Eagle stays in no one place for very long at a time.'"

Kenneth Anger asked Bobby to come to his house. "It was an old ornate Victorian place that'd been a Russian Embassy, and Anger had it converted into a sort of sorcerer's temple with all this magician regalia. There was this young handsome boy living with Kenneth, but when I got there, Kenneth told him, '*This* is Lucifer,' and he kicked the kid out. Kenneth then told me, 'You have to move into this temple and take your rightly place immediately — as you see,' he said, 'I've made room for you.' It was all necessary, he told me, so I could be the central figure in his masterpiece."

The filmmaker had special powers, Bobby says. He had strange, uncanny intuition, and he had a brilliant mind. "First he gave me this special gift," Bobby says, "a walking stick, a fist clenched for a handle with snakes carved up the sides and between the fist. This was one of the things that had belonged to Aleister Crowley, and had been stolen from the Crowley materials at an exhibit.

"To me, Devil-worship was a lot of shit. The friends Kenneth Anger had were weak, they were fakes to me, like if you decorated yourself with a lot feathers and paraded around telling everyone you were this fucking giant bird, so you have these creeps thinking you look good, so it makes you feel good — like you *look* good, but try to *fly*, man, and you do a crash right on your head. It was shit, to me, until I started heavily into the acid trips. This was pure acid — the Owsley Special tabs — that Kenneth had scored by the pocketfuls."

This was how it started, Bobby says, the metamorphosis of Bobby Beausoleil — from Lone Eagle, into the Angel of Disobedience. Into a devil. All that Kenneth saw in his head was later to be proven in fact. "Now, whether this was suggestion," as Bobby puts it, "or the *real* power of hypnosis, it makes a point, but still there was all this material to begin with which, in my case, was rolling faster as time went on. I was already a thief and an outlaw, and I had contempt for the world.

"Kenneth brought it all to a head. He made me the star of *Lucifer Rising*, and I *was* rising, and he made me believe that I had this power inside of me and that it radiated out of me.

"Maybe he was right — the movie and who I was were fused together. He was projecting me as the *angel of disobedience*, and this was the turning point in my life . . ."

He used purple, Bobby says. "This powerful color — this iridescent, vibrating purple. The walls were purple, contrasting with orange like the ceiling or the floor or the baseboard. This house had high vaulted ceilings with orange carvings, and each was painted a different vibrating color, every strip of woodwork would shimmer and vibrate. There was this psychological use of color as a disorienting factor. It *was* a sorcerer's temple, and what Kenneth was doing to my head, worshipping me as an evil god . . .

"Each acid trip became more and more an earth-shattering experience," Bobby says. "I was *experiencing* Lucifer, 'the angel on earth.' I believed that during the rituals, Kenneth was showing me myself, that this reflection of who I was and what I was doing was because of who *I* was, not that Kenneth was *making* me this, and here I could assume the role, in this ornate environment with its flashing colors, scrolls, fancy filigree, symbols — weird, *weird*, amulets, talismans, voodoo things, golden cat's heads, giant eyes, magic drawings, silver cocks and a human skull . . ."

"I remember the bathroom — orange, this bathroom. I was naked. I had this multicolored towel pressed to my face and I went into another room with all this purple in my head. The colors of the towel came alive.

"There was this altar bed in an alcove, closed in with these blue velvet curtains, drapes of velvet and flowing robes of color. I was on the altar bed naked and receiving great cosmic jolts. Everything around me was swimming on fire. I could hear Kenneth chanting magical words, and the sounds of his preparations as he read from the Crowley book. He was doing the *Invocation of My Demon Brother*, with all the fires of hell surrounding me. When the fires were pouring up over me, suddenly a great shaft of light above drove down and penetrated my chest. It kept pouring over me, this great shaft of white light. It was changing me. I died.

48

"It became everything, and I was like obsessed, experiencing all there was — all the blood and the killing, I was being killed. I was swimming in all death and destruction . . .

"I could hear the fires around me, raging, I was covered with this cape of blood. There were a million moving things — all the death and destruction. It was in my mind, in the environment. The voice of the magician kept on, and each word he said was the crackling of fire.

"I had no fear. There was no fear in me as I went through the most horrible deaths in the world. There was no fear, I knew I was the Devil . . .

"I was being born into all the events of my life — everything that had been was dead, and I was being reborn, being baptized by the tongues of fire. Great demon eyes were glowing above me, huge, vacant, no fear in those eyes. I was complete, all was complete, there was a great shattering completeness in the cosmic forces . . . And born into this Flash Gordon world, there was *I* — wielding the great golden sword of the Vikings."

Eight

From that point on, Bobby says, "Kenneth Anger was taking pictures of me — filming me in *Lucifer Rising* — the Birth of Aquarius." Everything he did, he says, was "automatic — in tune with the Devil's energy."

The first music group he put together after his relationship with Kenneth Anger began was called The Magik Powerhouse of Oz, formed to do the soundtrack for *Lucifer Rising*. "We were more insane than the other group. It was supposed to represent all the howling, the shrieking music from the pit of madness — each sound to represent elements like fire, wind, a baby crying, dogs howling, crazy laughter . . . And I was death. I was on the throne wearing the crown of death."

The blade was in his hand — that Viking sword. He was prepared to do the Devil's bidding.

But things were falling apart. The same energy vibrating through Bobby's body was no longer being mirrored on the streets. The legend of Haight-Ashbury was disappearing with each day, like smoke following a fired gun. "Christmas of that year," Joe Brockman says, "was a mess. Most of the people I hung around with, except Charlie Manson and some of them, were either in jail or had headed somewhere else. I woke up Christmas on a bad trip in a cellar with rats and stinking pipes all around me . . ."

It was over. The San Francisco City Supervisor made an announcement: "The real hippies of last summer are gone." And *Time* magazine was saying, "Love has fled the Hashbury."

Claiming he could see the collapse of Haight before it came, Charlie Manson says, "Being in jail so long as I had, it had left my awareness fairly well opened to what was coming, to what was going on around me and with the people I knew, those close to me. So I'd seen the bad things that were coming into Haight, the wild problems and the people all around me getting bugged and harassed in the doors of their own places. And there were all the problems on the streets. Wherever we gathered, the policemen were coming with their sticks and their guns and their badges, and they were running the kids up and down the streets like cattle being chased. It was chaos. Everywhere we walked, or tried to go to the parks, every time we tried to sit somewhere and talk or just sit and be and play music, the Man was there, breaking it up with his sticks, his guns, his badges, and he was there, he was everywhere . . ."

Manson and his group of followers left San Francisco on April 12, 1968. During the year on Haight, an "admirer" had given Manson a piano on which he composed many of his songs. Later he traded the piano for a camper and this, in turn, he used as partial trade on an old green and white school bus converted to include makeshift living quarters.

Joe recalls, "Charlie said that's what he wanted. I'd looked around, even over in Oakland, but I saw this bus on Turk Street. The thing was for sale and the owner was in Sacramento somewhere. They had it stored in the garage."

Manson says, "We got ahold of the school bus and I just wanted to get moving, to travel around. A road is the best place to be on . . . Just keep moving from one place to the next with nothing else in mind but just going on the road. I asked everybody around who wanted to go. I said, 'Anybody wants to go can pile in the school bus. We got plenty of room — we can eat and sleep and do our thing in here. Like it's not mine. This bus belongs to everybody, to anyone. Look, we'll put the pink slip right here in the glove compartment and that way the bus doesn't belong to anyone, dig, because the bus will belong to itself.' So what we did, we just turned off our minds and got the hell out of there. We traveled, just going around looking for a place to get away from the Man . . ."

Susan Atkins, one of the first to board the bus, explains, "There were four girls, one was Patricia Krenwinkel who I knew as Katie, and there was myself, along with three or four males. Just some of the men that came along, and we started traveling south."

Joe says, "They were all singing. Just going along singing songs Charlie'd put together." The bus was rolling and where it would end up none of them knew. "Pretty soon," Joe adds, "I was singing too."

51

One girl, Marie, was pregnant and slept through the first part of the journey, then took over the driving.

Another, known as "Skip," kept her face close to the window, staring at massive trees that seemed to pass by in "giant bundles of green gauze." She'd planned on being a poet and had majored in English literature at a junior college in Torrance, California. But in the middle of it, Skip recalls, "I split for the Haight. I got there, I was very straight, lived in a hotel. I even got a job in a furniture store which gave me a grubstake . . . But I was afraid of being alone. I was afraid of everything."

She got into the hippie scene, stayed with some other girls she'd met there and together they set up housekeeping. "We'd gone to the woods up in Mendocino and lived in a cabin there. We never messed around with speed, just acid and grass. What happened was that I lost all track of time. It just ceased to exist . . ."

She was on the old bus singing songs that Charlie'd dreamed up, stopping at nights to build a fire, then singing around the warmth. Part of a poem she wrote on the bus: "The nights reveal the whole universe in motion before your eyes — the magic of infinite pictures in multicolored dots — pin-prickly, thickly visual sensations that set you to laughing to image-making and then to drifting — to sleep with your mind projected, afloat in full emptiness . . ."

For Manson, "It was just a trip . . . When your mind is free there is really nowhere to go, and nowhere to be coming from, just grooving on the road because the road seemed to be the only place where you can be free when you're moving from one spot to another. I wanted to be able to breathe, just breathe! On the road like that you have the freedom of your movements to take a breath. There was nowhere to go. We were already there; but everywhere we went we kept running into the Man and the cops. We traveled to Seattle, Washington, and there was problems with the cops there. We went down into Texas and into New Mexico, too, and it didn't seem to matter where we went, the Man was everywhere . . ."

The girl Susan knew as Katie was to stay the duration of the "trip." Katie's parents were divorced. She had graduated from University High School in Los Angeles, then went to live with her mother in Mobile, Alabama. For a short time she attended Spring Hill, a small Catholic college in Mobile, then she returned to California and got a job as a file clerk.

"Until she met Manson she was a stable, conservative young woman," the father, an insurance agent, said. She met Manson one afternoon during her lunch hour. She boarded a bus with him, abandoned her own car in a parking lot, and did not even return to work to pick up her paycheck. Her father says, "She seemed to have vanished . . ."

Two weeks later, he received a letter from his daughter, postmarked Seattle. Katie wrote, "I have to be away from all of it . . . I am going to find myself."

She had found Manson and felt, as Skip said, that "he is magnetic. His motions were like magic. It seemed he gave off a lot of magic. Everyone was always so happy around him. But he was sort of changing. He seemed to change every time I saw him. He seemed ageless."

Katie's father was able to contact his daughter once again. He received a call from his former wife who related that Katie had called her and wanted $100. The mother gave him an address for their daughter in Sacramento, and he was able to reach Katie. He told her he would send a ticket for her to get back to her mother. "She said no, she wanted the money," he remembers. "I said I wouldn't send any." He was "convinced" Manson was "some kind of hypnotist. It was all so spontaneous." A long time would pass before he would hear from his daughter again.

The bus continued on its uncharted journey. But everywhere they stopped they were confronted with "the Man."

Susan says, "We traveled on and off for a long time . . . We went all up and down the coast to California, to New Mexico and Arizona, and then to Nevada . . ."

Joe says, "I lost about seventeen pounds. It might've been more. It all had started out as a fast, going on a fast. I felt better at first but then the fasting just went on and on, and then the people on the bus would get off and some others would get on. We had babies and dogs and a goat once. We picked up hitchhikers. Mostly young girls would get on . . . They'd stay for the ride or wherever we were heading. We'd ball at nights on the grass or just sleep on the hillsides.

"But the bus kept breaking down, and Charlie and me would be under it, doing things. He was really very mechanical, able to figure out right away what was wrong, almost by intuition. And if we couldn't fix it right off we'd just sit in the grass or fool around. Pretty soon someone would come along and be able to fix it up. Usually truck drivers. You could tell they figured we were creeps, that's what they thought. But I guess the

Man had told them, 'If you see any dirty hippies along the road, get 'em moving as far over the county line as you can!'

"I'd begun now to believe completely in Charlie. It came especially when the transmission seemed to sort of plop down out of the bus, and we were really stranded. I think it was somewhere in New Mexico. Susan had left with some guy — oh, that was after Marie had had her baby. Charlie delivered the baby himself, but Susan had helped and all . . ."

Susan would later say, "He didn't actually deliver Marie's baby, I did, and the baby was born breech birth but in perfect health."

Joe went on, "It was after the baby, and we hung up there with the bus. Charlie told me, 'Put it in your head that we'll be moving soon. See it right before your eyes that a guy's going to come along and he'll be able to get us moving — he'll have the tools.' So I sat on this big rock, smoking some grass, and waiting for the guy with the tools. What happened was the guy with the tools came along about sundown . . ."

Susan became pregnant in New Mexico. It was not by Charlie, but by the man she'd met and spent the day with.

"We were all called Charlie's girls," she explains. "But Charlie often told us, in fact every day he told us, 'You people do not belong to me, you belong to yourself.' But I personally thought that I belonged to Charlie. He had sexual intercourse with all of us girls. In the beginning I was jealous until I came to an understanding that he was only making love to the girls for the purpose of love and also to give them back to themselves. We — the girls — had sexual relations with each other. There was no limit to what I'd do for him. I was in love with the reflection and the reflection I speak of is Charlie Manson."

All of the girls were in love with Charlie, Susan believed, and they tried to prove themselves to him, though Susan says she cannot speak for the others.

"I did attempt to prove myself to Charlie and every time he would see me trying to prove myself to him he would say, 'You don't have to prove yourself to me. You don't even have to prove yourself to you . . .' They all did what Charlie wanted them to do, but if we didn't it's because we didn't want to . . ." Susan admits, however, that she did whatever Charlie wanted, because "Charlie is the only man that I have ever met — I'm not taking away from any other man — on the face of this earth, the only man that I ever met that is a complete man. He will not take any back talk from a woman. He will not let a woman talk him into doing anything. He is a man . . . He has more love to give to the world than anybody I have ever met. He would give himself completely to anybody."

In a small beach town south of Santa Barbara, Joe met an old friend, then traveling with a motorcycle group. He recalls his friend couldn't recognize him, was puzzled over his appearance and at moments thought he was "crazy."

Remembering the day, Joe says, "There was this hamburger stand and he was there with some bikers, he had a chopped Triumph. Right away I put it on him for some grass or acid, even some pills if he had any. He said he had grass up the beach, so we rode. Charlie was getting himself strung out behind one of the other bikes, oh, I think it was a Harley, all chrome, and we went up the beach a ways. When he got back with the grass the girls were painting the bus. They had black paint, everybody was splashing it on the bus, the bikers were helping them . . ."

The trip was being financed then on the credit cards Katie had brought with her — but how far were they going to go? How long was it going to last? These questions were not asked — it was completely up to Charlie.

"Why did they all do what he wanted? We had all left our old selves," Joe says. "I never thought about my old man or the rest. Oh, maybe a passing thought but — like Charlie said, 'It doesn't originate from where you're at, at the time you have thought. It's reflex to vibes in the air.' My head was clear and I was to the point where Charlie said he was, no thinking, no thoughts about what was happening. Charlie gave me to myself — whoever I was . . . It was happening and we were happening. I mean, out in the hills, I reach my hand out to pick a leaf or some berries, and I am my hand. There was nothing else to get in the way. And there were some times when we were all together that we didn't say anything or even talk to one another, I mean, *about* ourselves or what we were doing. It was, in all senses, that we were one big body together. And when I'd think of something funny, or when it would occur to me, something funny, I'd laugh and everyone else would laugh, and it wasn't just a catching-on laugh, because they *knew* what was funny and it was funny and it was funny for everybody. Shit, there were some times when I felt that *nothing* in the world could bother us, get in on our thing. Nothing could affect us because we were real and outside of us was not real . . ."

It all seemed vaguely *clear* to Joe. But there was nothing vague in Manson's ideas — he had rejected the "outside" world and was now making one of his own — even collecting inmates.

The bus was on the road again before the black paint was dry. Joe says the paint "looked like a weird velvet, with the dust and stuff blown up from the other cars on the road all stuck to the bus . . . I was very stoned and Charlie was singing. I looked around and saw some bikes following us and behind them, maybe a half mile, was the cops. They didn't have their lights going. We'd smoked all the grass so there was nothing to find. Just checking it out. Everywhere we'd been the cops checked it out — paranoid bastards."

Later, the right rear wheels of the bus sank into the soft shoulder in a weed patch south of Oxnard, California. The bus was out of gas, but even with gas the bus would have to be towed out of the slope. Instead of "sweating the situation," the group camped off the road.

"It was nice country," Joe recalls. "Charlie and I and Marie hiked about a mile. We found berries and stuff and took them back. As we were going back, I remember Charlie was smiling and he said, 'I'm going to cut a record in Los Angeles,' just like that. By then anything Charlie said to me made a lot of sense.

"We found a small snake and Charlie picked it up. He kissed it on its face, then he handed it to me. I kissed it, too, and then put it inside my shirt so it could get warm on my skin.

"The next day, I was sleeping with a girl in the shade behind the bus, and I guess the others were out and around. A big fat foot was pushing my leg and I looked up. Wow, it was the Man. The chick sort of yelped and put something over her tits. The Man in his big sunglasses got me up and against the bus, checking in my shoes and around my balls. I told him, 'There ain't nothing there but what ain't my personal property.' He said, 'Shut your mouth, scum.'"

The bus was listed on the sheriff's records as stolen, so Manson was arrested on the spot. Marie was charged with endangering the life of her baby, others were held for disorderly conduct. But few were charged officially. Joe said his name was "Tim Leary." Both Charlie and Susan were fined ten dollars each for possessing a fake driver's license. The sheriffs learned the bus had been recovered and resold, and then Charlie was released. Marie's baby was returned to her and everyone was warned to clear out of

Ventura County.

Joe says, "Before we left town, Charlie and I scrounged up two orange crates of grub, and after the sheriff's boys got us out of the ditch, we drove across the county line and stopped again. We made a big fire out near the beach and sang around it, and I put a lot of potatoes in the sand, under the fire. We roasted marshmallows, too."

Sometime later near Los Angeles the bus broke down in the Topanga Canyon area where more than a hundred "hippie squatters" had spread throughout the hills.

About that time, astrologer and actor Robert Aiken was working on a movie shooting in the hills and washes of Topanga. "It was a period picture," Aiken says, "and I was playing the part of an Indian Chief's son. The hills all around where we were filming were spotted with the hippie tents and rundown shacks.

The movie's assistant director had found some well-made tents and wanted to know where he could get some for use in the picture.

"It turned out," Aiken recalls, "the tents had been made by Beausoleil," the "Beautiful Sun" that Kenneth Anger had earlier picked for the role of Lucifer. "'Let's find him,' the director said. 'He can make some tents for us . . .'

"Beausoleil," Aiken says, "was living then in one of his tents with four young girls he said were his wives. He had two dogs, and a large hawk that perched on his shoulders."

As well as putting up tents for props, Beausoleil was hired to play the part of an Indian. The astrologer met him on a hillside that afternoon. "He stood there bare-chested with that big hawk on his shoulder," he recalls. "Its eyes were everywhere and it kept making wary sounds in its throat and ruffling out its wings."

To the astrologer, Beausoleil appeared as a *real* Indian. "He had an old truck which we talked about. He was making repairs on it and planning a trip somewhere, like far away, an excursion. He reminded me of a boyhood friend I had. We'd conjured up all sorts of fantasies like going off in buckskins into dangerous everglades. We'd always wear dungarees, never dress-up pants . . ."

Aiken recalls that Beausoleil needed money and wanted to sell him one of his tents, an especially good one. "The wood was like honed by his hands, but I had nowhere to put the tent, no way to haul it.

"'If the truck was going,' Beausoleil said to me, 'I could take it for you.' He was carving off branches to make a heavy stake. I always think of the knife he had," Aiken says, "A big bowie kind of knife with a hawk or firebird head on it — and he was in constant motion, his hands, feeling wood, testing the agility of branches, constructing things — a young man of outdoor action. But there was no role playing, no role. He was real. A primitiveness hard to describe and impossible to overlook. The girls with him were short, nameless types, like nymphs one would expect to find deep in the woods."

During Beausoleil's stint in the film he had sexual relations with one of the leading ladies and three of his wives disappeared into the hills, Aiken says. "It didn't seem to matter to Beausoleil. He had his dogs, his hawk, and his knife. He was the kind of man that could be stripped and thrown in the desert to perish, but by nightfall he'd be squatting in front of a handsome tent he'd built, dressed in buckskin and roasting fresh game over an open fire. He'd be content, having totally accepted his predicament as a way of life."

Though Aiken says Beausoleil was reluctant to discuss his past, he believed he got to know him as well as one could. "We talked at length about the Lucifer movie, the only other film that he'd been in, in which he'd played the Devil."

A film director friend of Aiken's had been a colleague of Anger's for twenty years. The astrologer suggested they get together, and a few days later the three met at a cafe in Hollywood and talked about *Lucifer Rising*.

"Beausoleil told us that Kenneth had stopped shooting the picture for some reasons, and during that time the footage, most of it, was stolen. He said he did not see Anger after that, as he [Beausoleil] left San Francisco with some friends. They just traveled around for awhile, and then he sort of settled in the Topanga area, built tents and was happy."

"Lucifer or not," Bobby says, "things had gone dead on the Haight and I had to be wandering again. I'd gotten involved with a thirteen-year-old girl named Cassandra who'd been attached to Anton LaVey's Satanic Church movement, and she was a regular on *my* altar as well as others . . ." Bobby claims she became pregnant, had his child, but having once been Lone Eagle, he took wing again. But not without some sketch of a plan.

"During a fiasco at the Straight Theater in the midst of the Equinox Show, I met another guy named Kenneth — this one named Kendall, an artist down in Hollywood and brother of a talent agent. This Kendall kept staring at me and then he proposed the idea that he was interested in painting a portrait of me whenever I managed to get down to L.A. So I had that in the back of my mind — a place to crash . . .

"I'd acquired an old Studebaker that had half the body sawed away and a sort of Hansel and Gretel gingerbread house built onto the rear section of the car." With this "cottage" stuffed with stolen musical equipment, lights, props, and cans of film from Kenneth Anger, and after a flop music tour of Berkeley with a new-formed "Devil's Band," Bobby drove out of San Francisco, heading south.

He wound up at Kenneth Kendall's house in West Hollywood, bringing with him two girls he'd picked up on the trip. Bobby stacked his loot and booty into a small shed to the rear of Kendall's studio, but seemed disinterested in the artist, and the portrait Kendall wanted to paint.

"But he agreed to it," Kendall says, "for the storage space and the use of a cot in another room. I never saw anyone in my life with such dirty fingernails," the artist says. "Bobby was restless, rude — surly — an untidy, arrogant child. He refused to sit still as I tried to paint a picture of him. He was too busy carving a death's head pipe in which he smoked enormous amounts of grass — marijuana. I could not get him to concentrate on remaining still for any length of time at all. Finally, he was too bored or busy with the silly girls to show up for the portrait, so I abandoned it.

"He stayed for a short time — sleeping on that army cot, and littered like an animal. He slept in his clothes and didn't bathe at all. Here is a young man gifted with an incredible handsomeness, and obviously of many talents, who seemed to have no interest whatsoever in what was happening in the real world . . . I knew he was a thief, and I worried about asking them to leave. Luckily, after a time, he took off with one of the girls. He left the other one behind as you'd forget something, and *I* didn't have any qualms about asking her to leave.

"Along with that girl, he did leave behind some of the things he'd stolen from Kenneth Anger, but the rest of it he either hocked or simply threw away — with an apparent, incredible indifference to the value of anything. It was very hard to tell — but he seemed to treat people the same way he treated objects he no longer had a use for, or that were simply too

59

burdensome to carry any further."

Next stop for Bobby was the offered sanctuary of the basement of Gary Hinman's house in Topanga Canyon.

According to Joe Brockman, "This guy Hinman was a straight dude, an Establishment person with a nice pad on Canyon Road. He was letting hippies stay there until they got themselves squared around. Hinman was a Buddhist, and into the Eastern religion stuff — the incense and crap, and into music and had all these Zen ideas that hippies were trying to get into their heads. He was okay — maybe a little *queer*, you know, and he liked to rap, and he could talk and talk and he was an easy guy to talk to . . ."

A week or so of freeloading at Hinman's, and then Bobby bummed his way down the canyon and wound up at a house in Malibu, "shacking on a woman's sofa and screwing her until I could scrape together enough bread to head north again. I knew I could put together another group — another band — maybe calling it the Zen-Bones Band, and make the rounds of Berkeley . . .

"Three — maybe four days or so," Bobby says, "and a few of these girls came around with this little guy who's Charlie Manson. One of the girls with this Manson is a girl I was sleeping with up at Hinman's. She was all over me again, and I was wondering what the situation was with this Manson, who said he was a musician and song writer. That, of course, made us click right away, and we talked music. I talked about the groups in the Bay area and we hit it off because he'd been on the Haight at the same time. I couldn't remember seeing him around but we'd run across the same people, and the same places.

"And yet," Bobby says, "there was something that just didn't fit together between us. Call it a clashing of wills — maybe it was always to be that way — a clashing of personalities. But in other ways we got along fantastically, even with that certain friction that was at the bottom of us getting together . . .

"The girls had told him about Gary Hinman kicking me out, and Charlie wanted me to come along with him since they were going on the road with a lot of girls, and we could talk about music, do something together about getting some recordings made.

"I said no, I had other things to do — I didn't travel with anybody. I could see Charlie liked that, even though it was clear he wanted more people to hang around him. But our relationship right from the start was what you might call 'open-ended.' And right from the start I was sure something going to be coming down. If we merged the two personalities, I knew, and so did he with that way he knew things, that we'd indeed raise hell on earth . . ."

Nine

Before hooking up with Charlie for the "helter-skelter express," Bobby made it to a club in Berkeley called the New Orleans House, staged a flop performance, then trekked north "to a sort of hippie ranch" near Napa. He says he'd sometimes sit for hours on a porch playing conga drums to the sun.

"It was the pure peasant life," he says. "Goats — milking the goats, drinking wine, we'd make earth music. Everything could be shrugged off except what there was to feed the instincts . . .

"We were a band of gypsies. There were dogs, birds . . . I rescued a hawk from a cage and it became a part of my life. I had three girls there and a cabin in the redwoods. Who the fuck could ask for more?

"There were always small matters, like check forgery, thefts, things like that — small crimes to keep a true gypsy life in Napa, plus the cops were looking for some of us. The people that ran this ranch were the same ones that owned the New Orleans House in Berkeley — and with the heat, cops being around, they asked us to move on."

Often, Bobby felt himself losing track of where he was — of where he was heading, where he'd come from. "I had to keep reminding myself I was heading where I was going —" which meant he'd put up a sail and the wind would fill it and he'd lean over the prow of himself, "watching for what was to come."

Drifting through Mendocino, a few girls there, "a few more over here . . ." Again through San Francisco, one particular girl he met seemed to connect to Bobby, she laughed and smiled and he laughed with her, "even though we didn't have a penny to pass between us . . ."

Her name was Leslie. They slept in an abandoned, burnt-out bus and brought another girl aboard. The girl he'd gathered in as his own — Leslie — claims that Bobby had the most beautiful face of any man she'd ever seen. "He was an angel," she says, "and I told him I would love him forever." She told Bobby, "I'll go anywhere in the world with you."

He said, "Would you come to hell with me?"

"Take me," she said to him.

Her last name was Van Houten, her parents were divorced, and she had one older brother. Her father was an auctioneer, her mother a school teacher. Like Susan Atkins, Leslie had been active in the church and a regular member of the choir. She'd been a girl scout and attended schools in Monrovia where she proved herself an above-average student, graduating in 1967 from Monrovia High. Her parents led active lives in the Village Presbyterian Church and were well-known for their work with the Parent Teachers Association.

The house Leslie grew up in was typical of the neat middle-class neighborhood, and each Christmas the front of the house was trimmed cheerfully with lights. Several years before, her parents had adopted two Korean orphans, a boy and a girl, to live with them. After Leslie graduated high school, she planned on becoming a nun, "more drawn," she later put it, "to the mysticism of Catholicism than to the Protestant way . . ." Then she met two hippie girls who shared their dope with Leslie, and the three ambled north to San Francisco and into the Haight scene.

Then she met Bobby Beausoleil. "I had about six girls with me by the time we got back up to Mendocino from San Francisco," he says, "and I played music around the area. Leslie had come up with us — I hadn't made love to her until we got up to Mendocino. We hadn't had sex on that old bus, nor did we on the way north of the city. I wore a top hat, and I had become Sir Hokus — a wandering minstrel, singing my songs and poems for a few coins . . .

"Leslie and I made love on acid. It was a tremendous experience. I was dressed in a Confederate soldier uniform. I had a sword. I had come back from the war — I was making love to Leslie and making love to all the women — making love to all of them is like making love to one woman."

From Mendocino, Bobby's band of gypsies flopped into a couple of hippie halfway houses in the Santa Cruz area. But by now, Bobby was using different disguises to keep one jump ahead of the law. "I wound up with a truck, an old beat-up that had been passed back and forth between dope deals, and I managed to trade it for a school bus. With Leslie and a couple of the other girls, we headed south out of Santa Cruz . . ."

Within days, Bobby traded the school bus for an old army weapons truck. He made a large bed in the back of the converted camper section and began to live alongside the railway tracks, "eating whatever we could," he says. "We were gypsies. I got good at stealing food from people's yards. I stole a sheep and I killed it and butchered it for us, and we roasted it over a fire — a few fires over a few days, and full of the lamb, we went on. Living alongside the railway tracks kept taking me back to my childhood. I kept thinking about that big old grey house I'd lived in by the tracks. The second house I lived in when I was a kid had a wooden — a board floor in the garage. I lost a frog in there, it went down into the boards. I used to sneak through holes in the fence to play with the little girls across the yard . . . One of them used to show me her pussy."

The wind was rising again for Bobby, and the sail climbed up — catching the motion. "The road just kept rolling south," he says, as his band of thieves and gypsies roamed southward along the edge of the ocean. "A few days maybe, and we were climbing right away from the coast and up into the hills of Topanga Canyon . . ."

A week? Maybe less — maybe more. Bobby was looking to steal something in a shopping center. "I see these girls running around — these were the ones that had been with Charlie Manson, and the one in particular that had come to Malibu that time. One of them was going back to Gary Hinman's house, and I said, sure, I'd tag along.

"They wanted me along with the other males — punks, is what these guys were. These girls could tell them what to do — like go sleep with the other men and we'll call you when we need something — go chop wood or fetch this, get something to eat for us . . .

"I wasn't about to do what any woman told me to do. My mother and I never got along. She had me declared incorrigible and every woman was the same as that. I never listened to a word she'd say, nothing anyone would say. It was her that had turned on me . . . It's a man's world but a woman's society, and that's what's the matter with society."

Bobby and his small band continued to squat in Topanga. He roamed free in the hills, surviving as "a man of the mountains," holding court over a small cluster of hippies squatting alongside their tents, until he met Robert Aiken, and managed to get some work through the movie production company.

"We had some interesting talks," Aiken says. "On another occasion, I accompanied Beausoleil and the director of the Topanga film to a friend's apartment in Beverly Hills. The minute Beausoleil saw the pool, he said, like a child, 'Oh, boy, a pool! That means I can swim —' and he threw off his clothes as he hurried outside to the water.

"When he was finished swimming, he and the director sat in the apartment and talked about Scientology until dawn. Bobby talked about a guy he knew named Charlie Manson, who was like 'a holy man,' and whose head was totally tuned in to Scientology. It was morning and the director was completely exhausted, but Bobby was fresh and ready to put in a good day's work.

"I could never imagine Beausoleil as being ordinary," Aiken says, "or normal, in any regular sense. He was apart from the main wheels of society. Perhaps that was what Kenneth Anger's perceptive eye had caught instantly . . .

"The movie in Topanga ended and we, the small crew, dismantled the property. When we left, Beausoleil was sad, sort of. It had been his ground that we'd stayed on, and he'd been very happy with all the activity . . .'

It was late June, the astrologer recalls. "Beausoleil had plans but the putting of them into action seemed distant. He didn't want to go down on the Strip where they'd call him 'Bummer Bob.' He was satisfied, he said, to stay in the tents in the woods with the hippies. But he was like being eaten up by the desire to move on — it was like a tide that was pulling at him. I could sense that there was nothing in the world that was going to hold him — except a steel cage . . .

"He had a lot of close people around there and he seemed to be waiting, like for a command or something to come out of the blue."

Bobby says, "It was in the air — like a storm kicking up. Ever since meeting Charlie Manson and feeling that kind of brotherhood between but all that fire and friction between us as well, it spelled something was going to be going down. When I used to say that blood was going to run, I now knew exactly what I was saying by that . . ."

Ten

"Helter-skelter is what it was," says Joe. "Charlie was all over like a queen bee, buzzing all around. He was changing, I should say it was more like a fever with his music ideas. He told us in the bus, 'You're all a part of it, we are going to have what there is . . .' But the only action I saw was his hanging around with music people. He was staying in a house on the hill. Some of us slept on the bus. Many that had come along — and then there were others there in the wash — and a lot had scattered around the hills, too.

"Charlie would have maybe half a dozen of the girls, all running around naked up there, and he would give them to guys to ball or whatever, and he'd give them around like that, pass them out to people he figured could get him into the music business. I wasn't doing much then because I wasn't feeling good, and when Charlie asked me to move up into this house he was staying in, I passed on it. I'd already been in this shack up behind the little shopping center in Topanga, with these girls and a couple of guys, and they weren't close or anything with Charlie. He'd gotten to know a guy named Gary Hinman, who was going to get something going, something to do with the music — that's what Charlie told me. Pretty soon he moved into Hinman's pad with some of the girls, I think a couple of the guys, too . . . The people I was with were on speed and after a week or so I was pretty sick. It was in my chest, and they took me to the General Hospital. They told me I was getting tuberculosis and had to stay there."

Manson remained at Hinman's house on the Canyon Road. Hinman was an active member of Nichiren Shoshu, a non-political Buddhist sect headquartered in Santa Monica. Hinman taught music at a school in West Los Angeles while working for his degree in political science at the

University of California. His friends say he was a man who loved to talk and knew something about everything. One says, "He was a genuine person, and took a keen interest in those with radical views. And he was one of the most generous persons I've known." Another musician friend of Hinman's recalls, "He was ready to relate to anyone . . . He wanted to know their thing. Hinman had many connections as well as friends in the music business, and that's what Charlie Manson wanted. Gary was sensitive to Manson's talents and his views, which I gathered were half-baked Zen, and enough Buddhist ideology to get Gary going. Also his ideas about music were you might say contradictory . . ."

According to Manson, "The Beatles confuse you with what they say. They trick you with distraction, with the beat. You get programmed from the front or programmed from the back. Music doesn't know time. Music is soul. And you can bring it in from the back. I can sing a song right now and when it's over you forget the words, the music, but it stays in your infinite unconscious. And then a few months later you hear another song, and it'll end with the same kind of riff . . . It's the same. You forgot the words and yet in the back of your mind, what it means comes back to you. And it meshes in your mind, like the advertising people do. Talking about a beer, Coors is great, Coors is great. Pretty soon you think of beer and you know that Coors is great. And that is what the Beatles do, they confuse you with cadence, and program you in the back, behind the beat, and this is what stays with you. Dig?"

Charlie would talk and Hinman would listen, then Hinman would talk and Charlie would sleep. One friend of Hinman's said of Manson, "You can't steal the show from that guy — he expects you to think over every word he's said."

For some time there had been another member in Charlie's group — "Tex" (Charles) Watson. He was the last of three children, and his parents operated a service station/general store in a small Texas town northeast of Dallas.

In high school Watson never made a grade below B, excelled in athletics, played halfback on the football team and was named all-district during his junior and senior years. He played basketball, was on the baseball team, and set a state track record in high hurdles. Active in numerous school activities, one of his jobs was sports editor of the yearbook.

After graduation he enrolled at the North Texas State University, though his goals were uncertain and he went along as a business major. But shortly his grades dropped to a C average. During that time, Watson was picked up by the police on suspicion of stealing typewriters from his former school. A grand jury was impanelled but dismissed the charge on lack of evidence.

Three years later, in the spring of 1967, the University let out and Watson decided to leave Texas. He told several friends he'd have "better luck" in California, and planned to attend the state university in Los Angeles. He moved into an apartment on Glendale Boulevard and began classes, but realized he no longer knew what it was he wanted out of college — except an army deferment, and continued with a business major. Something was "bothering" him.

One friend recalls his first meeting with "Tex" in Los Angeles. The friend was with a girl Watson's age, but on being introduced, "Charles stood up and called her 'Ma'am . . .' He had a very outgoing personality. When he [Tex] came here he had a pretty good job, making good money. I know he had at least a thousand dollars worth of new clothes hanging in his closet."

Another friend, a student and salesman who attended college with Watson, recalls, "he started not caring about his school work, not caring about the job. I think he quit and then he was trying to get some money somewhere. When he first came to Cal State he had been a pretty aggressive person, aggressive in a good way, what you might call success-oriented. But he was starting to withdraw from the people he knew. Someone getting himself into deep water . . ."

Watson was only to last the quarter at college. No one could say anything to him about it. He became edgy. "If you tried to encourage him, or get him to open up about whatever the heck it was that was needling him," recalls a girl, a classmate, "he seemed to withdraw more — or try to get away from you."

Joan Dreifus, of Glendale, dated Watson on occasion. She claims "Tex changed his manners and, you might say, his personality practically overnight. I said to him, 'What's wrong? What's gotten into you lately?' That was when he looked me right in the eyes and smiled in a strange way, and he said, 'Dope is getting into me.' I said, 'You're kidding,' and he said, 'I've been turned on to something that is way out —' And that's what it is, he said, that was happening to him. But I could see he was becoming a hippie . . . Because everybody around is either making marijuana or taking something, I didn't make a big deal out of it because Tex was. But then after a little while I saw that he was—was turning into something I just didn't know that well any more. He said, 'I'm finding out who I am,' and he said he'd become involved with an 'Infinitesimal Soul' — and he had a teacher, or guru as he called it — they were in a rock music group or forming one. And Tex said, just stating it like that, that he was finding out his own true self . . . I never saw him again."

The salesman friend reported, "He got deeper in the drug scene, and then I lost track of him for about five months. The next time I saw him, something had happened. He had hair down to here, and there had been a definite change. This nice guy who came out here became someone else, a completely different person. He was almost incoherent at times. He had very little communication with anyone he previously knew or anyone, I guess, in the so-called 'straight world.'"

Other "straights" who knew Tex said he was spending a lot of time with a hippie commune, and constantly talked about some type of guru, and a rock singing group he was associating with.

The "guru" was Charlie Manson, who, during his stay with Gary Hinman had met Dennis Wilson, a big name drummer and leader of a successful rock group, the Beach Boys.

It seemed the musician sensed in Manson an "original — far out" talent, and believed something could be done for him in the music business. Manson was invited to the performer's expansive home in Pacific Palisades, and it was not long before he was attending parties and associating with celebrities. Soon enough he was using the mansion as his own address.

One young woman, "Wallie" Sellers, although not part of Manson's crowd, was staying at Wilson's — "I was a friend, and then one day I was in the Palisades and Wilson came rolling by in the car . . . I was living in Malibu at the time, and he said, 'Hi,' you know, 'Come on down and see me sometime . . .' Others where I was staying in Malibu were on speed and I couldn't handle that other scene," she says. "And so I went down there to Wilson and I said, 'Wow, can I rent your guest house from you?' He said, 'Sure,' and I said, 'How much would you like?' and he said, 'Well, we'll talk about it later.' I moved everything down there, and then this old man who was staying there wanted the guest house, because, you know, he wasn't really part of the people. So, I had all my stuff there and then I took a room in the main house. Otherwise I never would have done that."

Wallie, then engaged to be married, had her own room and remained at the house about six months "about the same time Charlie and his girls arrived on the scene."

She says, "When I first met Charlie, and when I first looked at him, my first impression was that he was like people that I used to know in Hollywood, you know, they were just scammy people. They were nice, they were friends of mine and all this, but they were out to get what they could get, and this is what I first saw when I looked at him. I didn't even have to talk to him . . . But the more I got to know Charlie — the more I started to like him.

"Charlie cut an album," she remembers, "using the girls in the background, and it was really sort of an interesting album. Everybody thought he was a good musician, more or less, and he used to write a lot of songs. His one big one was 'Burn All Your Bridges,' that was one of his favorite songs, and everybody loved it, too . . . When I moved down there, there were these girls, one was only sixteen at the time," she recalls. "Charlie was definitely the kingpin, the head man. He brought his little harem over there, brought his girls to Wilson's and he got free rent . . . Charlie really seemed to believe in what he was doing, although I didn't go for it, because I couldn't believe him. There were too many things missing, you know, his great philosophy on love, and all this stuff, and brotherhood. I couldn't see how it would work if you're sitting in a $150,000 house and somebody else is paying the rent." Charlie's hopes "were not unrealistic at all," Wallie says. "He had some top musicians, and Wilson was backing him, and he had the free use of a recording studio. Charlie had a very nice voice. He sounds something like the voice in, what was that record about Martin Luther, JFK and Bobby Kennedy all getting killed — Martin, John and Bobby — sounds just like the voice of Dion.

"There was something peculiar when I first moved in there," she says. "They had a certain vibration thing around the house — I call them Charlie and the elves, because that's what I saw when I first went down there — the elf girls is what they were. They had long hair and stuff, and they sat there eating bread, and making bread and doing the whole bit, you know, in a big expensive house, and I kept thinking, 'Wow,' and they were so *calm, so* completely calm. And then Charlie came in on the scene, and I thought, 'Well, he's kind of doing a scam' — that's his thing, what he wants to do there. But about the vibrations there — he would say, 'Don't bring any people into the house that have got the wrong vibes. You know, don't bring any strangers in here.' He liked the set-up the way it was, under control, and I don't think he wanted to lose control of the atmosphere. He had control over everybody's heads, and he didn't want anybody throwing in any big questions." Charlie's girls "thought of him as their master, sort of," Wallie says. "It was kind of like a harem situation, and the girls all liked each other, they were sort of dykes, and Charlie was a little in love with Wilson, so everything worked out just fine," she laughed. "Everybody was happy . . . All these people wandering around, the elves, wore no makeup or anything else, and then there was Charlie as the kingpin man from Mars. Charlie thought Wilson was going to buy him and the girls a ranch, and was trying to promote this more than anything. Between trying to promote Wilson to buy them the ranch, and others to get him into music, that was about all he was interested in. He thought money from the music would enable him to support the ranch he wanted Wilson to buy. Everything seemed simple.

"One night we went out to visit some people in Topanga Canyon and when we came back down the mountain we went to the Self-Realization Fellowship Church and walked around. He got in a really serious mood for once . . . He knew I wasn't falling for his elf thing, and he was using different approaches on me, and I think a few times he let some of himself out. So we were walking around the church and he was saying, 'I don't think I've ever gone out and had a good time with a girl, just having fun, with a girl that has as much class as you do.' And he got into this big thing about 'class.' And about how nice it was to just spend a normal evening, you know, just drive in the car over to some people's house . . . you come back, you stop and you take a walk . . . it really impressed him that it was something normal, that he was able to do this with a girl that he thought had 'class.' And he said, 'You know, no matter what ever happened to you, you'd never lose that class.' Another time he said that, and he was almost mad about it. Definitely, he felt very insecure about this, that's why he surrounded himself with most of the girls . . . they were from very rich families . . . I'd just listen to the stories these girls would tell, about the psychiatrists and this and that. And it was really sort of sad, but I thought, well, Charlie seems to be doing more for their heads than the psychiatrists . . . I mean, he didn't surround himself with trash to start with. He picked from the cream of the crop, then brought them down to his level."

Wallie got to know Tex. "He had a very good sense of humor and he was just kind of like a big fuzzy dog or something, you know. He was always trying to make people laugh and trying to get attention and everything and he usually was successful in that. He had a fairly dynamic personality, and when he was exerting it he was very pleasant." Yet at Wilson's house Watson had always been known as "Square Tex." Still he was "sensitive" and "very sweet," though "kind of wrought up inside."

At the house, they were taking LSD "every once in a while," Wallie says, but the drugs were not "a regular pattern" in the beginning. "The first drugs that ever came down there, ever there for any amount of time, were brought by Watson," she recalls. "He used to bring pot, to get himself accepted and everything. He really wanted to be with it and he was really square . . . He's a fairly good-looking tall guy, and he's always been fairly popular with girls, and then there's this little runt, Charlie, and all the girls loved Charlie, and they won't do anything without his permission, without his saying so. He's number one, you know. So Tex really wanted to be into this scene, because he believed — in the philosophy — this is where he started, he wanted to believe in the philosophy."

Eventually, Wallie recalls, "Wilson sort of put his foot down because all these new girls would come around — freaky girls — weird. Wilson said, 'It's not cool around here anymore. There's too many people and I want you to split . . .'"

Some who had followed Charlie from San Francisco settled on an old isolated ranch one mile west of Topanga Canyon Road in the mountains near Chatsworth. Owned by George Spahn, the ranch had been the location site for the William S. Hart cowboy movies of the 1920's.

The façade of the main street, a cluster of rundown movie buildings, had become a ghost town with its Longhorn Saloon, the Rock City Cafe, some stables, weathered props and old trailers. Millions of moviegoers once viewed this old "wild west" setting, but the dust had settled. Rusted car parts littered the grounds and few visitors passed by, only some horse owners or occasional riders in the surrounding hills.

Charlie and several girls found the ranch by chance one afternoon while driving the black bus through the mountains. To Charlie, collecting misfits and rejects, the ranch seemed like a junked version of times gone by. Manson, who was later to say, "Where does the garbage go, as we have tin cans and garbage alongside the road, and oil slicks in the water, so you have people, and I am one of your garbage people," found the old ranch like water settling in a ditch. Tin cans, old bedding, teenage dropouts, anything rejected, he felt he could put to use. The Family could live rent-free, create an "inside" world within the "outside" world, while Manson pursued his dreams.

At first it came as a surprise to find the old black bus parked on the property, and the group was told they'd have to move, a ranch hand recalled. But Charlie talked with owner George Spahn, said the bus wasn't working and asked permission to remain until they could fix it. Then the girls started taking care of the ranch owner, and after that they just stayed. It was Susan, Charlie and some of the other girls who had moved the bus onto the ranch — "There was no other girls at the ranch when we moved there . . . We girls took care of old George Spahn, took care of his lunches and things like that, and managed to take care of ourselves as best we could," Susan said.

Susan, who took to sunbathing naked on rocks, describes the ranch as "very beautiful . . . The buildings are dilapidated and falling apart but the surrounding is like a wooded area. There's quite a few acres on the land and George Spahn, who is eighty years old and partially blind, still rents out horses for people to go horseback riding."

It was a new life. "In order for me to be completely free in my mind," Susan says, "I had to be able to completely forget the past. The easiest way to do this is to have to change identity by doing so with a name. I started to pick out a name, a very long French-sounding sexy name . . ." Manson later named her "Sadie Mae Glutz."

"Skip" says, "I had a shack of my own on the ranch. Some of the others stayed in the old trailer, a couple of the empty buildings. We cooked, really kept the place clean. The girls were so great. They seemed to be talented in womanly arts, sewing, taking care of the babies. They made it beautiful. Up in San Francisco everyone was having abortions. But at the ranch the girls liked the babies and the world seemed to revolve around them."

Susan's baby came in October. "Charlie delivered my son. He delivered him and one of the girls held me in an easy position. My son's name is Zo Zo Ze Ze Zadfrack . . ."

"Charlie delivered three babies. He was the midwife, so to speak, he was more with us women than he was with the men. At first," she says, "life at Spahn ranch with Charlie was beautiful, very, very peaceful." The elderly Spahn would leave the ranch in the late afternoons, and throughout the night it was a paradise for the family. "We called ourself the Family," Susan said, "A family like no other family . . . We all made love with each other, got over our inhibitions and inadequate feelings and became very uninhibited."

Skip says, "We'd sit around the fire and sing songs, cowboy songs, too. Some that Charlie would write himself. He'd play guitar. It started opening up after a while . . ."

Susan recalls, "As people would come and people would want to drop out of sight they'd give us mostly everything that they had and we'd usually give away — in other words, we never held onto anything, we always gave it away. In fact, we gave away more than we ever had . . ."

One new girl to Charlie's Family was Linda Darleen Kasabian. Her parents had divorced when she was young. Her father had worked in mills and construction jobs in New Hampshire, then migrated to Florida. Her mother remarried.

Linda had been a good student in school but was described as a "starry-eyed romanticist," unable to find whatever it was she was searching for. She had unhappy relationships with a number of boys, planned to marry one and quit high school. The marriage "didn't happen," and she married someone else. She was sixteen. One year later she was divorced. At seventeen she moved to Boston, met a young hippie and married him. She became pregnant and the couple traveled to California, where she and her husband split up, going separate ways.

According to Wallie, Linda joined the Family at Wilson's house "on her way somewhere and somebody picked her up hitchhiking. She said she was married, leaving her husband, and she seemed straight but just flits off to the ranch. Absolutely blew my mind."

She was told by Gypsy, another member of the Family, how all the girls had assumed new names and were known as witches, Linda went on, so she became "Yana the Witch." Linda says that since the girls said they were witches, she tried to become one. "It just sort of seemed like a little game," and Linda fell in as a member of the Family.

She said Manson later devised a "walkie-talkie" warning system to alert Family members, in the back part of the ranch, as they worked on

Charles Manson, age 14. Headline from Indiana newspaper reads:
"Boy leaves 'sinful home' for new life in Boys Town"

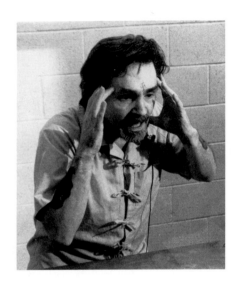

Manson today at Corcoran prison

Manson Family members at Spahn Ranch (Lynette "Squeaky" Fromme, front left)

ABOVE: Manson Family members at creek near Spahn Ranch
BELOW: Sandra Good in front of trailer at Spahn Ranch

Squeaky, Sandra, Gypsy, and other Family girls on a garbage run

Sharon Tate

Sharon Tate on set of "Eye of the Devil" as the sorceress Odile

Last photo of Sharon Tate alive, taken on the day of her murder.
Snapshot taken by fellow victim Voityck Frykowski; exposed film in camera found at Cielo Drive house

Tombstone of Sharon and unborn baby victim

ABOVE: Sharon Tate's body, left; Jay Sebring's, right; as left by the killers
BELOW: Abigail Folger on house lawn

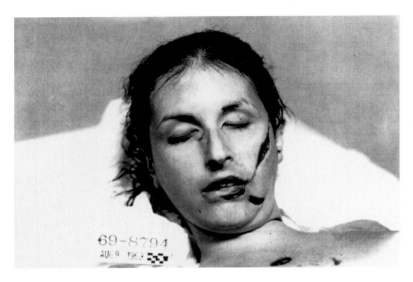

Abigail Folger at morgue

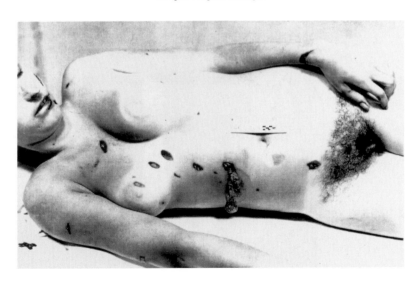

Steven Parent, death by gunshots

Voityck Frykowski dead on house lawn

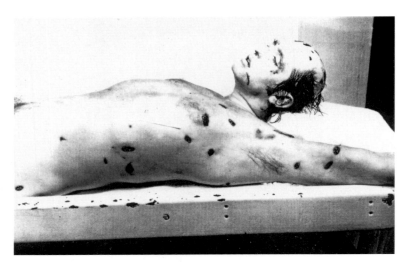

Frykowski at the L.A. County Morgue

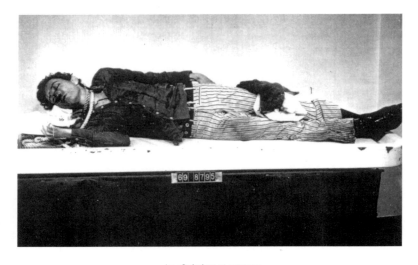

Jay Sebring at morgue

Movie director Roman Polanski, husband of Sharon Tate, being brought to identify body

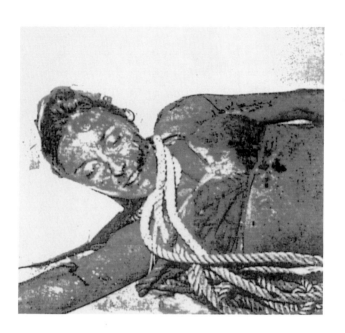

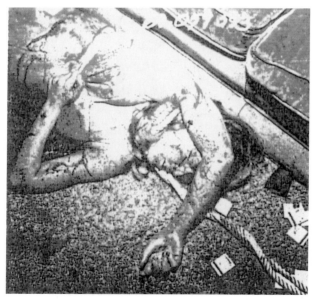

Sharon Tate's body in Cielo Drive house

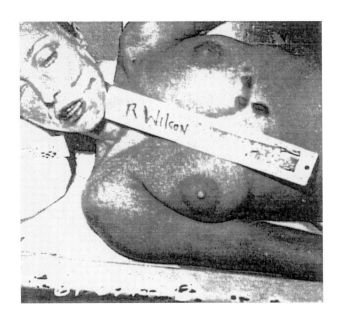

Sharon Tate's body at morgue

Murdered Leno LaBianca with fork sticking in stomach. Rosemary LaBianca murdered in bedroom

Head of Rosemary LaBianca

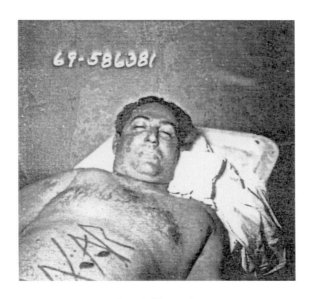

ABOVE: Leno LaBianca at morgue.

BELOW: Stomach of Leno LaBianca showing carved word "WAR"

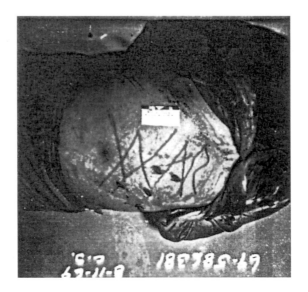

THE FLIGHT TO DEATH VALLEY

Barker Ranch

One of the dune buggies, on display
at an automotive museum

Door at Barker Ranch

Manson after arrest for murders, L.A. County courthouse

Susan Atkins, Patricia Krenwinkel, and Leslie Van Houten, charged with murders

Leslie Van Houten and Patricia Krenwinkel with heads shaved in emulation of Manson

Bobby Beausoleil, convicted in the Gary Hinman killing

Mary Brunner, Clem, and Family member at the courthouse

Clem charged with Family beheading murder of Spahn ranch hand Shorty Shea

Charles "Tex" Watson: "I am the Devil, here to do the Devil's work"

Manson in court

Manson in L.A. County Jail

Manson, convicted of multiple murder

Author John Gilmore, 1969 during Manson interviews

Satanist Anton LaVey (far left) and Bobby Beausoleil (far right)
during filming of Kenneth Anger's "Lucifer Rising"

Killer Bobby Beausoleil takes a bride in prison

Sandra Good, high priestess of the Manson movement, following release from prison

I HUNGRY KNIFE
SWEAR UPON THIS TREE
STUMP BEFORE MY UNIVERSAL
FATHERS TO KILL LIE AND
BRING THE SPIRIT OF THE
INDIAN BACK TO THE
LAND
                    RAISE FROM
WHITE MANS CONFUSION
AS EVEN MANSON &
CHILDREN CALL ME HUNGRY
KNIFE AND CREEP SILENT
WITH LOVE FOR EARTH
                    IPCR

Sandra Good's death threats to politicians and corporate leaders prior to Squeaky Fromme's attempted assassination of then-President Gerald Ford

Signed polaroid of Manson at Corcoran prison

Manson's business card (ATWA stands for Air, Trees, Water & Animals)

what she called stolen dune buggies, and "the girls worked sort of like a guard tower with the walkie talkies." Linda says the girls did "anything and everything. Oh, help the men with dune buggy parts, take care of the cooking, sewing . . . or other services for the men." The men, she explains, mostly worked on the dune buggies, although she "very seldom" saw Manson do any physical work.

Often Charlie would leave on trips to Wilson's and the "music scene," in pursuit of what had become an obsession. Meanwhile the Family would carry on, attempting to replenish itself.

"Scavenging became a way of survival for the family," Susan says. "The supermarkets all over Los Angeles throw away perfectly good food every day, fresh vegetables and sometimes cartons of eggs, packages of cheese that are stamped to a certain date. The stores are only allowed to keep them until that date, but the food is still good, and us girls used to go out and do garbage runs, is what we called it. Pick up the food and take it back to the ranch, and cut out the blue spots and check it over to see that it was good food. And we used to go out and panhandle. We went out on garbage runs and we went and panhandled, and one time one girl and I put on dark clothes and took it upon ourselves to do this — Charlie had no knowledge of it — we went out and creepy-crawled. It's moving in silence so that nobody sees us or hears us — wearing very dark clothes and move at night."

Linda recalls that sometimes Charlie told the girls how to dress, that "at night we were told to wear dark clothes." As for food, Linda also joined in the scavenging as the group "went on garbage runs . . . We used to go to the back of supermarkets, get the food they had thrown away, wash it up and fix it." The family ate "mostly vegetables, and never meat," Linda recalls. She said Charlie didn't give directions as to eating habits, "not really," although "he used to be big on zu-zus — candy and ice cream and things like that."

Manson, who says, "I have ate out of garbage cans to stay out of jail," was nonetheless in tune with the scene. "I live in my own world, and I am king in my world," he declares, "whether it be in a garbage dump or if it be in the desert or wherever it be, I am my own human being." And to Charlie, those who made up the Family on the ranch were the unwant-ed "people that were alongside the road, that their parents had kicked them out and that did not want to go to Juvenile Hall, so I did the best I could and I took them up on my garbage dump and I told them this, that in love there is no wrong."

Linda says she first met Manson on the Fourth of July, "Independence Day." She sought him out, she said, because she'd heard he was "the beautiful man we had all been waiting for." She had sex with him that second night there on the ranch, "in a cave." She says, "He felt my legs and seemed to think they were OK . . . He made love to me, and we had a slight conversation . . . I don't remember all of it, but he told me I had a father hang-up." She admits being impressed when Charlie told her she had a "father hang-up, because nobody ever said that to me before. I have no father, and I hate my stepfather." For Linda, too, Manson was to become the new father.

Susan was Sadie Mae Glutz. Manson says, "Sadie was the kind of girl that wanted to be something that she wasn't. And I told her, 'Sadie, you got to be yourself.' But all these pretty girls were with me, and making love to me, and she felt that if she made love with me she would be pretty like they were. And she is only — I only made love to her three times. She was pregnant most of the time I knew her, and once a girl is pregnant there just isn't any use to make love with her, dig. And anyway, she had these breasts that hung down to her waist. And I'd look at the line of girls waiting for me and I couldn't do it with Sadie. I'd look at the girls I'd had it with before and I couldn't go back, when I saw the others that were still waiting for me."

Susan said more girls came, following after the others, and moved into the ranch after visiting with Charlie. "He got to know them immediately."

Manson says, "These kids would come up to the ranch, young girls, and they'd say, 'teach us to make love.' And if I'd like them, we'd get some grass and go to the shack for a couple of days and they'd learn . . .

"If you want to get to people and unlock their minds, the basic way you get to them is through fear," he explains. It was a lesson he had learned. "A normal girl comes down to the ranch and she says she's looking for her sister — she's never been here. So I said to myself, this girl is not looking for her sister. She's looking to get involved with the people at the ranch and she's looking for 'nasty' things. Sex, which is nasty in her mind, and she knows as much as we do that she'd like to make love to her father, and she can't admit it to herself, yet her father in turn says, 'Don't go out screwing any other guy,' because he'd like to screw her himself . . . He doesn't want her screwing any other guy because of the society, and she

THE UNHOLY TRAIL OF CHARLIE AND THE FAMILY

has all these thoughts in her mind," Manson says. "She comes down to the ranch, and I said, 'Your sister's not here.' She says, 'What's in that dirty old room over there?' And I said, 'That's a dirty old room with a dirty old mattress, and you don't want to go in there because it's a dirty place, you know.' She says, 'I want to go in there,' and as soon as I open the door and go in there with her, she comes up against me and says, 'What are you going to do to me?' She's thinking in terms of wish fulfillment and she's already got it in her mind for me to rape her — she's already got it in her mind, all the nasty things, and she's got the excuses, already got it in her mind that this is a good excuse in case she gets caught by her father. So I put on my nasty face and I say, 'Come over here, come over here,' and 'put your feet up over here . . . Take down your pants — I want to play with your pussy.' I start playing with her, and when she starts to get hot, I put out my cock and show it to her. Then she really starts to get worked up, and I say 'Come here — touch it' She says, 'Oh, no, I wouldn't do that!' Then when she really gets warmed up, I say, 'Gee, I think I'll go out and get a cigarette,' and I walk away from her, to get the cigarette. And she starts growling and carrying on — 'How about — what's — come on, Charlie,' and she walks over to me . . . So I say to her then, 'Look, you never have to deal out of fear, don't let people run you out of fear — and don't be afraid of me acting like your father, and don't be afraid of your father —' I tell her sex is a beautiful thing, you can enjoy it without fear. 'So you go off and find some guy that's your equal, that's on your level, and have it with him,' and I send her off."

Charlie was claiming to have contracted with a rock group to buy two of his songs, one with a record company commitment. He also said he planned to accompany the group to Texas for engagements there, but couldn't keep the date because of parole restrictions.

One young man in the music field, Gregg Jakobson, tried to generate interest in Manson's songs and music. "Dennis Wilson — one of the Beach Boys — and I were interested in recording Charlie," Jakobson says, and arranged with a friend, Terry Melcher, the son of actress Doris Day, to accompany him out to Spahn ranch. "We wanted some financial backing to do a film to accompany the music. In other words, I was trying to involve Terry in recording and filming."

At that time, Terry Melcher lived in a rambling estate in the

Benedict Canyon area on Cielo Drive. The name *cielo*, Melcher says, "is Spanish for sky." He had been living there since April of 1966, and had known Wilson "a number of years, it must be the last six or seven now." At one of Wilson's parties, Melcher met Manson and Tex Watson. Melcher remembers, "Wilson drove me to Cielo Drive one day, and Manson was in the back seat of his car strumming his guitar, and they dropped me off in the driveway . . . One of my occupations is that of recorder-producer, and later I was asked to drive and meet Manson and his group, to see whether or not I'd be interested in recording them."

Melcher recalls that at Spahn ranch, "there were forty or fifty of them, it's hard to say exactly, they were everywhere, mostly young women, and they all seemed to be part of the same group, they all sang together with Charlie Manson. He played a guitar, and it seems to me some of the girls were playing tambourines. I was later told that they were all songs that Charlie Manson had composed. The type of music they were doing and the whole setting itself was rather peculiar to the pop music business, to say the least . . . I went back there approximately within a week after I had first been there, because a friend of mine was going to spend a summer traveling around the country recording various Indian tribes doing native songs and that sort of thing. I mentioned I had seen a group in Chatsworth that seemed something like an Indian tribe. They sat around and all sang together, and all participated — that perhaps that might be the type of thing he was interested in, and that was the reason for my second visit.

"Manson, he spoke to me," Melcher says, but there was no talk about arranging a time when they would get together with ideas of recording. "The reason I went back the second time . . . I felt sorry for those people. There were a lot of girls that were obviously young and I assumed that most of them were runaways, and when I went back with my other friend who had the trailer and it was set up to record out of doors, or anywhere that you might find people making music, the purpose of that visit was to perhaps show it to someone who maybe wanted to do something like that, but that wasn't exactly what *I* was looking for in music . . . After hearing them sing a dozen or so songs I may have singled out one and said, 'that is a nice song,' just to be polite," Melcher says. "When someone performs for you, you don't want to simply not respond to their whole presentation, and to be polite I probably said something. Usually that is what I say . . . There were all those people wandering around and I gave them $50, which is all

I had with me, so that they could buy some food."

Jakobson, who had arranged for Melcher to visit the ranch, recalls, "I think Terry showed some interest in the music, but there was nothing positive. There was never any, 'Yes, I will record you' talk going on. It was like that was the preliminaries and nothing ever came of it."

In fact, those who had shown interest in Manson's talents no longer found the time to review them. Charlie's "hobnobbing" and enthusiasm for getting "something goin'" in the music business had, finally, amounted to nothing.

Eleven

When she first heard Manson discussing his philosophy of the "Infinite Soul," Wallie Sellers recalls thinking, "This could be great if you really believed it. But I think what happened is that it was just a con — he was just doing it. He did *believe it* to a certain extent, but not completely. He was still interested in how to pay the bills like all men are. Girls aren't that interested because it's not part of their character. But here he had this family now and he had to support them, and when any man is put under that kind of pressure he can get very hostile. When he first went to the ranch there and things started going wrong, he was hostile. And he came back and the girls were all pregnant and everything. He thought that was great when he was at Dennis Wilson's — being with the Beach Boys, but all of a sudden the responsibility was all his — the whole thing, having to feed them, having to clothe them, everything. And I guess when his records didn't work out, and here were these girls . . .

"At that time he had gotten them so completely believing in everything, that I guess they turned around and completely convinced him. So here he was, he wanted to scream out and say, 'Don't you know this is just a scam, and that all of a sudden it's blown up in my face,' and they'd just say, so calmly, 'No, Charlie, it's not that . . . That's just the Establishment, they're just putting that into your head. We love you.' And Charlie sits there and he has nobody he can talk to — nobody he can say, 'Well, I really blew it, what am I doing out here?' to — because they're all giving him the same business that he's been giving them for a year. Tell me you wouldn't get frustrated. What happened is they convinced him of his own philosophy and then he blew his mind. Everyone is everyone else. I am you, and you are me, and so there's no ego. But Charlie had to have an ego, or he never would have been able to clothe and feed his family . . .

"Before, Charlie'd had it very well under control, because he never got mad. I was always wondering when he would blow it," Wallie says, "because everybody's got to get mad once in a while. They still kept coming down to Dennis Wilson's house, and I think three of the girls were pregnant at that time, and he was trying to tell 'em all to split and that they had graduated — they'd graduated and it was time for them to go on their own, and it was time for him to get a new following of girls. And they were *really* believing this, the three of them — all pregnant. He was really uptight, trying to give 'em this business about dissolving the group then, the whole thing, and he was going to start from scratch. He and Skip were going to start the new group. You know, that he and Skip would go and find a new Family, and I think that was Charlie's last dying effort to escape from having to follow through on his own philosophy. And when he went to that ranch he just had to believe it, because he just kept hearing it, like a record. Any one of the girls, you could ask them a question and they'd all give you the same answer. He had them perfectly trained, like Pavlov's dogs. I met Susan Atkins one time. I asked her about herself, and she gave me this routine, like a record, and I said, 'Are you one of Charlie's girls?' and she said, 'Yes, how did you know?' I just knew by the sound of her voice that Charlie'd been at her. So I think that Charlie either started believing it or he got so involved with it he just couldn't drop it, and he tried to change it a little to make it more interesting . . ."

Charlie began to talk more and more about a "bottomless pit," at first as though to himself, muttering about the bottomless pit. After his efforts to gain recognition in the outside world had all failed, his philosophy of oneness and love took a negative turn. He carried the Bible, cracked open and folded down to Chapter IX, Revelations, and he'd read knowingly:

"From the shaft of the bottomless pit . . . came locusts on the earth, and they were given the power of scorpions. They were told not to harm any green growth or any tree, but only those who have not the seal of God on their foreheads . . . Their faces were like human faces, their hair like women's hair . . . They have as king over them the angel of the bottomless pit."

And Charlie Manson was the "King" of his world. Wallie says, "He had a very aggressive line. He'd stare at your eyeballs, he'd just stare at your eyes, and he'd start in on this scam — this thing of his — he'd ask questions. He'd be very dynamic about it, just something a more normal man doesn't

81

normally do, you know, and tells you, 'I don't like your hair,' or 'I like your hair' or something, 'Why are you wearing makeup when it's not natural, where's your real face . . .' and all this, and 'What do you believe in?' and 'You should believe in this . . .' After a couple of hours of his talking and you're getting brainwashed."

"Once I had this movie star," Charlie points out. "She wanted me to make love to her. I told her that if she came up to the ranch, and took off all her makeup, and she was up there for a while, and I got the feeling, then I might make love to her. But she wanted to be released so bad, she said 'Charlie, you have to do it,' and she was really mad. And I told her, I was at her house, 'Okay, you go climb up that mountainside. If you want to make love to me you go climb up that mountain, and climb back down.' The reason I told her to go up that mountain and climb back down is because when she came back down again she'd be too tired to screw, she'd be too tired, maybe she wouldn't want to. Now I could screw her when I wanted to, not when she wanted to get it. That's the time — when she's tired, she doesn't want to do it . . . So when I start screwing her, and chomping on her, and she's so tired that when I finally get to her and build her up, and she starts moving, I can get to her mentally. She's so tired physically, I can get to her mentally and get inside her soul and body, and be inside her body and mind and control her." And the girls would put their minds and their bodies into the hands of "the master."

In his barren relationships, Charlie pretended to have "no wants — no needs," that he was self-sufficient. But after awhile he would manipulate, gear up the relationship to an area of confidence, or intimacy, to where he could take hold of whatever he wanted.

As head of the Family, Charlie manipulated. But what was it he really wanted? He wallowed in sex at the ranch, and in being worshipped as he had never known or even hoped for. Yet Charlie still couldn't be satisfied. It was as if the newfound affection wasn't really reaching Charlie the person but only the "ego" of the con man. It seemed Charlie, "the father," actually could love and seek to satisfy only himself, the loveless, fatherless boy who never grew up. As if in some strange way, among the many "put -on" faces of Manson, the "father" image was at the command of the son, at the command and mercy of Charlie's past. It seemed the boy within him was craving revenge on an incredibly indifferent world. With minds weakened by acid and amphetamines, Manson began to mold, as it were, the weapons he'd use in his war.

Linda, who said she'd been using LSD, peyote and "speed," claimed her chief reason for taking drugs was for "God realization . . . For one thing, I thought I could see God through acid. The acid told me it was God," she said, though adding, "I realized you don't have to take LSD or peyote to discover God." She said the Family used drugs regularly. It was a part of the life. "We lived together as one family, as a father . . . and the children."

Charlie recalls, "I may have implied on several occasions that I may have been Jesus Christ, but I haven't decided yet what I am or who I am. . .

"When you take LSD enough times you reach a state of nothing, of no thought," he admits. "An example of this, if you were to be standing in a room with someone and you were loaded on acid and the guy says, 'Do you like my sport coat?' And the guy would probably not pay any attention to him and say, 'I bought this sport coat at Penney's,' and then he still would not pay any attention to him. About two or three minutes later the guy loaded on LSD will turn around and say, 'My, you have a beautiful sport coat,' because he is only reacting — he is only reacting . . ."

His "children," Charlie says, are "everyone that loves me, anyone that will return my love." He says, "I would like to be a good father and do what my children would like me to do," but then, sometimes, the "children" would have to be punished. He recalls that one member of his Family was "kicked out of her house when she was thirteen. She always liked to get attention from her father . . . So she would do things like drop coffee and spill things and do childish little things so her daddy would come and spank her on the hand. So she brought that problem to the ranch," he says. "She asked to be spanked several times. She came close to burning the ranch up and I would tell her, 'Would you quit doing that,' I says, 'If you don't stop doing that I'm going to spank you. I'm going to whip you.' And she would keep doing it, so as any father would do I conditioned her mind with pain to keep her from burning the ranch down or to keep her from doing something that she may have done that would affect everyone."

But Manson had his own plans that were to affect others. He continued programming members of the family, preparing them to carry out his orders without question — the drug effects began to blur distinctions among the many faces of Charlie — it was not really the "father" anymore — as much as an extremity of the "Infinite Soul" which was, of course, everything and everybody in Manson's inside world. He treated them rough, in a manner similar in theory to the army breaking away a young person's individuality. "I did all sorts of nasty things to the girls that I could think up." Manson says, "One girl — I picked up this stick and threatened her, and I used the goddamn stick on her. 'Don't act out of fear' I said, and don't get hung up on the father. She'd say she wanted to make love to some guy but was afraid of daddy and society, that they'd find out about it."

A young attorney who knew Manson was later to comment on Charlie's authority at the ranch. "Charlie needed to express the power and leadership, he had to be the father. When he 'liberated' these young girls he was still expressing the power — he is the father. I asked Charlie, 'What about the mother and son, and what you call the equal relationship — the brother and sister — isn't there an equality in here somewhere? Couldn't you be one or the other — you're always talking about the one extreme, the father and daughter relationship . . .' Charlie said to me, 'A woman came to us, she was bringing her fifteen year old daughter to me. I said, "We don't want you lady, you're too old, you couldn't hack it here. You'd sit around and everybody would see your flabby stomach and know how old you are, know all the hang-ups you have." And she says, "Whatta you mean, my layers of defense mechanisms?" And I said, "Yeah," and the fact that the daughter's — she doesn't have the pure relationship, she's just had one relationship — with her father. The old woman's had other relationships with men that have hung her up in various ways over the years, for so many years, and also her body, she couldn't hack it. But the fifteen year old has just had the relationship with her father. She's clean — she's fresh. I can get to her still, she doesn't have the "layers" around her.'

"Charlie liberated them from the father image," the lawyer says. "He uses them but then tells them 'don't be used.' Then he tells them, 'Go out and do beautiful things. I told one girl to go out and be beautiful. Next time I saw her she was riding by on a horse — it was beautiful. When they find out their fantasies are not what they really wanted, then they just want to liberate their souls, and I do this . . .'"

One dropout from a motorcycle group, twenty-one-year-old Carl Foster, became part of the Family at the ranch. "At first," he said, "It was hard to figure these women around Charlie. He once said to me, women must live for men, that's why they're put on the earth, they must serve men, have to die for men, and kept saying how they were like batteries, when they run down they must be recharged by loving them or they had to be dumped. It got so five or six girls a week would be coming up to the ranch in these cars they'd borrowed somewhere or probably stole — some junk with doors half coming off, and a few of these girls were so damn young they should've been in grammar school. Here, gradually, a lot of stolen cars started to pile up around the place, and Charlie told them, and told all of us, that nothing was important there except that the only way for us to be happy on earth was to serve him — was to become his slaves . . ."

Charlie had no use for "old ladies" or mothers around the ranch. Yet, it seems, in some strange way, his basic needs differed little from the girls who sought in him a guiding force — an authority replacement they could love intimately. Manson, who as a child knew neither love, compassion nor his mother in any meaningful way, finally found a host of young girls competing to "mother" and care for him intimately. But for Charlie the love had come too late — he had no use for an emotion he could not humanly understand. And if he could not "love" these young girls, running from pressures they could not understand, certainly he could use them.

Men visited the ranch. Linda says during these visits Charlie "told us to make love to them and to try to get them to join the Family. If they wouldn't, not to make love to them."

Speaking for other men on the ranch, Foster said, "The girls were all around the place and you were always welcome to share them or take whoever you wanted. But when you did, you then became part of Charlie's property, too. He'd said that he'd need to have men around, because, as he put it, there was no limit to what a man could do. But then, the women held power over the other men — that way, the women were the key to everything, and Charlie had it all sewed up."

Wallie recalls that Charlie "was always trying to find some man, some guys he could put on the Family — he wasn't at all pleased with the men that were out there. That's why Charlie wanted Tex there.

"But Tex was kind of wrought up inside," she remembers. "At first he was sitting there with his ego perfectly intact, saying, 'Why do the girls love Charlie better than me?' I guess," Wallie says, "later it just started building up and building up. 'Why can't the girls love me?' You know, 'Why do they have to like Charlie?' I guess he finally had to prove himself."

Marge Smith says, "Watson was impotent, he couldn't make it in a straight manner with a chick. And he was also very peculiar, brutal in a quiet way, if that can make much sense . . . I have seen him on occasions just sitting, very high, and cracking his finger knuckles and staring at Charlie."

"During the day," Susan said, "We would all gather and go through our changes and do what we were doing that day. By changes, I mean like if I didn't like what one of the girls was doing, you know, I'd go over and I'd move about and say, 'You're stupid for doing that.' That is what a change is, and what she did she did because that is what she did and what I thought about it was irrelevant to what she actually did, it didn't matter . . ."

There were times Susan seemed to disappear. She'd desert the ranch and family as though in moments of panic, as if the "liberation of her soul" was not yet complete. She'd rush off in one of the junk cars, or hitchhike south to Hollywood.

Manson said, "Sadie was taking things from me, and disappearing for weeks at a time. Like I had some hash, and she took it and was gone. And when she came back I told her, you didn't have to take it. If you wanted it, I'd give it to you. I give anyone anything they wanted, if I had it. They didn't have to take. Another time Sadie took the records I had and sold them. I didn't ask her what she did with the money or anything . . . At the ranch I told her to sweep the floor and make me one of those sandwiches, because that is all a woman is for. That is why God put them here, and no girl is going to stand in my way of my thing . . ."

Susan says, "We'd get programmed to do things, like stealing, which I took upon myself, really . . . The Family would get programmed by Charlie, but it's hard for me to explain it so that you can see the way — the way I see the words that would come from Charlie's mouth — would not come from inside him, it would come from what I call the Infinite. Like, he just said we needed credit cards and we need that and we could use some of this," and Susan would assume she'd have to go out and get them for him. "And also anything that we saw that we needed, it was up to the girls. We knew this, to take care of our men . . ."

Susan recalls when "we hitchhiked over into an area and we were scared to death," it was something Susan hadn't ever "experienced, and wanted to experience it because everybody else in the Family was doing it — creepy-crawling. They never actually took anything, I don't think, inside the residence other than money. I never actually saw any money that they got from inside any of the residences. This girl and I . . . there was an automobile parked on the side of the road. I opened the door and looked inside the glove compartment and saw some credit cards. I reached in and took them. I turned them over to Charlie."

The girls continued doing everything Charlie wanted them to do, Susan says. "Charlie always told us, 'You do what you want to do. If you do not want to do it, do not do it.' But when he would ask me to do something, I felt I had to go ahead and do it because I knew he would do the same thing for me, otherwise he wouldn't ask me to do it . . .

"Then we'd all gather at night and sit down and start singing, and Charlie would always play the guitar and we'd always sing songs and he used to make up the songs. Songs that I have never heard before or words that I have never heard before put together in such beautiful manners. Some were happy, some were very — some left me with an open head, left me just sitting there like I was dead."

As the Family went through its "changes," Tex, in particular, was changing radically. Stuart Guthrie, a Los Angeles actor, remembers when his brother, Mike, and Tex came to California together. Both had gone to high school and college, and they stayed with Guthrie when they first arrived from Texas. He recalls how Watson was upset at the prospect of Mike going into the army. "The psychological relationship was very much Mike the leader and Tex the follower," Guthrie said, "and when my brother got drafted I think that's why Tex went with Manson, like he didn't have any place to go."

Guthrie explains that when Tex went for his own army physical exam, "he came in and wanted to clean himself up, so he cut his hair off. Then he went down to the draft board and they didn't take him. That's the last time I saw him until some months later, when he came down from Spahn ranch, and when I saw him again he had changed from a rational human being to a vegetable." Guthrie attributes the change to LSD. "He had been taking drugs every day for a long time, not just smoking grass. He was taking mescaline, acid, speed, acid, acid, acid, acid, acid . . . So far gone, it's like I said, 'Call your mother, Tex, call your family, they haven't heard from you in over a year. They don't know if you're dead or alive. Call home.' And I had to tell him where his mother lived, and what her phone number was. He couldn't even remember where they lived. He was just a bleeding vegetable, moving around, doing whatever Manson told him to do, like a robot."

Carl Foster, feeling that on the ranch he was "sinking more and more into a dope-head," recalls, "the girls — they'd do absolutely anything Charlie told them to do. Well, at first when I'd first gotten to know them, I thought it was mostly because he was really an expert at making love. I'd never seen one person, one man, have such control over other human beings. It was just like they had a built-in machine in their heads, and it was Charlie that ran the controls. It was, you see, he had taken over the control of so much of our feelings, and emotions, and even what we'd eat, our drink, the money we had, or whatever we had and he seemed to control our drugs and our sex, too. The girls groveled at his feet. That's a fact — Charlie programmed them like you would a computer. He'd feed suggestions into their heads without them really knowing that he was doing it — he might say to them, 'I need some money. This is what I have to have — some money.' He wouldn't come right out and tell them to steal it, but that's just exactly what he meant for them to do. Like myself, later on, he'd never give me an order outright, like to steal something, but he'd buss it into my head by telling me how he needed this or that. Then, the next thing I knew, I was out somewhere stealing and it would be for Charlie . . .''

Foster believes that Charlie is "an insane genius. I believe to this day he is just about capable of anything and he could work miracles and all. I really think there were times when he didn't believe he was a human being — but he thought of himself as a superman or something put on the earth to be worshipped . . . And he would talk to you in a soft, soothing voice like someone lulling you to sleep, and even though he'd later on suggest things that would seem impossible, yet you could not stop yourself — even if you were in a straight world — from going out and doing it."

In short, life for the Family was becoming the will of Charlie.

Susan remembers, "Starting about a year or so ago, Charlie said, 'I have tricked you into doing what I want you to, and I am using you and you are all aware of that now, and it is like I have a bunch of slaves around me.' And he often called us sheep."

The Family members who lived at the ranch believed now that they were in paradise; but their lives were no longer their own. They were part of something else — being swept, gliding on a volition other their own. Charlie told them all, "I have brought you to paradise." It didn't matter that he'd tricked them. "There is no beginning now, and there is no end," he preached. "There is no past. There is only now in this infinite time . . . We are all one member — one force."

Twelve

A leader of the Straight Satans motorcycle club, Danny DeCarlo, first met Manson in March, 1969. "Charlie had a motorcycle, a three-wheeler that had a blown engine on it, and he wanted me to fix it. He wanted me to rebuild the engine; on Harleys, I am an expert." DeCarlo fixed the motorcycle at the ranch and stayed on. "I spent seventy-five percent of my time at the ranch. My house was the bunkhouse," which he shared with Bobby Beausoleil. His reason for remaining: "there were a lot of pretty girls up there." DeCarlo was interested in one particular girl, but also he got to know the others. About Susan, he says, "We didn't get along too good." As for Katie: "We talked, that is about it, but I never did nothing, you know, snatched her up or anything." He got to know Tex. DeCarlo said he also met Beausoleil at that time. DeCarlo got to know two other girls — Linda Kasabian, "I know we got together once," and a young girl — Leslie, who'd been with Bobby Beausoleil. DeCarlo says he wasn't interested in her, though "she was interested in me some, but I wouldn't . . . She chased me around a lot."

Leslie had arrived at the ranch with a couple of other girls, and with Bobby. The change in Leslie — the substitution of families — was almost instantaneous. One member of her new family — of Charlie's Family — says, "Leslie just drifted in one day along with some others, like they'd come up on a fluke, a joke. She went in the trailer with Charlie and after that she was part of us."

"But the thing was," Carl Foster says, "she didn't want to ball Charlie. She wanted to be with Bobby — not Charlie, physically, that is. She was more jittery than the others — something really determined about her, and like she didn't have any sense of what it was, so of course Charlie'd steer her straight. He had that over her, and she was going to fit in like she was being locked down."

DeCarlo had brought a child to the ranch, and says, "I took my little boy up there to the ranch because my wife had him but she wasn't taking care of him, so I went to Venice and brought my boy back up there." His boy was a year and a half old.

After DeCarlo rebuilt the three-wheeler for Charlie, he says, "Manson was on a motorcycle thing whereas he wanted to do this thing with motorcycles but he decided on dune buggies . . . So, me being an expert motorcycle mechanic and plus I belong to a club, a powerful club that he knew — he wanted my club to come up there, but they didn't want nothing to do with him. His idea, what he wanted to do with my club, was to scare the public away, you know, and they didn't want nothing to do with him."

Joe Brockman had been split off from the Family for some time. He recalls, "While he'd been at Wilson's and then the ranch, I acquired a '66 VW and made some scores along the Strip . . . Looking around for Charlie or Bobby. Up in the canyon I got hold of some of the others, Freida, Skip, I saw a couple others and Gypsy.

"Most had gone to Charlie's ranch. So, with my mild case of TB, I went out to the ranch and spent some time working on the VW, busting it down to a dune buggy for Charlie. There were a lot of old cars in Chatsworth and we tore them down on the ranch, converting them. We had a couple motorcycle guys helping. One was putting together a three-wheeler Harley for Charlie who'd got the bike exchanging the rights to a song. It was a better song than a bike, but Charlie said he didn't care.

"A lot of times Charlie and I would go off by ourselves. I spent almost three hours in the afternoons. He took me up to this water hole and told me about the people — there was plenty of girls, and then the guys that wanted to join up. I saw some of the bikers that came up, a lot of others. They wanted to get at the young girls. Two that I knew up there were just fourteen years old," he went on. "Charlie would never let them. He'd stand between them like a door, making a door of himself. One afternoon he said to some guys, 'You got to go through me if you're after them, and I have no fear.' I'd seen big dudes get scared of Charlie when he'd come on that way. He told me, 'I don't give a shit for anything and I'm taking these guys for a ride in the dune buggy.' He took them and spun around curves at eighty and ninety miles an hour. Charlie said, 'You see they just walk away from me because they are afraid, because I don't give a shit whether I get killed or not.'

"Others came down to the ranch to join up with us. Charlie'd say, 'In order to join up with our bunch you have to have experienced fear, lived with it.' So we'd take them down to the water hole on a trail, and then stake them out on the trail which was a byway for snakes to get to the water. Me and a couple others, Carl Foster was one, we tied Charlie down on the trail and all the snakes crawled over him. He dug it. The snakes had no fear because he wasn't afraid. Others that we staked out were screaming their heads off. And one guy, of this bike group, a real bust-out beer head, he screamed and fainted and came to and was screaming. He pissed all over the ground and cried like a child. We had to get him off there or he'd have gone nuts."

Manson, Joe, and some of the others would make long excursions north out into Death Valley to an area called Goler Wash, north of Shoshone, California. Joe explains: "Charlie'd been up there before and took the bus up. He wanted to find the place where nobody was and nobody wanted." There was an old house there, occupied at that time by a couple of miners. "It was called the Barker Ranch," Joe says, "and Charlie wanted to know who owned it and the land around there. Mrs. Barker owned it, we were told, but she wasn't around the place very often. She didn't live in Death Valley. A couple of miners were doing claim work in the wash. One, Buck Johnson, a sort of caretaker called 'old Buck,' said he was a gold miner.

"Just a little ways from the Barker place, maybe a quarter mile, was another house and it was owned by the grandmother of one of the girls Charlie had in the Family. We stayed there on and off and after a couple of weeks Charlie said, 'The animals around here are a lot smarter than most people we know,' and he said they hadn't lost the ability to love or be real, but that people had lost that. They couldn't love. He said even the wild burros were more aware and able to love than man could."

Manson says, "I studied the animals, I know how they get moisture from the sand. I've seen them do it. I'd watch the rodents burrow and exist in places where no one could live, how they'd go down deep, and get the water, even store it. I didn't eat meat. I didn't eat meat and I could communicate with the coyotes. The coyotes would come along and they would smell my crap and could tell there was no meat in what I ate, so they had no fear of me. They knew right away that I meant no harm to them."

Earlier he had located Arlene Barker, owner of the property in Goler Wash on the edge of Death Valley National Monument. Mrs. Barker recalls, "He [Manson] asked me if he could camp at Goler. There was a girl with him, and he told me he was associated with a group in the music business. He said the Beach Boys. I was under the impression from what he said to me that he wrote music for the Beach Boys. He gave me a golden record. I told him if he wanted to stay over there a few days it was all right with me." At that time, Mrs. Barker had two men living at her ranch, "doing assessment work in the claims, and they told me that there was a couple from Arizona and a little boy, and a couple of what they described as hippies, staying at the ranch."

The Family made several trips back and forth between Death Valley and the Spahn ranch, Joe remembers. Manson continued to rule over the Family that was growing in number. "At nights the new girls would wallow around Charlie," Joe says. "He was the ringleader of the circus that was happening. Some of the people were really turned on to love — strung out behind the physical thing. One night after a camp fire and singing, Charlie and I walked around the rear of the old bunkhouse. He said, 'Making love is the most basic experience, to me the only real experience.' He said love means a lot of things to different people, 'Like the guys in jail read stories about some goddamn love, to them all a love story means is a big cock on one page that gets bigger on the next page and bigger on each page after that. Love isn't like that,' Charlie said. 'Love involves beautiful emotions.'

"Then the next thing he's laughing and sort of crouching in the shadows. He talks about the thirty girls doing anything he wants," Joe says. "He said, 'I screw anyone I want, get it all I want — I got a Rolls Royce over here, I got a sports car over there. I got dune buggies and anytime I want I got the mountains.' Meanwhile the girls are waiting on him hand and foot. They are all puppets he controls. Charlie wrecked up the Rolls and he wrapped the sports car and he just left them laying there at the side of the road. And I said to him, 'You just going to leave the cars racked up here?' 'Yeah, sure,' he said, 'Who needs it?' What did he care about the cars?

"He said, 'When I was your age I used to spend an hour every day with a girl making love to her. Now when the sun goes down,' he said, 'I just think of screwing, I can start screwing any one of thirty girls, and I can screw all night long.'"

Linda admits that the girls were on the ranch to serve the men, and particularly, Charlie. She recalls one occasion about mid-July: "There was one particular girl, I don't remember her name. She was very young, maybe fifteen — sixteen. She was very shy and very withdrawn," Linda recalls. "She was in the middle of the group and Charlie took her clothes off and started making love to her. She was pushing him away — at one point she bit him on the shoulder and he hit her in the face. And after that she just fell back . . . Then he told Bobby Beausoleil to make love to her and he told everybody to touch her and make love to her." No one touched the girl until Charlie told them to, and afterward, "then Charlie told everybody to make love to everybody . . . We all shed our clothes, and we were on the floor and it didn't matter who was beside you, a man or a woman, you made love and touched each other and it was like we were all one." Everyone was nude and had sex with each other, she remembers. In the Family philosophy, "everything was all right" and "there was no wrong," she says.

Joe claims, "I had two girls that slept with me during my stay at the ranch. One had stayed with Beausoleil before he split. Tex and one of the girls stayed over at the Longhorn Saloon that they were making into a nightclub. Charlie stayed practically a different place every night with a different girl. He told me he didn't like the girls to take aggressive parts, he had to be strong, and he was aggressive. 'I don't like a girl to be aggressive when they're screwing you,' he said, 'because it tends to bring out the female in you. And I don't like to be submissive. It's a woman's part in life to be submissive and to take care of men. You see,' he said, 'That's why it's so great with these young girls because they take care of me like a mother . . .'"

Charlie had other demands to make of the family. Linda recalls that one day at supper time, Charlie told Bobby and another in the group, Bruce Davis, "to go with credit cards and to buy all types of clothing for us and the children and certain parts for the dune buggies . . . He wanted each of us girls to have two sets of clothing, sort of like a straight dress to wear on, like weekends at the ranch, or when riders would come by, and each of us to have a pair of moccasins and Levis and a blouse or whatever, and clothes for the babies, and he ordered sleeping bags. We got sleeping bags and there were a whole bunch of pocket knives for each person . . ."

Freida King had been living at the ranch for some time, always barefoot, but never without a knife at her side. "People wore whatever shoes they could find," she says. Freida was painting the saloon. "Painting and fixing it," she says. Inside the saloon were two old Sparkletts water bottles, which had been painted along with the walls and some old chairs. Freida put the words "Helter Skelter" on one of the water bottles, she says, "because I listened to the Beatles, and they told me to paint the jug so I just put it on there . . . I don't know if Charlie told me directly, it was just getting everything ready and the jug had to be painted."

Manson says about "helter-skelter" that the words come from a Beatles song. "It is not my music," but he adds, "I hear what it relates . . . It says rise — it says kill."

In some of the songs Charlie wrote, the word helter-skelter was used, and, Susan says, "he'd talk about helter-skelter. We all talked about helter-skelter. You must understand that all the words had no meanings to us and that helter-skelter was explained to me by Charlie then — I don't even like to say 'Charlie' — I'd like to say the words came from his mouth — that helter-skelter was to be the last war on the face of the earth — it would be all the wars that have ever been fought built one on top of the other, something that no man could conceive of in his imagination. You can't conceive of what it would be like to see every man judge himself and then take it out on every other man all over the face of the earth."

It seemed no one but Charlie knew what was in Charlie's head, if Charlie himself knew. But Linda remembers "a certain passage in one song where he said he thought he heard, or did hear, the Beatles calling him, saying, 'Charlie, Charlie, send us a telegram' — he thought the Beatles were calling him."

Another family member recalls that Manson told the family how certain lyrics of the Beatles called for the black man to rise up. In one Beatles song, Manson believed he heard machine gun fire and the oinking of pigs, he said. The young man, who remembers being under the influence of LSD when he first met Charlie, says he later thought Manson was Jesus Christ and that he once tried to die — at Manson's command — by attempting to stop eating, thinking and exerting all physical effort. He said that out in the desert, Manson told him, "Give up your thoughts. Die. Because it's all unreal."

Just as throughout history some have been willing to die for

Christ, some of the Family were supposedly willing to die for Charlie. Or kill for him.

"A guy worked at the ranch — worked for old blind man Spahn," says Foster, "named Shorty Shea, a kind of ranch hand guy who pictured himself being an actor like some sort of John Wayne. He'd married a black chick that Charlie didn't like — because she was a 'nigger,' he said, and advised me to stay upwind. This Shorty'd been bummed out with Charlie running the ranch as he was, and he'd even talked to the old man about kicking Charlie and the hippies out of there, and Shorty was the guy to do it, or so he thought. This guy even had some of the license plates on the swiped cars. Charlie said, 'It's too bad he's breathing. He oughta stop breathing and let live, right?'

"Old George, the old man, he liked the girls, especially Squeaky who was at his side half the time when she wasn't making garbage runs, and she was like this blind man's — walking him here and walking him there, and the old man dug it — dug her. And Squeaky didn't trust or like his hired hand — this Shorty guy — this dumb fucking cowboy . . . who was digging his own grave."

Charlie had been talking about death, says Linda. "I heard him say, 'If you are willing to be killed, you should be willing to kill.'"

A boy Manson drove into town with one day, recalls an episode after the two left an ice cream parlor. He asked Manson to drive him by a relative's house, and when they arrived, the boy says, Manson wondered if the family had a dog, then suggested, "Why don't we go in there and tie them up and cut to pieces." The boy said he told him "No." In his wildest dreams, he couldn't have taken Charlie seriously.

A few afternoons later, Joe says, "I was sitting at the Longhorn in the shade and Charlie came out. He'd been painting the inside of the saloon. I hadn't said a word, and he looked at me and said, 'You're changing and going away.' I said, 'Where?' and Charlie said, 'You are going into yourself, dig. We have been through a lot of shit and a lot of it hasn't flown yet. And you have always been going out of yourself, haven't you?' And I said, 'Yes.' He said, 'Go in all the way, it's where you're heading.' He said why didn't I go back to the desert, and I said I wasn't sure about it out there, to which he sort of laughed. He said, 'You've gone in by yourself and nobody's pushed you, and what you're doing is right, it's perfect, dig, because that is what you're doing.' He said whatever had to be done, had to be done, and the thing of being done would make it perfect."

Joe stayed on at the ranch, "maybe another week or so, I don't have any idea about time. I didn't see Charlie every day — he stayed all over, with a different girl all the time." In Joe's mind, time was disconnecting itself from his thought process. In Death Valley, Joe says, "On a couple occasions in Shoshone I'd walked for miles with him on the desert floor. I'd seen him squatting in the noonday sun without a hat, figuring things for himself, when not even the animals would go in the sun. Maybe I'd been affected by the heat. But I had lost track of clock and calendar time. Anyway, I stayed at Spahn ranch. We all got up when Charlie did and ate whenever he did and what he ate, and he was a clock we all watched to check things out and see where we were."

Yet Charlie himself told the family, "I have never lived in time." He said that in reform school, "A bell rings. I get up. The door opens and I go out. A bell rings, and I live my life with bells. I get up when a bell rings and I do what a bell says. I have never lived in time.

"Things are relative," he told them. "I haven't got any guilt about anything because I have never been able to see any wrong. I have never found any wrong. I looked at wrong, and it is all relative. Truth is relative to the way you want to think. My reality is my reality and I stand with myself on my reality. Whatever you do is up to you . . ."

But Charlie's time and Charlie's law was becoming the absolute. One girl says she once saw him slap another girl across the face twice, angrily admonishing the two girls and Tex that they were not to go to sleep until he [Charlie] had gone to sleep. Another girl, seventeen, says Manson struck her with the leg of a chair, kicked, hit and even whipped her once with an electrical cord.

"Charlie preached love," Joe says, "but he was saying something else. He used the love he showed in all kinds of ways to strip us down to the bone, and then we were ready to do whatever he wanted. I stole, we all stole. I hit so many supermarkets and drugstores I lost count. We made almost daily raids into the 'pig pen' (shopping centers). And when I couldn't get the stuff in my clothes, stealing, I was out in all the garbage cans. We spent a lot of time in people's trash and we even had a song about The Garbage Man we'd sing at the ranch . . . We were all part of the garbage man — all the great garbage man — and we were really people of what you could call the true garbage can . . .

"One day," he recalls, "I think Leslie was in a car with a couple of girls, and we went to do some prowling in the pig pen, and the car broke down. The fuel pump just sort of busted up. Also there'd been no oil for the car for a long time, not since I'd stolen a case from a Chevron station. The girls got some of the stuff Charlie'd wanted them to bring back, and they started hitching. Some dudes picked them up and said, 'No, the guy can't ride,' and this made the girls sort of laugh because none of it mattered one way or another. So I just started walking and then I saw this sheriff's car — pulls up and I had pills in my pocket, so he said, 'Let's go . . .'"

Manson's music and financial hopes had taken him nowhere, and the more desperate he became the more he began to scheme — using the family to execute his plans.

Foster says, "Charlie got whatever he wanted. He got it out of everyone, a kind of suicidal loyalty . . ." He indicated that cars would be stolen and brought to the ranch. Often a car would appear and then disappear. "If they were stolen," one girl said, "I think they were taken out to the desert, and stashed there. Charlie said we'd all move there later on."

Reportedly there was talk at the ranch about a Volkswagen and a Fiat that belonged to Gary Hinman, and Charlie had told one young man that Hinman was planning to turn over the pink slips to those cars.

While in jail, Joe thought about Charlie's music. Charlie believed he and his music could not be separated, and "that was his whole strength . . . But Charlie is wrong," Joe says. "I had always hoped that something would've happened, that something would've worked. But it didn't. I don't know why, except that Charlie's real talents were not in music as much as in a sort of magic at getting people to do exactly what he wouldn't go out and do himself."

Bobby claims he was at the ranch because of the music — "the chance that something might come of it." He says, "Charlie first talked to me about the ranch — living there and taking care of the music part of it. We'd talked about forming this group — actually had it together, though our ideas were quite different. He had this idea about the unity of everyone at the ranch — everyone joining in and he had the primitive side of it, like a lot of Indians or natives chanting. But Charlie had a good voice and he played well, and he could bring everyone together and get a real session of it — even if it was singing around a big campfire . . .

"He had this idea of coming out to the desert. He said it was a new world — one that he'd found for us and for himself. He wanted to record this music about the desert so the rest of the world would do the same thing — 'Come out to the desert' sort of thing. That's how he thought it out. I tried to set up a recording for us, for that part of it and for the ranch songs. We had motorcycles and the choppers, and Charlie had it in his head that we'd do motorcycle songs, too.

"I went down to Hollywood to set up a recording for the sessions. Kitty was into it and so was Gypsy, and we had these tapes. Charlie had the idea that we'd be able to get the money out of that Buddhist guy — Gary Hinman, that Hinman had told Charlie he'd loan him the money against a percentage of the sales. So he'd get Hinman's money . . ."

Bobby ambled back and forth between the ranch and recording studio in L.A., but claims that every time he'd try to get Charlie to make some commitment as to a date so Bobby could set it up, "Charlie'd seem to drift off," Bobby says, "more concerned about building up a weapons supply — stealing guns, getting dune buggies together. All this in preparation for the Death Valley life we were all going to have — setting up a community out there . . ."

While living in the bunkhouse at the ranch, DeCarlo of the Straight Satans got "very friendly" with Bobby. DeCarlo says, "Manson didn't live in no particular place. There were two little shacks that he mostly stayed at; but nobody had one particular place to stay except for me, because I do a lot of drinking, you know. I sit and drink and play the radio and Charlie didn't like nobody to drink, and I also got the girls to cash in Coke bottles to buy beer and he didn't like that so he kept away from me."

Bobby, he recalls, "left the ranch for about three days in the middle of July. He returned, and one night while I was drinking beer and listening to the radio, Bobby began to brag . . . He became very talkative," DeCarlo says.

Manson had been trying to gain title to the two cars owned by Hinman, because Hinman no longer wanted to finance a recording session. Also, Charlie was after the money, but Hinman was planning a "pilgrimage" to Japan. Bobby knew that Hinman was going to make the trip and believed he had the money stashed in his house.

What Bobby "bragged" about, according to DeCarlo, was that he and two girls had gone to Hinman's thinking Hinman had the money there, and it had been Bobby's intention to rob him. Marie O'Brien, mother of a child fathered and delivered by Manson on the black bus in 1967, also says she and Susan went with Bobby to Hinman's house to force him to turn over the money, and to get the pink slips.

Bobby and the girls met Hinman outside his house with a 9mm pistol and a large knife with a thunderbird handle. Hinman said he didn't have the money, but they forced their way into the house, and then, after talking with him at length, they decided he didn't have any big money, though he offered to contribute $100 or $150. Then they called Manson. Later, Manson and Family member Bruce Davis arrived at Hinman's. Manson, Bobby says, was carrying a sword and told Hinman he wanted "to talk about that money" and looked "very fierce." According to Bobby, Charlie feared Hinman would go to the police, and promised that if he joined the Family there'd be "lots of girls to take care of him, and that he'd be able to live like a king." And Manson asked Hinman, "If we gave our world to you, would you leave?" But Hinman told Manson he couldn't give up his own way of life or belief in Buddhism. Charlie said, "That's about what I figured." Hinman told everyone to leave and Charlie threatened him with the sword, and they struggled over it. Manson slashed Hinman across the face, almost cutting off his left ear and wounding him deep in the jaw. Along with Davis, Charlie then left in Hinman's Fiat, after forcing Hinman to give him the ignition keys. Bobby says Charlie then ordered the girls to clean up Hinman's wounds. When this was done, they slept, except Marie who held the gun and kept watch over Hinman.

DeCarlo says Bobby told him they tortured Hinman for six or seven hours and then called Charlie up and said, "'Gary isn't cooperating' — so Charlie told me, 'You know what to do. Kill him — he's no good to us.'"

Marie was in the kitchen, she recalls, "and Sadie was in the bedroom. We heard a noise — a commotion — and ran into the living room. Gary had been stabbed and Bobby was standing behind him . . . Hinman was bleeding badly," she says, and "Bobby was holding the knife . . . Gary was bleeding from the chest . . . He walked to the bathroom, he looked like he might be in shock." Then, she says, Hinman "began chanting" and came back into the living room and collapsed in "sort of a coma."

DeCarlo says Bobby told him the first time he'd stabbed Hinman, "it didn't kill him right off. So I hit him again and again . . ."

Marie says while stabbing Hinman in the chest, Bobby shouted, "Society doesn't need you — you're a pig! It's better this way. I'm your brother!" Then, she says, Hinman fell near a makeshift Buddhist shrine. He had been stabbed five times in all, twice in the chest and head, once on the left side of his face, but the blow that was to kill him had entered his chest and directly pierced the heart. For moments, Marie recalls, they listened to Hinman breathing "real loud," and "someone put a pillow over Gary's face," to silence the noises he was making. Bobby then instructed the women to clean up the "bloody mess."

DeCarlo says, "After Hinman was dead, they took the blood and put a panther paw on the wall with the words 'POLITICAL PIGGY,' to divert suspicion toward the Black Panthers." Then, after attempting to clean up the fingerprints and other evidence, the three "hot-wired" Hinman's other car, the Volkswagen, and drove to the ranch. Bobby later returned to Hinman's house to remove more fingerprints, and "check it out." When he came back he told the others that the body was still there. A few days later, Bobby left Spahn ranch.

On July 31, three friends of Hinman went to his house as "no one had seen him for several days." The mailbox was jammed with mail. The house was surrounded with flies. "They were thick," a friend said, "And there was this buzzing of them in the air."

Inside the house, which was splattered with blood, Hinman's decomposing body was found.

A homicide officer later recalled "there were flies and maggots all over the face, neck, ears, and eyes, in the nose and apertures of Mr. Hinman's body."

Bobby was arrested in San Luis Obispo on August 4. He was driving Hinman's car which had been reported stolen, and the police found a thunderbird knife in the tire well of the car. He was taken into custody and charged with the murder.

Thirteen

During the early part of 1969, Terry Melcher moved out of the house on Cielo Drive after arranging to sublease it. The new tenant was movie actress Sharon Tate and her director husband Roman Polanski. They took occupancy of the house in March. Coincidentally, astrologer Robert Aiken had visited the house on Cielo Drive the year before. He says, "I knew some people who were friendly with the persons that had leased it, and I drew up a horoscope on the house. It was very badly aspected in a certain area — friends, or a group, or a gathering, could run into bad situations there. It was like an airplane, a group of people on it, and there is an accident . . ."

Polanski had a film commitment in Europe and Sharon Tate joined him in London that summer. When she returned to the States in mid-July, she was eight months pregnant. She planned to remain at home to await the arrival of her first baby, with close friends nearby such as Abigail Folger, daughter of the president of Folger Coffee Co. Another friend, Voityck Frykowski, a Polish writer, was working on a project for Polanski, and remained at the Cielo Drive house.

The estate forms the dead end of Cielo Drive. A fence stretches across the secluded road, and beyond it several clustered buildings sprawl along the graded property. It was once the home of Cary Grant, and had since been rented often on short-term leases to celebrities of the movie colony.

A gate is opened electrically by pressing a silver button on a waist-high length of pipe extending up from the shrubbery. Though the estate has been valued at more than $200,000, there are signs of neglect: a wood fence along the drive has been shattered by bumpers, paint on the main building is cracked and flaking away in patches. An old buckboard, once a movie prop, that serves as a decoration near the gate, has been chipped and splintered by motorists maneuvering around on the asphalt parking area.

At the opposite end of the property is a smaller guest house, and during the summer it was occupied by nineteen-year-old William Garretson. He had been hired as a caretaker by the landowner of the estate.

On August 8, 1969, Mrs. Winifred Chapman, housekeeper for the Polanskis, washed the front door of the house "because of the finger marks and the paw prints from the dogs, and I also washed the windows," she recalled. "I had cleaned the door with soap and water . . .

"There had been a carpenter working on Friday morning, and there had been men in and out all week. The room was being done over . . . making a nursery out of it. There had been a lot of work in there."

The housekeeper finished her work and left for the day between four and four-thirty. "It was still daylight," she said. "I left with two of the gardeners who drove me down to the bus stop."

About 8 o'clock that evening, Garretson left his guest house and walked across the property to the gate. By the time he had hitched a ride down to Sunset Boulevard to buy some groceries it was shortly after nine. He talked to a couple of friends on the Strip, then headed back to Benedict Canyon.

He saw Sharon Tate's car in the garage when he returned, and Abigail Folger's Pontiac near the old buckboard.

Everything was quiet inside the house. Well-known hair stylist Jay Sebring, an old friend, was visiting.

Garretson didn't remember what time it was when his friend, Steve Parent, came to visit him. The boy parked his Rambler on the property and carried a new clock radio to Garretson's guest house.

After visiting Garretson, Steve made a telephone call to another friend he wanted to see that night. Garretson walked him to the door and said "goodnight."

Outside, Parent got into his car and released the brake.

About an hour earlier, at Spahn ranch, Susan gathered up her "creepy-crawl" clothes and a knife. She says Charlie "told me the type of clothing I should wear should be dark clothing that I would take along with me — didn't matter, just a change of clothing. Wear dark clothes."

She does not recall getting any actual instructions from Charlie, "other than getting the clothes and knife," and was told to "do exactly what Tex told me to do."

Susan got into a car at the ranch with Tex, Katie and Linda. The car belonged to the hired ranch foreman. "It was a four-door Ford, yellow and white," Susan says. "Johnny frequently let us use his car. He had no knowledge of what we ever used the car for . . . It was an older car and it didn't have a back seat, just the floorboard . . . I just remember sitting in the back of the car and waving goodbye as we left the ranch — to Charlie and there were other people out there . . . There was a rope in the back of the car when I got in there. There was a set of bolt cutters . . . Tex had a gun. I had a knife. Linda had a knife. Katie had a knife, and to the best of my knowledge, I believe Tex had a knife . . .

"I couldn't wear shoes. I had a few sores on my feet from infection."

Tex drove the car, Susan said. "He told us that we were going to a house up on the hill that used to belong to Terry Melcher, and the only reason we were going to that house was because Tex knew the outline of the house. He told us about it as we were traveling." According to Susan, Tex described the house and said "He and Charlie had been there once talking to Terry and I think he said, with [Wilson]." She said Tex mentioned that Melcher no longer lived in the house.

There were movie stars there — Charlie had visited the house after Melcher had moved out. He'd said they'd treated him like a piece of garbage. Charlie'd told Tex, "They looked at me not like I was a human being, but like I was a piece of scum to be sucked into a toilet . . ."

"We sort of got lost on the way," Susan says. "I think we took a wrong turn and ended up somewhere in Mulholland and we went directly there . . . Tex did most of the talking in the car. In fact, to my recall, he did all of the talking. He told us we were going there to get all of their money and to kill whoever was there . . . it didn't make any difference who was there, we were told to kill them. It was late at night and it was kind of like we were all confused.

For Katie the auto ride was "like you're driving into a monstrous, like it was a monstrous stomach, and you watched like veins and arteries . . ."

Susan says, "There was a lot of confusion at that time because I didn't know what was going on, but I know that Tex got out of the car . . . got the bolt cutter, went to the power pole. He climbed back down, told all of us to get into the car, put the bolt cutter back in the car, and drove back down the hill and parked on a side street. Then he told us to get our changes of clothes, and we all walked back up the hill and walked to this fence . . . We walked up to the gate but didn't want to touch it or go over it because we thought there may be an alarm system or electricity running through it. We looked for a way to get over the gate and we noticed that — we walked over this way — there is a hill that goes up like this next to the fence. We walked up the side of the hill and could see that we could get over the fence easier there than getting over the fence where the gate is. I was told to go over first. So I threw my change of clothes over the fence and held the knife between my teeth, and climbed over and got my pants caught on part of the fence and had to kind of boost myself up and lift from where I was caught, off of the fence and fell into the bushes on the other side. I was followed by the three others, Katie, Linda, and Tex. Then we were going to move forward toward the residence, and saw lights coming from, apparently a car . . . I didn't actually see the car, just saw the headlights. Tex told us girls to lie down and be still and not make a sound. He went out of sight I heard him say, 'Halt!'"

The car had been coming down the driveway as the four were climbing over the front gate, Linda recalls, and "Tex jumped forward and stuck the gun to the man's head. The man pleaded, 'Please don't hurt me . . .'"

Susan also heard him say, "Please don't hurt me, I won't say anything." Then, she said, "I heard a gunshot and I heard another gunshot and another one and another one. Four gunshots. Tex came back to us and told us to come on. I saw him go to the car . . . He reached inside, turned off the lights, and then proceeded to push the car to where it stopped. Then we walked. I walked past the car — could see someone inside the car — I couldn't see the face, I just saw the head and it was leaning with the face toward the right to the passenger side. I didn't pay too much attention to it," Susan says. "We walked toward the residence, past the garage . . . We walked past that, came down to the walk but got off the walk. We came and walked over to this window — to the right of the front door . . . Tex opened up the window, crawled inside and the next thing I knew he was at the front door opening the front door — only two of us entered — Linda Kasabian stayed outside. Tex was already inside . . .

"As I walked in, Tex was in front of the couch and there was a man lying on the couch and his head — the back of his head was facing me and he was facing the opposite direction. It was — I was standing here and he was lying with his head here and his feet extending thát way . . . The man stretched his arms and woke up. I guess he thought some of his friends were coming from somewhere. He said, 'What time is it?' Tex jumped in front of him and held a gun in his face and said, 'Be quiet. Don't move or you're dead.' The man said something like 'Well who are you and what are you doing here?' Tex said, 'I am the Devil and I'm here to do the Devil's business . . . Where is your money?'

"The man said, 'My money is in the wallet on the desk.' And Tex told me to go over and look at the desk. I went over and looked at the desk, but I didn't see a wallet and I told Tex I didn't see one. Tex told me to go to the other rooms, go in and see if there was anybody else in the house. I went into two bedrooms, walked past one room and saw a woman sitting wearing glasses reading a book. She looked at me and smiled and I looked at her and smiled — she held her glasses down, and looked. I looked at her and waved my hand and smiled to her and went on to the next room, and saw a man sitting with his back to me and the woman lying on the bed, apparently pregnant, and they were talking. Neither one of them saw me, and I walked back into the living room and acknowledged to Tex that there were three more people . . . I had no idea who they were. When I first saw them, my reaction was, 'Wow, they sure are beautiful people.'

"Tex told me to tie up the man on the couch, so I took the rope (this was the rope that was in the car) and very loosely tied the man's hands . . . I had put his hands together in a crisscross fashion, and his wrists. I have never been very good at tying knots and I wrapped the rope around his hands a couple of times and I was shaking and everything was happening so fast that I did a very poor job of tying him up. I stood back and Tex instruct-ed me to go back and get the other people."

Susan did not learn until the following day who they were, but uses their names here in recollection: "I walked back to the room and went into Abigail Folger's bedroom, put a knife in front of her and said, 'Get up and go into the living room. Don't ask me any questions. Just do what I say.' She then proceeded to get up out of bed and walk down the hall and was met by Katie . . . And I went into the other bedroom and stood to the left of the door and told them both to get up and go into the living room [this was Sharon Tate and Jay Sebring].

"Shock. That was the expression on all their faces. Once he got

106

into the living room, Sebring said, 'What are you doing here?' and Tex told him to shut up. He told him to go over to the fireplace and lie down — Sharon said something to the effect that she is pregnant. Jay Sebring said, 'Can't you see she is pregnant, let her sit down.' Sebring didn't follow Tex's orders and Tex shot him. Sebring fell in front of the fireplace and Sharon and Abigail screamed.

"Tex asked the two girls if they had any money. Abigail said she did. Tex told me to take her into the bedroom. Abigail Folger walked into the bedroom. She reached into her purse and pulled out a wallet and said, 'I only have seventy-two dollars, I just went to the bank yesterday,' and asked me if I wanted any of her credit cards and I shook my head no. I took the money and put it in my pocket and walked her back to the living room where Tex had me re-tie Frykowski with a towel that I had gotten from the bedroom . . . I didn't do a very good job of that either.

"Abigail was standing and Sharon was sitting. Tex went over to Sebring and bent down and viciously stabbed him in the back many times with a knife. Then he told Sharon and Abigail to lie down next to him . . . and told Katie to turn off the lights and all the lights went out . . . There was enough light from the outside lights so that we could see on the inside. I looked over and saw a dog in the window. The dog ran away.

"The people got down on the floor," Susan says, "And they lied down and they were crying, and they were saying, 'Please don't hurt me.' Each one of them kept saying 'Please don't hurt me, we won't hurt you, we won't call the police, please don't hurt me, we won't call the police.'

"Tex proceeded to tie a rope around Sebring's neck then to Sharon Tate's neck, then to Abigail Folger's neck and threw the rope — he threw it over a high beam which he pulled which made Sharon and Abigail stand up so that they wouldn't choke to death, and then — I forget who said it, but one of the victims said 'What are you going to do with us?' Tex said, 'You are all going to die.' And at that time they began to plead for their lives — Frykowski and Sharon and Abigail — Sebring was dying on the floor.

"They were pleading, I would have been, too — and Tex ordered me to go over and kill Frykowski. I went over to him and raised the knife in my hand. I looked at him and hesitated. I hesitated long enough for the man to jump up. He knocked me down and I grabbed him as best I could . . . I tried to stop him and he kept pulling my hair and I was kicking at him and I was fighting him — it was like I was fighting for my life, it was like I never fought before, something I never experienced. He had hold of my hair and pulled it very hard and I was screaming for Tex to help me, or somebody to help me, and Frykowski, he was also screaming. Somehow he got behind me and I had the knife in my right hand and I was — I was — I don't know where I was at but I was just swinging with the knife and I remember hitting something four, five times repeatedly behind me . . . I just kept swinging. I kept swinging the knife, I would swing the knife backwards, it was like . . . I didn't see what it was that I was stabbing — I never stabbed a human being before, but I just know it was going into something . . . Then the man — he let go of me, got away from me and started running toward the front door, which was open, and screaming bloody murder, yelling for his life, for somebody to come help him . . . And I went to run after him, and then I looked over and Katie was calling 'Help!' She was fighting with two women. And the dark-haired woman Abigail had hold of Katie's hair and was pulling on it and Katie was fighting and she called for Linda . . ."

During it all, Linda "heard a man scream — then just screams. I don't have any words to describe how a scream is. I never heard it before. It was unbelievably, terribly horrible."

Frykowski got to the door, Susan says. "Tex hit him over the head with the gun butt . . . I believe the handle of the gun broke . . . He was stabbing him as best he could because Frykowski was fighting."

Linda, outside the house, saw "there was a man who had just come out of the door and he had blood all over his face . . . We looked into each other's eyes.

"I said, 'Oh, God, I'm sorry,' and he just fell into the bushes."

Soon after, Linda says, "the man had gotten up and moved away. Tex was hitting him and stabbing him and he was on top of him. The man was struggling with him . . ."

Inside, Susan says, "Sebring, he was dead I believe, lying on the floor . . . Although I heard moaning, I don't know whether it came from Sebring or not — Abigail had gotten loose from the rope and was in a fight with Katie."

Katie says, "It's all the picture-like motion, reaction, it's hard to explain, trying to describe in detail . . . I remember looking up and Sadie was — and Sadie was — was fighting with like with two women, and I —

108

I guess I just got up and ran — and ran over and started fighting with a woman over there. And I can remember finally like Sadie was fighting over here, or something, and I was fighting."

Susan says, "Tex went over to help Katie, and I saw Katie be released from Abigail's grip, and I saw Tex stab Abigail and just before he stabbed her — maybe an instant before he stabbed her, she looked at him and let her arms go and looked at all of us and said, 'I give up, take me.'

"Tex stabbed her again and she gripped her middle section of her body and fell to the floor . . . And then I saw Tex go back outside."

Abigail crawled up and tried to run from the house, Katie recalls.

Linda says "Katie came running out of the house and I said, 'Please, make it stop — people are coming.' She said it was too late . . . then I saw a girl run and Katie chasing after her with an upraised knife, and I just turned and ran to the car down at the bottom of the hill . . ."

Katie remembers: "I had a knife in my hands, and Abigail took off running, and she ran — she ran — she ran out through a back door . . . And I went through that door, and was chasing her on the grass and we started fighting and I stabbed her and I kept stabbing her."

Inside the house, Susan says, "I can remember seeing Sharon struggle with the rope. Tex told me to take care of her, and I ran to the pregnant woman because she was starting to take the rope off her neck. I went over and grabbed her by the hand and put my arm around her neck . . . and I had her head in my arms, and then I saw Tex come back to the man on the floor with the rope around his neck [Sebring] and he was stabbing the man.

"Sharon looked at me and begged to let me have her sit down and I was told, before we got there, no matter what they beg don't give them any leeway," Susan says. "Anyway, I went over and put her down on the couch and looked into her face, knowing that anything that I would say I was saying to myself, in a sense reassuring myself. I looked at her and said, 'Woman, I have no mercy for you.' And I knew at that time I was talking to myself, not to her.

"She said, 'Please let me go. All I want to do is have my baby.' She still had the rope around her."

Suddenly, Susan says, she found herself alone in the living room with Sharon. "She kept pleading, 'Please don't kill me, please don't kill me, I'm not going to say anything.' I just looked at her like, 'Shut up!' I told her to shut up, I don't want to hear it. She said, 'Please, let me sit down.'

I said, 'I'm not going to let you do anything, just be quiet!' I threw her down and held my knife at her, and I said, 'Don't move, don't move.' She said, 'Please, all I want to do is have my baby.' I said, 'Don't move, don't talk to me, don't say anything to me. I don't want to hear it . . .'

"Tex came back in and he stood over and he looked at her and he said, 'Kill her!'

"It was just there to do," Susan says. "I didn't relate to Sharon Tate to be anything but a store mannequin . . . She sounded like an IBM machine — words kept coming out of her mouth . . . Begging and pleading, begging and pleading. I got sick of listening to her, so I stabbed her. And I just stabbed her, and she fell, and I stabbed her again . . . just kept stabbing and stabbing . . ."

Susan says she could feel the knife jab through the skin and strike bone — feel the "razor-sharp honed" blade hit bones and strike past into the deep soft organs. She would later claim it was the most exciting sexual experience she has ever known — that knife driving deeply again and again into Sharon Tate's flesh and body.

"Sharon put her arms up, and then her arms fell . . . I don't know how many times I stabbed her. I don't know why I stabbed her."

Then, Susan recalls, "Tex came back in, said, 'Hold her!'" And Susan saw "Tex stab her in the heart area around the chest. Sharon fell to the floor off the couch and we went to the front door. I believe Tex said, 'The gun doesn't work anymore. I broke it over his head.'

"Then I ran outside and Katie was just getting up from in front of the woman on the grass." They had gone out the front door, Susan says, "and I saw Abigail on the lawn . . . I just saw her nightgown, a see-through nightgown and I saw blood on it, and I saw Tex go over and stab her three or four — I don't know how many times."

Frykowski was laying out in front of the house. Tex was stabbing Abigail, Susan recalls, and "while he was doing that, Katie and I went looking for Linda because she wasn't around anymore. In fact, we started calling for her. We didn't want to call too loud." Tex walked over to where Frykowski was, Susan says. "He was lying with his back to me. Tex kicked him in the head, and the body didn't move very much. I believe it was dead at that time. Then we walked up to the gate. We walked around there, looking for Linda.

"Tex was walking toward Katie and me — he told me to go back

110

into the house and write something on the door in one of the victim's blood. He said, 'Write something that will shock the world.'

"I had previously been involved in something similar to this where I saw 'political piggy' written on the wall, so that stuck very heavily in my mind," Susan says. "I didn't want to go back anywhere near the house, so I just blanked my mind and walked into the house. I picked up the same towel that I had tied Frykowski up with and walked over to Sharon Tate's body — she seemed to have been cut up a lot more than when I had last seen her. I never actually saw her face. Her hair was covering her face and there were sounds coming from her body . . . Gurgling sounds like blood flowing into the body out of the heart.

"I picked up the towel and turned my head and touched her chest and at the same time I knew she was pregnant, and I knew there was a living being inside of that body and I wanted to cut it out, but I didn't have the courage to go ahead and take it. And I got the towel with her blood, walked over to the door and with the towel I wrote 'PIG' on the door — outside on the front door — 'PIG' in Sharon Tate's blood. I held the towel in my hand and stood there for a few minutes. I did not know what to do . . ."

Susan would later confide how her mind "reeled with pictures . . ." How she was impelled to drink of the spilled blood — to take her fill of it like a vampire. She would later describe the feeling of beautiful Sharon Tate's blood on her hands. "It was slick and I brought my hand to my face and I could smell the blood. I opened my mouth and I licked it on my fingers . . ." Again she thought of cutting the baby from the dead woman's body — of wrapping the unborn in the same towel and taking it to Charlie. "How proud Charlie would be if I presented him with the baby cut from the womb of the woman . . ." She thought of cutting Sharon Tate's heart — of cutting it from the wounded chest cavity, and how it could be eaten — as the hearts of enemies were eaten by the Indians. She thought of eating the baby — of skewering it at one of the family's bonfires — each eats of the flesh of the unborn and are reborn themselves.

But, Susan says, "I turned around and threw the towel toward the living room where the bodies were lying . . . I walked out the front door at a very rapid pace up to Tex and Katie . . . We had left the change of clothes at the gate. We picked up these clothes before we left. There was a possibility I had blood all over my body . . . I'm pretty sure Tex had a lot of blood on him. Tex pushed the button that opened the gate. We proceeded to walk down the hill to the car."

Linda was alone and didn't enter the car at first, she said. "I guess I was in a state of shock." The "first thing that came to my mind . . . was to go to a neighbor's house to call the police." As she remembers, Susan said she'd left her knife inside the house, and "I think she started to run back in the house," while she herself returned to the car. After "just a few minutes" then, Tex, Susan and Katie returned to the car. "All three of them" were bloody, Linda went on. "I was sitting in the driver's seat. Tex pushed me over and got behind the wheel. He seemed really uptight because I had run back to the car."

Susan recalls that Linda started the car and Tex said, "What do you think you're doing? Get over on the passenger side. Don't do anything unless I tell you to do it." Then, Susan said, "we got in the car and as we were driving, we changed our clothes inside the car. We started to drive all over. We drove somewhere along Mulholland Drive, somewhere up in the canyon, I can't say for sure where. All we did was drive along and all of the weapons except for one weapon, I believe it was my knife, was handed to Linda who was sitting up in the front seat along with the gun, and we drove along the road until we came to what looked like an embankment going down like a cliff with a mountain on one side and a cliff on the other. Tex asked for something white, some sort of piece of cloth. In other words, if there happened to be a car behind he could throw out the white stuff as a diversionary."

As they drove on, Linda says, "They complained about their heads, that people were pulling their hair and that their heads hurt, and Sadie said that a man hit her in the head, and Katie said her hand hurt . . . She said that when she stabbed, that there were bones in the way, and that she couldn't get the knife through all the way, and that it took too much energy or something like that, and that when she stabbed, it hurt her hand. Katie said one of the girls inside was crying for her mother and for God." As they drove on, all had changed clothes except Linda. "I held the steering wheel while Tex took off his top and he changed his pants later on. They wanted to go hose off the blood from their bodies," Linda said. She doesn't know where Tex eventually stopped the car. "I don't know the name, but it was the street where we had spotted a hose when we were coming up the hill. And we stopped and parked the car to use the hose." It was "not very far . . . maybe five or ten minutes" from the Tate residence, on a hilly street.

"We went to a street that looked dark, it didn't have any lights on it," Susan says. "We went there to wash the blood off us. Only I didn't know that until we actually got to a house. We were so much one with each other that we really didn't need too many words spoken. Everything we did from the time he cut the poles to the time we got back to the ranch was spontaneous. It was done with no thought. So we were looking for a house to wash the blood off ourselves, because that is what we did.

"We found a very dark house and there appeared to be nobody home. Tex found the hose. We took and turned on the hose and took it out into the street and started washing ourselves off, our feet and our arms and our faces. We had already changed clothes, so — and I heard a man and a woman come out of the house and they were yelling 'What is going on?' And the woman was yelling something about 'My husband belongs to the Los Angeles Police Department and he is going to see that — blah, blah, and blah, blah,' I don't recall what she said.

"Tex looked at him and said, 'Gee, I'm sorry, I didn't think you were home. We were just walking around and wanted a drink. We didn't mean to wake you up or disturb you.'

"And the man looked down the street and said, 'Is that your car?' and Tex said, 'No, I told you we were just walking.' The man said, 'I know that is your car, you better get in it and get going.' And at that time the woman said to get the license number and she was frantic and she started calling us filthy hippies and tramps and calling us girls sluts and prostitutes and all those crazy things that people do.

"Tex told us girls to get into the car, so we walked to the car and got in . . . Tex had already started the car and the man reached in to turn off the car ignition."

Linda says, "Tex fought him, and then just 'jammed,' and I thought the man's arm would come off" as they sped away. They just drove, she said. "It was like a country road, sort of . . . winding and hilly . . . with only a few houses — there were very few lights."

After about ten or fifteen minutes, Linda says, "I remember we came to a sort of level part of the road, and there was a dirt shoulder, and Tex handed me the clothes and told me to throw them out — the clothes that Tex, Sadie and Katie had changed."

She got out of the car to throw them away. "They were just in one bundle," she remembers, and she threw them over a hill at the side of the road. "We drove off, and then Tex told me to wipe off the prints on the two knives," using a rag. "After wiping them off, I threw the knives out . . . while the car was moving. One landed in the bushes but the second bounced off the curb, and I could sort of see it on the road." She remembers tossing the knives out about "three, four or five minutes" after throwing away the clothes. The buck knife wasn't there, she said, because that was the one Katie had left behind. "I just reached my hand, and threw them out. I may have thrown out the revolver, but I don't remember." She recalls, however, that "the right part of the grip no longer was on the gun . . . I think Tex said when he hit the man over the head, it shattered the gun . . ."

They continued driving, Linda says. "We came to streets with lights and traffic, and we stopped at a service station. Tex told Sadie and Katie to go in and wash themselves off. Then he went in himself. He ordered some gas before we left."

Susan says, "I think the gas station was located on Sunset Boulevard. We went into the bathroom and checked for any other blood spots. In my fight with Frykowski, I had opened the sores that I had on my feet and my feet were bleeding and very sore."

Linda stayed in the car and got into the driver's seat, while Tex was then "on the other side, in front." Sadie and Katie got back into the back seat and they returned to Spahn ranch, arriving about "an hour and a half after leaving the service station."

As they returned to the parking area at the ranch, Linda says, Charlie was in "about the same spot where he stood when we left."

Susan says, "I remembered being in the Tate house — I recall either hearing twelve chimes or seeing a clock that said twelve . . . So we probably got back to the ranch somewhere around two o'clock in the morning. Charlie said, 'What are you doing home so early?' Charlie changes from second to second," Susan says. "He can be anybody he wants to be. He can put on any face he wants to put on at any given moment. Tex was nervous like he had just been through a traumatic experience . . . Katie was very silent. I almost passed out — I felt as though I had just killed myself. I felt dead.

"All the things that happened after that are very foggy to me. All I know is that I got out of the car. I had seen blood on the car at the gas station and I went into the kitchen."

Linda recalls Charlie had "instructed Sadie to get a sponge to wash off the car, and told the rest of us to go through the car." Susan says she "got a sponge and a rag and went back out to the car and wiped it off . . . The outside of the car, door handles and the steering wheel. I don't think I did anything to the inside of the car . . ."

When the car had been checked and the blood removed, "Charlie said to go in the bunk room," Linda recalls. She went into the bunk room with Katie and Sadie, "then Charlie came into the bunk room with Tex, and Tex told him, what he told the people at the house — 'I'm the Devil, here to do the Devil's work.'"

Susan says, "Tex told Charlie — basically just what he had done. That it all happened perfectly. There was a lot of — it happened very fast — a lot of panic, that they were panicked, and Tex described it, 'Boy, it sure was helter-skelter.'"

Linda says, "Tex said there was a lot of blood — it was really messy, and that there were bodies all over the place, but they were all dead . . . Then Charlie asked us if we had any remorse. He simply asked us, 'Do you have any remorse?'" Tex, Sadie, Katie and Linda each replied "No." Then, she says, "Charlie told us not to talk this over with anybody at the ranch, and to go and get some sleep." They'd done a good night's work. It was only the beginning.

Fourteen

On Saturday morning, August 9th, Mrs. Chapman arrived at the Polanski house to start her day's work. Immediately she noticed the wires at the gate, cut and hanging down. "I opened the gate and went on in . . . I picked up the paper and snapped out the outside lights, unlocked the back door with my own key and I went in, and I went to the kitchen phone and picked it up. Since our electric was on, I surmised it was the telephone wires, and I picked up the kitchen phone and it was dead, and I started up front to waken someone . . . That is when I saw the bodies and the bloody clothes — I ran out."

The woman ran, screaming. She did not return to the Polanski house.

Six patrol cars soon arrived at the scene, and officers went through the property with guns drawn.

A dog was barking behind the guest house and a voice called out, "Quiet!" But the dog continued to bark. "Christopher, be quiet!"

Within moments the police burst through Garretson's door — he sat stunned on his bed. He was immediately taken to a patrol car, and didn't even recognize the bodies of the people he had known as he passed them on the lawn.

At ten o'clock, Detective Manuel Granado passed the police cordon that kept back the newsmen and spectators.

Sharon Tate's theatrical agent had been called from an early tennis match to identify the bodies. He left in tears, refusing to speak to reporters.

Detective Granado, having entered the house, observed the three pieces of a pistol grip, two large pieces and one very small. "The two large pieces," he said, "I found inside the living room. The small piece was immediately outside, approximately a foot away from the front door . . . I picked them up with my tongs and had them fingerprinted," giving instructions to "be careful with some blood that was on the pieces of the hand grip."

Homicide Detective Michael McGann recalls on his arrival shortly after Granado's, "I entered the property and observed Steven Parent slumped over the seat of this Rambler, which is this two-door . . . I continued onto the property, entered the walkway, and observed Voityck Frykowski lying on the front lawn on his side . . . I continued toward Frykowski's body, at which time I observed Abigail Folger lying on her back. . . I went back to the front of the house . . . The window was open and the screen was sitting beside it leaning against a window . . . A vertical slit had been made in the screen . . . I observed numerous blood splatters about the front porch and on the front door. The word — the door was partially open and 'PIG,' or 'P-I-G' is written in blood.

"Then I entered the entryway and continued into the living room of the Polanski residence. I continued over to this couch . . . and observed Sharon [Tate] Polanski lying on her left side directly in front of the sofa. I also observed the body of Jay Sebring lying on his right side in front of a chair."

Detective Granado had observed the rope around Sharon Tate's neck. "It appeared to be wrapped around and then around again and it didn't appear to have a knot in it but was just wrapped around the neck. It extended over to Jay Sebring, around his neck. It went around the same as Sharon Tate except that the rope went in and tied. His face was wrapped and he was face down . . ." The rope Granado described had "three large strands with multiple smaller strands. This rope went along with the body to the coroner. It was severed by the coroner at the scene, and Sharon Tate's portion stayed with her body and the other portion stayed with Sebring's body."

Sergeant McGann said, "The interior of the house did not appear to have been ransacked . . . The wallets of Abigail Folger and Voityck Frykowski were loosely found in one of the sofas in the Folger bedroom but they did not appear to — the house itself did not appear to have been ransacked . . . There was currency inside Abigail Folger's wallet."

Garretson was charged with five counts of murder on the basis that he had been the last living person on the premises. The housekeeper was taken to the UCLA Medical Center in a state of shock. Later, she was brought to the police station where Garretson was being held. He kept repeating that he had seen nothing, heard nothing. He had put on his record player, removed his shirt and stretched out on the bed. He remembered closing his eyes. When he opened them again it was near dawn. He picked up his telephone but the line was dead. All the lines seemed dead. He wasn't sure what to do and it made him feel "a little bit frightened." He went back to sleep. The next thing he knew the dog was barking and then the police were there.

Later, the bodies lay in the County Morgue, six in all.

Steve Parent was identified by his parish priest, who went to the morgue after the boy's father told him Steve was missing.

Chief Coroner Thomas Noguchi examined the body of Abigail Folger, and also directed and supervised the autopsies performed by another medical examiner. Folger's death came from "a stab wound of the aorta, that is the large blood vessel originating from the heart, causing massive hemorrhage." Dr. Noguchi found twenty-one stab wounds on the body and said they appeared "caused by the same type of cutting instrument." As to depth of the wounds, he said, "I would say that five to six inch stab wounds were observed."

There were no gunshot wounds in her body.

Frykowski's death was attributed to "multiple stab wounds of the body causing massive hemorrhage . . . There was one gunshot wound," Noguchi said. "A total count of the stab wounds found on the body was fifty-one." The coroner found a total of thirteen cuts to the scalp. "I would say the wound characteristics were totally consistent with injuries caused by blunt force," he went on. There were five stab wounds in the back and eleven wounds to the chest, up to the side of the chest, and these wounds were caused by a bayonet-type instrument, the same instrument that caused the wounds in the fifty-one parts of the man's body, he said. There were sixteen stab wounds to the left arm, eight stab wounds to the left leg. Describing the gunshot wound, he said the bullet entered the left armpit, more toward the back, and "the direction of the gunshot wound track was almost horizontal" as if Frykowski were in a standing position. "Then the bullet was found in the back at the fifth dorsal vertebra . . . the fifth backbone column below the neck bone."

The autopsy of Steven Parent showed death by "multiple gunshot wounds of the chest, causing massive hemorrhage . . . There were two gunshot wounds in the chest . . . One gunshot wound was also found on the left face. I should, perhaps, say cheek, and another gunshot wound was found on the left arm, which was a through-and-through wound," the chief coroner said. He reported one stab wound and one cut to the left hand . . . "It could be considered a defense wound," incurred as Parent sought to prevent total injury.

Dr. Noguchi concluded that the gunshot wounds to both Frykowski and Jay Sebring were non-fatal. The cause of Sebring's death, Noguchi said, was determined as "exsanguination . . . massive hemorrhage, caused by stab wounds." He said the body suffered six stab wounds generally in the left side of the chest. "The organs that were involved which caused the hemorrhage were aorta, a large blood vessel coming out from the heart and left lung, and also other injuries which are apart from the stab wounds . . ." He said Sebring's face "showed bruises and swelling . . . contusion. Such as the bruise on the nose, and the left eye. There were cuts found on the left hand . . . As far as we can determine there was a gunshot wound on the left side of the chest penetrating to the left lung, and there are spattered fragmented bullet along the area of the central portion of the chest." There were two gunshot wounds, he said. One on the left side of the chest and another in the lower back. "The fragment was found . . . on the back and just — I think between the skin and the shirt he was wearing."

The autopsy on Sharon Tate was performed by Dr. Noguchi himself. He said death was caused by "multiple stab wounds of chest and back penetrating heart, lungs and liver, causing massive hemorrhage." The rope around her neck had left no abrasion or scarring mark, and, he said, "there was no indication of strangulation . . ." There were sixteen stab wounds on Sharon Tate's body. In the chest area, Dr. Noguchi found four stab wounds, and eight stab wounds to the back. "And," he said, "certain wounds to the arms and other areas of the body."

Had death come instantly?

"In my opinion," Dr. Noguchi said, "based on the study of the previous cases where a person receives stab wounds to the heart causing massive hemorrhage, the average person would first receive a profuse hemorrhage into the body cavity, thus causing a sudden drop of the blood pressure . . . It is quite possible still that the person would be able to move to escape from the location where he or she was injured, but most likely the person would be incapacitated very shortly after infliction of the stab wound through the heart . . . As the blood pressure decreased to less than one third of the normal blood pressure," he went on, "then it is very unlikely the person would be able to move and probably suffer a short period of coma and death usually within fifteen minutes."

Dr. Noguchi said a number of the wounds in Sharon Tate's back and chest "penetrated through the ribs." He was asked if this would require a great deal or moderate amount of force, and if the assailant could be male or female. Dr. Noguchi answered that "this type of wound could be caused by a number of factors. One, the instrument has to be reasonably sharp and . . . heavy enough to have a momentum so that it can continue penetrating into the deeper tissue of the body, and the person has to have the strength to give a strong thrust into the body. I would be probably speculating too much if I would differentiate whether male or female. The strength of male, female, sometimes is equal and sometimes depending on the circumstances," Noguchi continued. The examination of Sharon Tate revealed that she "was eight months in pregnancy stage and the male fetus was found." However, Noguchi said, "there was no injury to abdominal area nor the unborn baby . . . I performed an autopsy on the unborn male and there was no congenital abnormalities and maturation of the baby was entirely consistent with eight months pregnancy."

The death of the unborn baby, he said, "would not be simultaneous . . . we know . . . a number of cases where after a maternal death the babies have been saved by emergency Caesarian sections. We feel that the fetus is resistant to lack of oxygen to enable it to survive a period of fifteen to twenty minutes of cessation of the maternal circulation."

The perfectly formed baby boy made the sixth victim of the slaying.

Dr. Noguchi gave a brief statement to the press, saying, "This crime was so weird and bizarre that we are showing photographs of the bodies to a psychiatrist and a psychologist who are consultants on our staff in an effort to determine from them a behavior evaluation of the killer . . ."

One detective said that since the telephone lines had been cut the murders were apparently premeditated. He suggested the victims were "caught unawares" and that an escape attempt was apparent by the manner in which the bodies were found. "It was a weird homicide," he said, "but I don't think we have a maniac running around loose."

Garretson's attorney disagreed with the police. "I think there is a maniac running around," he said. His client underwent an hour of polygraph tests at central police headquarters that Sunday afternoon, but detectives were "not entirely satisfied with the results," and Garretson was released with "insufficient evidence to detain him any longer."

Both Linda and Susan learned for the first time who "those people" were "the next morning on the news and TV, in a trailer next to George Spahn's house."

Linda says, "It seems I had slept most of the day, and then when I got up, Sadie told me to come and watch TV."

"The Soul sure did pick a lulu," Susan recalls saying, "But the Soul did a good job, or something to do with the Soul, not meaning Charlie Manson picked a good one, meaning the Infinite Soul . . . I believe the words came from my mouth, I'm not sure because I don't know, I just know that something to that effect was said. And I said something to the effect that it served its purpose — to instill fear into the Establishment."

Susan says, after the news, "Some of the girls talked about it and that — I don't recall exactly what they said, but they were aware of the fact that we had gone out the night before . . . At that time they weren't aware of the fact that we had done it but we didn't actually have to say anything. The Family was so much together that nothing ever had to be said. We all just knew what each other would do or had done . . . I got the impression that they put two and two together."

Linda doesn't remember seeing Tex that day, although the whole family was together for dinner later. Then, she says, "I was in the kitchen, cleaning up, and we were all sitting around, and Gypsy came in from town with a whole bunch of zuzus, you know — candy — and she was going to take a bunch of us up to the water hole and I was hoping I would get to go. Then Charlie came and called Katie and Leslie and myself aside. He told me to get a change of clothes . . . my driver's license . . . and to meet him at the bunk house." Soon after she met Manson and others at the bunk house, "I can't remember exact faces . . . but eventually we were all there. Myself, Charlie, Leslie, Sadie, Katie, Tex and Clem."

That night, Susan says, "Charlie told me to go get two changes — get a change of clothes. I looked at him and I knew what he wanted me to do, and I gave a sort of a sigh and went and did what he asked me to do. I didn't pick up any weapons."

Linda says Charlie told them then, "we were going out again tonight, that last night was too messy, and he was going to show us how to do it. No one said anything to Charlie then," she recalls, though at one point "Tex said we needed better weapons, that the ones we took were not good enough." She remembers seeing "two long swords" then in the bunkhouse, though she didn't notice if anyone picked them up.

The group then went to a car owned by a ranch hand, the same car that had been driven the night before, Linda says. "I sat between Charlie and Clem in the front seat with Clem on the right. Tex was directly in back of Charlie, and Leslie sat on Tex's lap, and then there were Katie and Sadie . . ."

Then, Charlie handed Linda "a leather thong he had been wearing around his neck." It was rolled up, Linda recalls. "I put it in my pocket. It was sort of decorative . . . it was wound around . . . it looked like a hangman's noose."

Twenty-four hours had not passed since the killings. Susan says, "I was still in a state of shock from the previous night . . . I know it was in the early evening. It was after dark. Charlie drove. There was a gun in the car, and Charlie had it." But she knew it was not the same gun that had been used the night before and was "thrown over a hill."

"We just started driving," Susan says. "The only discussion I can recall, sticks in my mind, is that we were going to do the same thing we had done last night only two different houses, there was to be two sets of — two groups consisting of one man and two girls to go to two different houses. That is why there were two men and four girls . . . I don't know if these were Charlie's exact words, but basically that is what he said."

They drove to a gas station and bought some gas, and Linda believes Charlie went out and got some cigarettes. Then, she says, "Charlie told me to take over the driver's seat, sitting beside me . . . I drove on the freeway, a long way. Charlie gave me directions." Tex was quiet, and only Charlie gave the directions.

Linda recalls Charlie directing her "on the freeway and then we got to a turnoff, and he told me to turn, and I remember it was Fair Oaks in Pasadena." Eventually Charlie told her to stop. "We stopped in front of a house. Charlie got out of the car and told me to drive around the block." When they returned to the house, "Charlie was standing in front . . . We sat in the car for awhile because there was a man and a woman sitting in a car nearby." Charlie said "something like the man was too big, and told me to drive off." Linda started the car.

When Charlie got back in the car, Susan says, "he said he saw pictures of children through the window and he didn't want to kill anyone because of the children. He said, 'You realize that if you have to take the life of a child, it would only be to save the children of the future . . .'

"Somewhere in the same neighborhood we stopped at one house and we stayed in the car. Charlie stayed in the car. We just watched . . . about two, three minutes.

"We drove on and then we just continued driving around and I fell asleep. I was thoroughly exhausted, and when I woke up we were in front of another house and I seemed to recognize the house — not the house, but the particular area." Susan had been to that area "about a year previously . . . I was there with about fifteen people." The house she recognized was next door to the house in front of where they parked. There had been a party there, she recalls. "We had all took an LSD trip together," she, Charlie, about fifteen others. "And the reason why I couldn't see the house was I was sitting in the back seat, like I said there is no seat to the car and I was slumped down because I was sleeping, and when I looked up, I just woke up from a dream and I dreamed that Charlie had gone into a house with Tex and killed the people."

Linda says she drove through a "modern, expensive area" but Charlie gave instructions to drive on because "the homes were too close together . . . We came to a church. There were lots of trees. Charlie was going to go in and find a minister, or a priest or whoever was there . . . but all the doors were locked." Then he drove for awhile, to Sunset Boulevard in Los Angeles, before instructing her again to get behind the wheel. For awhile they had driven up a dirt road, Linda recalls, stopping at another house before driving back through the city down Sunset Boulevard. Linda says she followed a white sports car through a residential area. They went up and down many dark streets. Finally Charlie told her to park.

Susan, in the back, saw Charlie get out of the car. He went in the house and was there a long time. She said, "After a while, then Charlie came back and he said, 'Tex, Katie —' and he looked at me and he could see that I didn't want to go into the house. Then Charlie turned away from Susan and said, 'Leslie — go into the house.' He said something to the effect that last night Tex let the people know they were going to be killed, which caused panic, and Charlie said that he reassured the people with smiles in a very quiet manner that they were not to be harmed — just that they were not to be harmed.

"He said he had the people already tied up." Then, Susan remembers, "Charlie said 'paint a picture more gruesome than anybody has ever seen.' And so Tex and Leslie got out of the car." Susan says Charlie told them they wouldn't wait, and to hitchhike back to the ranch.

Susan stayed in the car with Linda, Clem, and Charlie. She says, "Charlie also had a wallet he supposedly got from the house. When he got back in the car — after he sent Leslie, Tex, and Katie into the house — he said it was the woman's identification.

"We drove off," Susan says. "We drove around and Charlie said we were going in the opposite direction than we came from. We drove in a predominantly colored area. I don't know the area, but this is what I gathered, seeing Negroes . . .

"Charlie gave Linda the woman's wallet and told her to put it into the bathroom in the gas station, and leave it there hoping that somebody would find it and use the credit cards, and thus be identified with the murder. Linda said she did it — I didn't see her leave it but she didn't come back with it either. Then we drove around for a long time and I went back to sleep. It wasn't like I was asleep, it was like I was drugged. I felt very heavily drugged. I was not on drugs at the time . . . I just felt like that I had been shot with morphine, or something, or fell asleep . . . or passed out."

Linda, wide awake, stared at passing headlights until there were no more approaching and everything was dark. They were at the beach, and Charlie was asking them whether they knew anyone around there. Linda says they replied "No," but Charlie turned to her, she says, and said, "'What about the man that you and Sandy met? Isn't he a piggie?' And I said 'Yes, he's an actor.' And then he further questioned me, and he asked me if the man would let me in. And I said, 'Yes.' He asked me if the man would let my friends in, Sadie and Clem. And I said, 'Yes.' He said, 'OK. I want you to kill him,' and he gave me a small pocket knife. And at this point I said, 'Charlie, I am not you, I am not you. I cannot kill anybody.' I don't know what took place then at that moment, but I was very much afraid."

Charlie then told her, Linda says, "'As soon as he opens the door, slit his throat' . . . I said, 'Charlie, I'm not you, I can't kill anybody.' He had the knife in his hand and started telling how to kill him. 'As soon as he opens the door, slit his throat.' He told Clem to shoot him."

Linda had met the man before, she says, while hitchhiking with another girl, and the man had taken them to an apartment building in Venice. There she had showered, had something to eat and had sex with the man.

As Charlie directed them to Venice, Linda says, "he started to tell me how to go about it, killing him, and I remember I had the knife in my hand, and I asked him, 'With this?' And he said, 'Yes' and he showed me how to do it." It was a kind of digging motion. And as they neared Venice, Linda recalls, "Charlie said, 'As soon as you enter the house, as soon as you see the man, slit his throat right away.' Again he told Clem to shoot him. He then said if anything went wrong, you know, just hang it up, don't do it, and hitchhike back to the ranch."

In Venice, Linda says that at first they couldn't find the apartment building. They drove around many streets, finally parked, and she and Charlie went on foot in search of the location. Linda recalls that as they walked through the dark streets she told Charlie she was pregnant and that Charlie kept talking to her and "sort of made me forget about everything . . . he just made me feel good." They continued their walk while Clem stayed in the car trying to rouse Susan. It was on this walk, Linda says, that they met a policeman and Charlie had a "very friendly conversation" with him, trying to find the building where the actor lived.

When they finally found the building, Susan and Clem joined Linda, while Charlie returned to the car. Linda went inside the building with Clem and Susan, although she knew she would not lead them to the actor's apartment. She says, "I knocked on the door, which I knew wasn't the door, and a man said, 'Who is it?' And I said, 'Linda.' And he sort of opened the door and peeked around the corner, and I just said, 'Oh, excuse me, wrong door,' and that was it.'"

Afterwards, Linda says, they smoked some pot down on the beach, and Clem buried the gun he had in the sand. Then the three thumbed rides back towards Chatsworth. It was the same night, Linda says, that she began to make secret plans to leave the Family.

The house that Tex, Leslie and Katie had entered earlier that night, as Susan remembered from the rear of the car, was on a hill in the

Los Feliz area.

The property belonged to Leno LaBianca, wealthy owner of a supermarket chain. He and his wife, Rosemary, had been married "about eight to ten years," says Roxie Lucarelli, a Los Angeles policeman and personal friend of the LaBiancas. "I have known Leno about forty-five years plus and Rosemary about ten years . . ." Leno LaBianca had lived in the area since he was a boy, and the two had been in their new home there "a matter of months . . . We attended a Christmas party at his former home," Lucarelli says.

When he arrived at the LaBianca home that night, other police officers were there and he recognized Detective Danny Galindo, from L.A. Homicide. It was about one o'clock in the morning, Galindo says. He'd been able to determine that the LaBiancas arrived home after dropping their daughter off and buying a newspaper. He couldn't tell exactly when the two returned. However, he could establish that the LaBiancas had died sometime before 10:30 p.m.

Later, recounting what actually occurred in the house, Susan says: "Katie told me that they took the woman into the bedroom and put her on the bed, and left Tex in the living room with the man and that her and Leslie stayed with the woman, and reassured that woman as Charlie had told them to do . . . that everything was going to be all right and that everything was good, and they wouldn't be hurt and everything was going to be all right, and Katie told me this herself. She said, 'I wasn't talking to that woman, I was talking to myself.'"

After they had entered the house, Katie found the man and woman sitting on a couch. "The man's hands were tied," Katie says. "And we just looked at him, we looked, you know, it was like there was no thought. We just looked at him."

Leslie remembers that "the woman looked up and said, 'We will give you anything.'"

"The woman started talking," Katie says, "started saying something about, oh, something about 'We won't call the police, we won't call the police,' you know, something like that." Katie says she and Leslie then took the woman into a bedroom, where, as Leslie recalls, the woman again was saying she wouldn't call the police.

"I remember I came out of the room," Leslie says, "and I ran to a kitchen and I opened a drawer, and I grabbed out a whole bunch of utensils out of the drawer . . ."

In the bedroom, while she looked in the closet, Leslie says, "the woman picked up a great big table and she picked it up and it looked like she was going to throw it. And I looked through the corner of my eye and I saw a lamp coming down, so I blocked it I got it away from her, and we fought for a few seconds and I got her on the bed and ripped the pillowcase off the pillow and I put it on her head . . ."

Katie returned to the bedroom. "I had a knife in my hand and I remember Leslie picked up the knife," she says. "Like Leslie, I guess, put a pillowcase on her head, and then she [LaBianca] started. She kept saying something about the police — 'Just leave!' — or something like that —" and then, Katie says, "the woman heard her husband being killed and started to scream, 'What are you doing to my husband?'"

"I asked her to lay still," Leslie recalls. "Then she got at the lamp shade again and I took one of the knives and Katie had a knife, and we started stabbing and cutting up the lady."

Susan says Katie told her they "then stabbed the woman with a fork she got from the kitchen . . . Leslie was helping Katie hold the woman down because the woman was fighting all the way up until she was dead.

"And [later] I looked at Katie," Susan recalls, "and I'm not sure in my own mind whether Katie said this or I said this — that is what the woman would carry with her infinitely, 'What are you doing to my husband?'

"Katie said after that they went out by the living room and wrote things on the front door . . . 'DEATH TO ALL PIGS.' I'm not sure whether she said they wrote in blood on the refrigerator door or on the front door. I think she said they wrote 'HELTER-SKELTER' in blood. In the corner of the living room somewhere they wrote 'ARISE' in blood . . . Then, she said, they all took showers after they killed the two people, and changed their clothes inside the house.

"Katie said she went into the living room with a fork. She brought the fork from the kitchen. She looked at the man's stomach and she had the fork in her hand, and she put the fork in the man's stomach and watched it wobble back and forth . . . fascinated by it. 'WAR' was carved on the man's chest.

"She said when they came out of the shower and on the way to the kitchen, the dog came in and wagged her tail in front of them and Katie bent over and petted the dog and was kind of surprised the dog wasn't afraid of her, and the dog followed them into the kitchen. They were hungry and decided they wanted something to eat . . . They ate something . . . they got food from the refrigerator.

"Katie said the bodies would probably be found, on her own assumption, just from the type of people that they were and the neighborhood, they probably had grown children, usually they would probably come over for — like Sunday dinner, or Sunday afternoon, or sometime during the weekend the children would be over and would find the bodies.

"They had changed their clothes in the house, and on the way back to the ranch they dumped the old clothing in a garbage can."

Detective Galindo says, "As I entered the living room I observed the body of Leno LaBianca, laying in an east-west direction beside the couch and just a little bit angled with his left leg underneath the massive coffee table."

There was a fork protruding out of his stomach, "sticking just above his navel, approximately two inches, and just to the left of the midline . . ." The detective observed "some rather angry scars on his stomach area and what appears to be either 'W-A-R' or 'X-X-A-R,'" carved into the skin. LaBianca's hands were tied behind his back with a leather thong, "like the leather shoelaces, tied around the wrists." His head was covered and there was an electrical cord around his neck.

Dr. David Katsuyama, Forensic Medicine, examined the bodies. When the pillowcase was removed from Mr. LaBianca's head, Katsuyama recalls, "there was a knife still found in the neck. The knife was present in the neck and the pillowcase was pulled loosely over it . . . the knife was a kitchen knife or steak knife . . .

"There were four or five stab wounds," he says, "some rather irregular, and there are four in the anterior portion of the abdomen and there was one in the mid-back . . . One of the stab wounds of the neck had caused severance of the right carotid artery, which is one of the main vessels that feeds the structures of the head. The stab wounds into the abdomen had perforated parts of the bowel, the colon and the portions of the tissue that hold the bowel to the abdomen."

Galindo states, "Beginning with the remains of Mr. LaBianca, I observed a large amount of blood that had gathered on a cushion seat on the couch beneath which Mr. LaBianca lay. I observed in what should be the den area just north of the living room a crumpled piece of paper that appeared to contain smears of blood.

"In the living room on the wall, on the north wall by the door . . . I observed the lettering 'R-I-S-E,' and it appeared to be in blood . . . On the north wall of the living room, facing north and just left of the archway into the den there was lettering 'DEATH TO PIGS,' in rather large reddish letters on the wall, and it appeared that a picture of some sort had been removed from the wall. This appeared written in blood.

"In the den — through the den and into the kitchen, again on the north wall, of the kitchen there was a refrigerator on which on the door the lettering 'HELTER-SKELTER,' had been written in blood. 'HELTER' across the top right hand door and right underneath the word 'SKELTER,' in a combination of capital letters and lower case letters.

"In the bedroom at the southeast corner of the premises," Galindo says, "I observed the body of Mrs. LaBianca . . . She was lying on the floor, face down, on the outside of the bed . . . She was obviously dead."

Dr. Katsuyama performed the autopsy on Rosemary LaBianca, and attributed death "to multiple stab wounds to the neck, the trunk, causing massive hemorrhage . . . There are nine major wounds in the back and on the upper portion of the back and on the lower portion of the back were numerous small superficial, relatively superficial, cutting wounds over the lower portion of the trunk and on the buttocks." One investigating officer says, "it appears as though the back area has been shredded or ripped extensively." Dr. Katsuyama also states finding "wire also wrapped around the extremities, hands tied together and the lower legs tied together, and also wire wrapped around the neck . . ."

Galindo surveyed the entire residence. "After approximately five or six hours' search it was our determination that a large amount of valuables still remained within the premises, including several diamond rings, two large jars of coins, several coin collections, (and two bags of mint nickels, about $200 worth), many guns and rifles. There didn't appear to have been any ransacking of any sort. Underneath the washbasin — in the bathroom — there was some paper towels that had been water soaked and appeared to have blood . . . the only possibility of ransacking would have been the evidence of watermelon rinds in the kitchen," eaten and scattered about.

What dumbfounded the deputies was that nothing of value was

taken; many costly appliances, as well as currency and coins, had been left untouched — "as though the killer or killers didn't even recognize the articles as having any mortal use. It seemed their only concern had been to butcher up the people like that. And to see the garbage scattered about the kitchen, the watermelon rinds slung around . . ."

Fifteen

"About a day or two after August 9th," Danny DeCarlo says, he noticed Tex limping around the ranch. "They used to have karate classes up there," he recalls, "and the thing was to kick, you know, with your foot, so he was limping. I said to him, 'What happened to your foot?' And he says, 'Me and this guy got into it.' And I said, 'You hurt your foot?' He says, 'Yeah.' I said, 'Well, what did you do to him?' He says, 'I took his money.' I said, 'How much you get?' He said, 'Seventy-five dollars.' I figured it was just maybe a bar fight, those were pretty common."

DeCarlo says, "Tex was really quiet. He never said anything except when Charlie wasn't there. Well, then, he jumped up there where the king's throne was. He took over until Charlie got back and then he retreated back like a little mouse, just like the rest of them did."

Then DeCarlo had a brief conversation with Clem. DeCarlo says, "I saw no calendar, no clock, so I can't give exact dates, but I said, 'What did you do last night?' And he kind of looked at me and smiled but then he looked over my shoulder and Charlie was standing behind me. And so he kind of looked at Charlie and Charlie looked at Clem just as if to say — not to say anything, and so Charlie more or less said, 'Well, so we took care of business,' something along that line. So Charlie turned around and walked away from me, that is, away from my back, see, and then I turned to Clem and Clem looked at me and turned around and walked away and said, 'We got five piggies,' and that was what he said. That was the first time I ever heard 'five piggies.' I just let it go at that because I never thought nothing of it."

Tex and a couple others left the ranch heading to the desert, and about a week later, the Straight Satans rode their bikes up to the ranch.

131

Susan recalls, "His club members wanted him back in Venice and they didn't care what they did to us to get Danny back to Venice . . . So they all talked to Danny in private. The men threatened to rape all of us girls, and they told us that if Danny wasn't back in Venice by five o'clock the next night they would come out and kill us all, including the children, and start a fire and burn the ranch down, and we proceeded to look at them and said, 'Go ahead. Danny does what Danny wants to do. If Danny wants to stay here that is up to him, you can come out and kill us all, we won't even fight back . . .'"

DeCarlo says, "My club brothers — they'd come up there to visit and Charlie would sit down there and run this thing down to them about tearing society apart, and they thought he was nuts and figured he was brainwashing me and they came up here that night to get me, and they were going to take him and wad him up in a rubber ball . . . Me and one of my brothers was outside on the boardwalk out front there and everything was pretty well commotion. They took a gun off Clem and was going to tear the place apart, and beat all of them people to pieces, and Sadie said, 'We can take care of the Straights like we took care of them five piggies.'"

As Manson recalls, he told Clem, "I'll talk to them," but Clem said, "No, they're going to take the place apart."

Manson said Clem told him then, "Here is an idea. We put the gun tucked in your belt, behind you, then you talk to them with your hands spread apart, they will see you don't have any gun and I'll be behind you, so if you need to be backed up, I'll be there."

Then, Charlie says, "We did that and these six big guys came down on us, and I spread my hands and they said they wanted all kinds of bread, they were going to tear down Spahn and the people there. We had about fifty kids up there then and they were all living in the hills and in the caves . . . I told him you can't do that, they haven't done anything and he can't want that. And this guy behind me is so scared he isn't behind me anymore, he is off in the corner shaking. And I asked the big guy, and I'm just a little guy, I looked up at him and asked what is it that you want, why do you want to bother us here? And he was going to do it anyway. So I said, 'Look man, how much is it worth to you to break everybody up, and break the place down. Is it worth a life?' The guy answered, 'Yeah, it's worth a life.' And I took this gun out from behind my belt and laid it down on the ground, and I said, 'If it's worth a life, take mine.'

"He didn't take up the gun, and I said, 'Mister, that was your judgment, not mine. And I don't ask for anything unless I can offer it.' So I picked up the gun, and I said, 'It's your life or mine . . .'"

DeCarlo recalls, "It was pretty much in turmoil, I wanted to hurry up and get the people out. I said, 'Let's go down and have a beer.' So I made everybody get in all their cars and get on their bikes and shoot down there into the Valley so I could get them away from the ranch. I didn't want them to start no trouble up there." There was another reason they didn't want "no trouble" at the ranch. The sheriff's deputies had been coming around, "snooping, buzzing," and finally decided to make some arrests.

About 6 a.m. the following morning the deputies came in what appeared to Manson as "an army of law — raiding the ranch." Within a short time, they had arrested everyone except George Spahn. The first to enter the vans were Manson, Clem and DeCarlo, handcuffed to one another. Then Susan, along with twenty-seven others of the straggly group, was transported to the Sheriff's Department in Malibu where they crowded the cells. Some were later transferred to the Los Angeles County Jail, held on various charges from prostitution to possession of narcotics.

Although some marijuana was found, most of the Family were held for only seventy-two hours. "The night I got out," DeCarlo says, "I went back to the ranch. About four or five days after that I went up to Death Valley. I drove the truck up there."

After the Family was released, Wallie Sellers recalls, she visited the ranch to see Charlie. He wasn't there, she says, but Sadie, Leslie, Katie, and other girls "were sitting out there in this freezing cold place, and they had absolutely no feelings of guilt or anything — no feelings of anything, except this mask of childishness."

According to Foster, this is when Charlie "lowered the boom around the ranch . . . Inside this little family inside the bigger family, you had these vibes happening, and what Charlie tuned in on was that his enemy — Shorty Shea — had brought the law on them. And then they were figuring Danny DeCarlo and his fucking Straights were going to get everyone nailed, so Charlie made the decision to get rid of Shorty, who he knew knew too much about what'd been going down . . . You know, the situation with the dead piggies . . ."

DeCarlo was quick to learn of Shorty's shortcomings, and his disappearance from the ranch — as though this was a warning directly aimed at Danny.

"They got a bunch of bayonets and a sword," Foster says, and managed to get Shorty off by himself down the trail. Each one had a razor-sharp knife and they went to work on him fast — each of them sticking him, and carving him up like he was a piece of meat on a table. He didn't do any screaming cause he went down fast, though it took them a little while to dismember his body. They cut off the arms and the legs, and one of the legs they cut in half, I think, and then they cut his head off . . .

"Cutting off the arms and the head was so they wouldn't know who the body was whenever it was found. What they did — covering it over with leaves and brush at the time, and planned on getting back to bury the pieces separately — some of them they got in garbage sacks — that's what I was told. The whole thing was a joke — and Charlie had a ball having Shorty's dead body taken apart piece by piece."

The point was then to get the dismembered corpse to decompose as quickly as possible, so the girls went out to shop for a sack of lime.

A few days earlier, Linda had left the ranch. She had borrowed one of the cars and drove off, leaving her baby daughter behind. A day later she reached New Mexico, hoping to find her husband, Bob. But the car broke down outside Albuquerque, and Linda hitchhiked north to Taos.

Meanwhile, up in Death Valley, DeCarlo says, Tex was there, but he didn't see any girls at the Barker ranch. "I was the first one to get out," he says. "Manson came in a car, all the young girls were with him. All the younger ones . . . We was going to stay at the Barker ranch, but someone was living on the Barker ranch now, and you know, Charlie couldn't live there. One of the girls, Katie Meyer, her grandmother owned the Meyer ranch about a quarter of a mile down the road, down the little wash there, and when we first got to Death Valley we went over there to the Meyer's ranch and stayed there . . . I was there for about four days, and when I left Death Valley that was it." DeCarlo then rejoined the Straight Satans in Venice, while others leaving Spahn ranch drifted northeast to the desert.

Charlie says, "Nobody wanted Death Valley. I said, I'll take it. Pretty soon I had about thirty or forty kids, and no one wanted them. They were kids that their parents didn't want, that society didn't want. I wanted them, like I wanted Death Valley." He scooped them up, it seemed, like salvaging garbage. They settled onto the wasted property in the dust and heat on the edge of Death Valley, hoping to live as well as the lizards and desert animals. Some envisioned it as "perfect," as perfect as everything in Manson's philosophy. Between sitting on rocks and scavenging in the old house, in the dusty cupboards, for whatever goods could be found, Skip scribbled writings. In one note she described the setting:

"A stone house sat in a valley, up a wash. It was a house traditionally open to passersby, miners, and prospectors, yet a couple of the girls had, a year previous, gained permission from its owner to live in and care for it. They had returned from the city at the end of the summer. All of us came flocking in to the desert at various times, stopping by the house, using it as a get-together for singing, and a warm place for babies, and a water hole."

While Bobby Beausoleil appeared for his preliminary hearing in the Hinman murder, Joe Brockman, released from jail, joined Manson and the Family in the desert. He doesn't remember Goler Wash as being as pleasant as Skip's description. "That's where life was stripped down to being no different than the animals around us . . . We roamed in small packs across the desert floor and all through the hills, hiding what we could and stashing things for later. Charlie had changed. He was now like a hard piece of bone and we were all puppets. We knew it, each of us, but the strange part was that we couldn't conceive of another way of living. He gave me the name 'Scorpion.' It was complete. My past had been amputated and my future was happening at the moment. We carried knives and ate with the dogs. I humped girls on rocks or took them standing in the brush. Later, we built secret dugouts, and had supplies stashed in various caves throughout the desert."

For Manson, it was "a whole new world . . . Before, I had never been around many animals in my life, being locked up. In the desert I got to looking at the coyotes, and I got to be close around with the dogs and the snakes, and the wild rabbits, goats, and mules . . . they'd roam around the desert in small packs, and in herds that sometimes were only maybe a couple of burros, four or five in a pack, and they were afraid of man. You could tell he'd been around and cracked sticks on them, and beat on them whenever he could, and they were afraid of anyone going close to them. But I could do it. I'd approach them and I would sit down, and with all the strength I had I'd begin to cry out loud so that they could hear me. Just weeping and sobbing, and pretty soon one of the mules would come sort of close, then closer, trying to figure out what was wrong with me. Then when he was right in front of me, pretty soon he'd reach over, he'd rub his nose against me, nudging me as if trying to understand. Very slowly, hardly making any motion at all, I'd touch him and before long he understood that I could love him and he'd be willing to do whatever he could for me, because he had it in his mind that I did love him and meant him no harm, and we were the same.

"Some of us went around the desert for weeks trying to get as close as we could to all the animals, to try to learn from them how to live out there, how they did it, and to be part of them, you know . . ."

Charlie told his followers no animals were to be killed in the desert.

"In Goler Wash," Carl Foster says, "even an insect or a scorpion that is deadly, that crawled up and sat on your arm . . . if you brushed it off you were going against what Charlie wanted. He said, you have to let them crawl on you and you have to learn from them. They are the same as you. We're all here together . . ."

On one occasion, Foster was walking through the desert and a rattlesnake crossed his path. He was about to jump aside but Charlie said, "No! Sit down and look him in the eye." Foster squatted down and tried to conceal whatever fear he experienced.

"After a while," Foster says, "the rattler stopped rattling and he didn't strike or come any further in my direction. It was like he knew I was going to just sit there and do what I was doing. Then he turned the way he had been going and went off real slow." Foster believes Charlie caused the snake to go the other way. "He had power over the animals, like he could hypnotize them . . ."

Freida King arrived in Death Valley with several other girls. "We always wanted to go to the desert," she says. "At first, we camped up behind the Meyer's ranch and I slept with the baby . . . A lot of us slept in the bus . . ." Then, about living at the Barker ranch a short ways down the wash: "We lived outside, we just wandered all over the desert. I don't think anybody ever left to buy groceries. I think more people came and brung them up."

One of the young men says, "The women around the place were treated like dirt, it was the dogs that got the real good treatment."

Charlie says, "Don't treat the dogs like people. Treat the dogs like dogs. They are better than people."

"I remember Charlie," the boy continues, "how he'd sit sometimes for hours at a time, just looking into the face of one of the dogs, feeling their teeth with his fingers and talking to them. Whispering . . ."

The dogs would eat first, and then the men would eat whatever
the dogs had left behind. Then the women would get what was left over
from the men.

"None of us were really ourselves out in the desert," Foster says.
"We were just reflections of Charlie. We were him and it was impossible
for us to think of life without him."

The group soon spread through Death Valley in clusters of camp-
sites and makeshift dugouts, and these shifted from day to day. Like burros, they roamed in small packs through washes and hideaways, and
stashed whatever they could find where they might need it later. Stolen cars
were camouflaged to become clumps of dried brush or boulders. Tiny
lookout stations were linked from one point to another with portable
phone lines connecting a few army surplus field phones. Unless they had
run out of gasoline, the idea was to be able to mobilize within minutes.
Manson learned the importance of water. He says, "Lots of times I'd
camped out all night, sometimes for days at a time. I remember that on
one of the first times I'd stayed out more than a day, I set up camp at a
water hole, and then when I had sacked out for the night, I began to hear
the coyotes howling and I noticed that it was not an ordinary howl, but
going on and on, a peculiar kind of howling. Then it was like a flash, as
though they were talking to me, telling me they were thirsty, needed water
and I'd put myself right at that spot where they came for their water. They
don't carry canteens and there are no drinking fountains in Death Valley
so I put my gear together and camped off away from the water hole, oh,
maybe a quarter of a mile, sort of up on a slope and I could still see the
hole down there. After that they grew quiet and pretty soon they began to
come down out of the desert to their water hole. And I knew, when they
were howling again, only it was a lot different, that they were thanking me.
That's what they wanted.

"I never carried a canteen, because I had stashed a canteen here,
and a canteen over there, and they'd find me or I'd find them. They were
put around in different places. Everybody would be so worried about me,
'Where is your canteen? How are you going to get water?' But I knew that
I'd find it, and it would be out there waiting for me when I needed it. That

part of the desert was mine. And I knew it. If they chased me they'd have to carry a canteen, they'd have to carry a gun, and they'd have to carry a pistol, they'd have to have four other guys with them. And my canteens would be out there."

As to Charlie's commands, Foster says, "He had been saying that 'ours' was a democratic setup — that everyone had a voice . . . but that he was receiving instructions from God. No one moved unless Charlie knew about it. You woke up and you didn't know what to do until he told you what to do. And in what he said — there would be certain words he'd implant and these words and the gestures he'd make would reach right into our subconscious minds . . ."

It was as if Manson had changed after the killings in Los Angeles. Out there he wasn't any kind of "saintly" father. About that time, a visitor recalls, it was as though "the electricity was pouring out of him. His hair was standing on end. His eyes were wild. He was like a cat that was caged. He was like an animal . . ."

"Old Buck," the itinerant handyman, had settled on the Barker ranch before Manson's arrival. Calling himself a "longtime student of human nature," he said he carefully watched Manson while he lived around the Goler Wash area. "There were snakes all over the desert. They got in the cabin and everywhere . . . They picked up snakes in the house and carried them outside and turned them loose."

The man kept apart from the Family, though on occasion he discussed Manson with other miners in the area. "Manson believes that he — and all human beings — are God and the Devil at the same time. He believes all human beings are all part of each other. You see what that means," Buck says, "it means that human life has no value. If you kill a human being, you are just killing a part of yourself so it's all right . . .

This sort of power takes a long time to work an effect . . . Motions are tied to emotions. Certain motions create certain responses if you know how to use them."

One day in September, Boyd Taylor, a U.S. commissioner, was driving through Saline Valley with his wife and son in a camper truck. "We drove to the Warm Springs and camped that night. But about two o'clock that morning we noticed headlights approaching and two vehicles drove up, one a very streamlined dune buggy and another a Toyota four-wheel drive vehicle . . . I was awake so I leaned out of the door of my camper and talked to the driver of the dune buggy [Manson]. He asked about the Warm Springs and I told him there was an Upper Warm Springs, and he said they'd go up there and try to find it."

The next morning, Taylor says, the two cars returned and Manson and "another tall, thin gentleman walked over to where we were and talked to us . . . His [Manson's] hair was long and he wore a pair of shorts, no other clothing. The cars were very, very dusty; so were the occupants." Taylor said Manson told him he was unable to find the Springs. "I asked him about the dune buggy. I said, "That's a pretty fancy dune buggy. Did you have it built or did you buy it that way?" He said, no, he had bought it already made that way and that he was with the Beach Boys. He said he wrote arrangements for the Beach Boys . . . that he was a drummer, also. He made $50,000 that last year and was just taking it easy and enjoying himself. He said they were going to meet some friends up at the 'race track,' a big, flat dried lake area, and try out the dune buggies and have a race . . ."

Near the Barker ranch, Joe says, and above the wash, "I lived in one dugout above the ranch site and slept during the day." As a "sentry," he searched the area through binoculars — for an invasion by the law. "Sometimes I'd wake up with a snake near my face, trying to get close to my heat. Soon I could pick them up without fear. I milked a couple of rattlers and kept them around me on my night patrols. Me and Charlie stole five-gallon cans of gasoline from the rangers and hid them in another dugout across the wash. It was primarily a stash of auto stuff and cool enough to store the gas." At that time, it appeared that Joe and those in his dugout were preparing for war. They had weapons, Joe says, and "Charlie had our minds at his disposal. He had convinced me that he was getting messages from God . . . and these messages became our thinking process — like tape in a computer."

But Joe's health had been failing. "Finally, I believed I was dying," after frequent collapses — "or I would have died if some of the girls hadn't arranged for me to get to Bishop," he said.

Later, he was to say, "My tuberculosis has cleared somewhat. But I feel I am 'Scorpion' and I am insane because Charlie had controlled the most basic things about my character. I am still crazy — I don't have the past I'd had when I was in San Francisco. There is nothing behind me but

139

a sneaking knowledge that I have played the role of a minor hero in a super issue of Mad comics."

A few nights after Charlie's meeting with Boyd Taylor, he camped with two girls near the ridge of the racetrack. In the morning, he said, he stood up and a "big coyote came across the flat and up to me. He stopped just in front of me and was looking at me dead ahead with no fear. He kept it up for maybe half a minute, and a few times he kept looking back over in the direction he had come. And then I was looking out that way and I saw some rangers. They were coming across the desert floor. The big coyote was warning me!"

He packed up his gear into the dune buggy and drove off behind the ridges.

The Highway Patrol officer entered the wash, accompanied by a park ranger. They were looking for a Toyota involved in the burning of some park equipment. The officer, James Pursell, reports that on September 29th they arrived at the Barker ranch, probably shortly after noon. Pursell drove up and two girls met them midway between the car and the house. He recalls they were dressed in "clothing obviously much larger than they were, sloppy, dirty, baggy clothing, pants, shirts, and hats . . . they were not too communicative and said they were just out traveling through the desert more or less." However, they did say that old Buck lived "down the wash a ways."

Pursell followed the wash until they found the miner, "perhaps a mile, maybe a half mile from the ranch." After talking to old Buck the patrolman "felt it wise to return with him to Barker ranch and have a little more detailed talk . . . Buck was driving a military pickup truck," Pursell said. "In the back was a load of miscellaneous automotive parts, new. Batteries, the acid for the batteries, tune-up equipment or parts, headlamps, a new tire and wheels, Volkswagen. Also he had a movie camera. We asked where these items came from and why he had them, and he said he was taking them from Rock Falls in Goler Wash up to Barker Ranch for another individual. I believe he simply stated, 'an individual named Charlie.' I asked why he would be doing this if it were not his, and he said he felt his life might depend on his doing what Charlie advised him to do.

"We went to one of the out buildings at the ranch," Pursell recalls, "and all of us had lengthy discussions about what was going on in the area. We received some rather unbelievable information. There apparently was a large group of people that could be described as hippie-type. They had a number of dune buggies, a red Toyota. They were engaged in more or less war games, like Rommel of the Desert Rat Patrol at night . . ."

Soon after, Pursell and the deputies entered the Barker ranch region to make arrests on charges of auto theft and arson. Deputies found stolen cars in camouflaged hideaways, not far from where Pursell met a dozen young women, some nude, sprawled on the rocks, sunning themselves. They were not embarrassed, Pursell notes, but said they were "taking the sun, getting away from the smog for awhile."

Sometime later, near nightfall, Pursell approached the ranch and opened the kitchen door. He stood there for several moments, his pistol in hand, peering into the dark. There was a single candle burning in the room, and Pursell made out "about a dozen" people sitting around a wooden plank table, just starting on an evening meal of sugared Rice Puffs, caramel popcorn and chocolate candy bars.

He ordered them out with their hands above their heads, "the male suspects one at a time backwards, and the three females to come out together." He then entered the cabin, took the candle, and began searching the rooms. He found another suspect standing in the bedroom. Then, in the bathroom, pausing at what appeared to be a dirty mop hanging out of a tiny cupboard beneath the wash stand, Pursell bent down and opened the door.

"Hello," Manson said to him.

The cupboard, Pursell says, was "perhaps three feet high, twelve to eighteen inches deep, perhaps eighteen or twenty inches wide." He was amazed at how Manson had crumpled himself into the small hole, knees bunched up beneath his chin. He ordered Manson out of the cupboard and waited. "It took him a little while to unwind."

All the suspects had been handcuffed and loaded into two pickup trucks. In two raids, the deputies made twenty-seven arrests. They had found eight children in a state of malnutrition. Manson, Susan and the other adults were charged with auto theft and arson.

Some of the family were released, including Katie, after brief "checking out," as one deputy said. And "we saw this Susan Atkins was wanted for questioning — one of "possibly three young women" named in warrants issued following Bobby's arrest in August. So she was held at Inyo

County, then returned to Los Angeles and arraigned in Justice Court on murder charges in the Hinman case. Bobby was waiting in County Jail for his trial to begin in early November.

Katie, with others in Death Valley, was soon picked up again in nearby Lancaster in connection with the Hinman case. The Sheriff telephoned her father in Inglewood. "They were holding my daughter on some sort of suspicion of murder," he says. "I left for Lancaster right away." Upon arrival, he learned she had been questioned only "briefly — something to do with the stabbing of a man that befriended hippies," and he managed to talk deputies into releasing Katie into his custody.

"On our way back down to Inglewood, her reaction was so unemotional," he says. "I don't think we spoke twenty words by the time we had hit the San Diego Freeway." They stopped to eat, and Katie began to talk. "She didn't say anything significant, but just enough of a gesture so that it appeared that all was well again." She spent most of the next two days around the house, and "some of the time visiting friends." Krenwinkel deliberately avoided questioning her. He says, "I'm not the kind to use third-degree . . . And I didn't want to preach 'You did wrong.' I just felt, I didn't think I could win her back that way."

A week later he got a telephone call at his office. It was Katie. "She told me she'd talked to her mother in Mobile and she wanted to go there, to see her mother. She was entitled to that." He bought his daughter a plane ticket that evening and drove her to the airport. He watched the plane leave, taking Katie to Alabama.

About the same time, Linda had traveled across the country and arrived in Miami with her eighteen-month-old baby girl, and pregnant again. Linda had earlier been able to gain the help of a man who ran a Zen Buddhist retreat in New Mexico. She was able to return to California and arrange with a lawyer to get her daughter out of a foster home, where the baby had been placed after Linda left her at Spahn ranch.

Linda then returned to New Mexico. "Three weeks later," she says, "I was able to get my daughter back." Finally, from New Mexico, Linda hitchhiked with the child to her father's in Miami. She tried to erase the murders from her mind. "I didn't want to remember it anymore," she says. "I just wanted to forget about it . . . I couldn't, and I kept reading newspapers and seeing horrible things." She said she once thought of turning herself in, or getting in touch with relatives of the victims. But, she said, "I just couldn't — I was too much afraid, and too much pregnant, and I had the baby with me. So I didn't do it." Her father, Rosaire Drouin, says Linda "showed up in Miami around the first of November." It was the second time in the fifteen years since he had separated from Linda's mother that he saw his daughter again. "I remember the first time she came to Miami," he says. "She stole a lot of things from my apartment, and was buying dope with the money. The only time she ever wrote to me is when she was in California, and only when she needed money. I sent her some."

Drouin, a bartender in Miami, says Linda "was not a bad girl, and she was not a good girl. She was pretty happy. No, I wouldn't say she was depressed or unhappy or anything like that. She was happy as hell. In fact, I kept looking through her luggage to see if she had any drugs. I wondered if she was high." He recalls her "always talking about the good life out in California, about living in the woods and all that . . ." He says both Linda and her baby had sores on their arms. "I guess they got those living in the woods . . ."

In Santa Monica Superior Court, Susan had been made a co-defendant with Bobby, but would not stand trial with him. She was extremely "talkative and cooperative" with police — she provided details of the efforts to rob Hinman. He had been stabbed and tortured, she said, the "knife was stuck into his heart." Among the girls who had gathered in the "reflection of Manson," it seemed Susan, in particular, had been searching for punishment . . . as if even her earliest violations of the law were committed to bring down authority upon herself. Though she'd followed Charlie's orders, her compulsion to confess demonstrated that he had failed to give her the treatment she needed.

In the trial, felony charges were dropped against DeCarlo, an arrangement for testimony against Bobby. But DeCarlo said he was testifying because "a man was killed for no reason at all. That's my motive for being here."

Susan's new obsession to divulge what she knew was not limited to the Hinman case. She was sharing a cell with some young women, and one was Ronnie Howard. "One day," Ronnie says, "Susan told me, 'I don't think anything in life shocks me anymore.' And I answered, 'Well, few things shock me, either.' Then Susan said, 'I bet I could tell you a few things that would shock you . . . What if I told you that I was at the Tate house and that I was the one that did it — murdered Sharon Tate?'

143

"I didn't believe her at first," Ronnie says. "It was too fantastic — I couldn't believe an innocent looking girl could be involved in all this. I just thought it all fantasy — until she went into details. Then I asked her, 'Who really killed Sharon Tate?' She told me she did. And again I thought it fantasy. So I asked her, 'Where did you stab her, in the stomach?' And she said, 'No,' she didn't want to hurt the baby, so she stabbed her in the chest. She couldn't remember how many times, she said she just stabbed until Sharon Tate stopped screaming."

Susan "enjoyed telling me," Ronnie recalls. "I didn't have to press her too hard because I was her friend. She loved telling me about it, and loved to brag about it. Still I thought it too fantastic, and that she was talking fantasy, until she told me about leaving her knife behind at the Sharon Tate house. Later I told police, and the police went back and found it."

Susan bragged, Ronnie says, that eleven murders had actually been committed, and that the murders so far "'was just the start of it,' that there were many more murders to come. Susan said even if she never got out, that I should go see Charlie because he would be out anytime." She remembers Susan telling her the "family" had planned a lot of killings.

"They were going to just jump into their bus and go across the country and stop at different houses . . ."

At the time, Manson was being held on auto theft charges and Ronnie feared his release. "It was fantastic. Especially when Susan told me how the murders so far was just the start of it." It was so incredible, Ronnie admits, that in jail she couldn't get any authority to listen to her.

"It was the hardest thing I've ever tried to do in my life, to get anyone to listen to me," she says. "I never tried so hard to get a phone call, just a phone call to police. I knew that people here [in jail] had committed the Tate-LaBianca murders, and were going to kill many others. And I said, 'Please, let me make a phone call.' But I couldn't — I don't think anyone believed me. I tried to tell the lieutenant, and I went through her deputy. But the lieutenant said I didn't give the deputy any basis to the story, 'So why don't I just forget about it.'

"Finally, I was going to court and was allowed to make one phone call, only a few seconds. I called Hollywood Police Department and told my name. I know I tried so hard to reach the police, and if they didn't send anyone out to see me I was just going to forget about the whole thing. But the same day they sent out a couple investigators to see me, and they got after her.

"I was kept over in jail longer, supposedly for my own protection, though I said I knew how to protect myself better outside.

"I had a very hard time in jail," Ronnie admits. "There is a code about informers, and everybody in jail was against me. Everybody I thought was my friend, was my friend no longer. And even when I left jail, Sadie told me, with a smile — but then she always smiled, and I think she would still talk to me if she could — she said, 'Ronnie, I have no ill feelings toward you, but it's the rest of the Family.' And she said, 'You know, our people are everywhere, in every state. No matter how far you go, you have plastic surgery done or whatever, how many thousands of dollars you have, you're going to die, Ronnie, you're gonna die.' I just smiled back at her and said, 'Well, we all have to die sometime.'"

Later Susan wrote to Ronnie, "When I first heard you were the informer I wanted to slit your throat." But, she added, "I snapped that I was the real informer, and it was my throat I wanted to cut."

Another cellmate of Susan's, in jail on charges of forging a narcotics prescription, also said Susan bragged to her about the murders — boasting — "many more were going to die." Susan told her, she says, "They felt the stabbings and the brutal cuttings would release the souls of the victims . . . the more they stabbed, the more they enjoyed it. They got sexual gratifications from the stabbing." The cellmate told her lawyer, and soon after others who had been jailed with Susan related similar stories.

Sadie loved to talk. She later told another girl, "It was in their eyes — wide and scared as I told them what I'd done and how it was, and how much I loved doing it. I said it made me come to think about it — to remember it was like licking honey — like licking blood . . . I liked to look in the eyes of girls while making love and tell them what it's like to kill with a knife . . ."

In mid-November, a full-scale investigation was ordered. Two lieutenants and sixteen policemen were assigned to the case, and a week before Bobby's trial ended, Deputy District Attorney Vincent Bugliosi accompanied detectives to Death Valley in search of physical evidence to support circumstantial evidence linking Manson and the others to the murders.

The day before Thanksgiving, the jurors in Bobby's trial deadlocked, and a mistrial was declared. Bobby beamed at first, but the public defender, acting as his counsel, then informed him he would be retried along

145

with Susan.

On November 25, the police transferred eight prisoners from Independence in Inyo County to County Jail in Los Angeles on subpoenas. At this time, murder complaints were filed and fugitive warrants issued for the arrest of Linda, Katie and Tex.

Deputy District Attorney Aaron Stovitz said a grand jury would be impanelled to investigate the murders. At the same time, Susan gave to her newly appointed attorneys, Paul Caruso and Richard Caballero, a lengthy account in which she said she acted under Manson's "hypnotic spell" during the time of the murders. Further, she would waive rights against self-incrimination and give testimony to the grand jury, gambling that her testimony might save her life. Caballero said, "She will tell the jury exactly what happened in the Tate and LaBianca houses."

When Susan's father learned of his daughter's arrest and the claim of her being "hypnotized," he said, "I think she is trying to talk her way out of it. She's sick and she needs help . . ." He said Manson's family visited him in San Jose. "I thought they were just a slap-happy bunch of kooks, dumb hippies . . . I should have been more firm with Susan, demanded more. I loved her, and still do. She once did some very beautiful things, but that was a long time ago. And now the horror has come. And I know where she's been. Everywhere people died when they were there . . ."

Sixteen

Watson reached his hometown in late October, where people observed the "change in Tex." One friend remarked Tex seemed to "have a tornado in his head . . ." The elder Watson, who ran the general store, junk shop and gas station, soon learned of the charges against his son — sought on a fugitive warrant. He brought the young Watson to the deputies at McKinney, Texas, "for the detectives from California." Though he did not understand what the charges were all about, he was to scrub the name "Watson" from the storefront as publicity of the crimes soon spread.

And while Tex spent his twenty-fourth birthday in the McKinney jail, his family appointed a former county attorney, William Boyd, who immediately said Tex was unable to decide whether to fight the extradition.

Stuart Guthrie recalls that after Tex's arrest, his brother Mike "went down there in the courtroom and sat ten feet away from Tex — who had known Mike all his life, but didn't seem to know who he was that day . . . So I'm of the opinion that Manson could have told Tex to stick his head in a buzz saw and Tex would have done it with a smile on his face, without even knowing what he was doing."

After further meetings with Tex, lawyer Boyd requested psychiatric examinations, saying, "I personally have some serious doubts about this boy's mental state." The lawyer then decided to fight extradition, and detectives who had come for Watson returned to California without the prisoner.

Meanwhile, the house near Mobile, Alabama, where Katie had spent most of her early life, had been staked out by the police. Katie was wearing a big floppy hat, jeans and a baggy checkered shirt when she was arrested on December 1, by a detective named McKellar. While driving in

147

a car with a teenage boy, she pulled the hat down over her face when she saw the police "as though we wouldn't be able to see her," McKellar said. But problems arose over the fugitive warrant and it became clear she would resist extradition to California, the same as Tex.

Soon after Thanksgiving, Linda Kasabian left Miami on a plane to Boston. From there she set out for New Hampshire, to remain about a week in a small industrial town near Concord where her stepfather and mother lived, and where she had spent her childhood. Linda's mother says, "She loves children. She was never, never violent . . . There was no hate in her at all. She was searching for something — love, I guess."

The first week in December, friends of Linda's arranged for her to surrender to New Hampshire police. In custody, she said, "I won't talk. Not now, not ever," as though parroting Manson's law — "you never squeal, you never snitch . . ."

In Los Angeles, Charlie and five others were indicted on seven counts of murder and conspiracy to commit murder. A week later, he was brought into Central Jail in Parker Center, where he was to say, "I asked someone once about the way he is going, and I told him, no, he was going the wrong way. He answered and said, 'Are you going the right way?' And I told him, 'Yes,' I was going the right way. And he said, 'You mean the only way is your way?' and I said 'Yes, that's right. I'm going the right way, and everybody else is going the wrong way.'" Charlie laughed.

He then proceeded *en pro per* with plans to represent himself — his way. An attorney told Manson that "relevant means the weight of the point to the distance from what is being brought out." But Charlie didn't feel that the judge knew really what was relevant.

"What is relevant? When I go in that courtroom," he announced, "I've got twenty-one objections that are relevant. I don't believe the judge knows — it is his word, his reality which is not my reality. And my reality is not his." He was informed that "the rules and the tricks and the things the district attorney can do, will be much against you." But Charlie showed little fear. It was as if all he needed to solve his problems was his day in court.

One attorney, Brian Reese, assisting Manson independent of the court, offered to buy him a shirt for his next appearance. "Yeah," Charlie said. "You can get me a red shirt like a Shakespeare-type long collar, full sleeves, and V-neck. I used to have one just like it. Make it devil red," he laughed. "Real devil red."

Superior Judge George Dell, who had anticipated a three-minute hearing for Manson to enter a plea, abided Manson's discourses on law and philosophy for forty minutes, dealing patiently and politely with Charlie's motions, the like of which he admitted he had never heard or seen before. Among them, Manson sought to form a corporation with six other jail inmates, "The Family of Infinite Soul, Inc.," to handle his plea for freedom on a writ of habeas corpus. It explained that "the People of California has the defendant outnumbered in legal assistance," and asked that fellow prisoners be allowed to assist as co-counsel with Manson "in the interests of Just-Us."

Fondling a half-dozen long yellow pencils, he offered the judge his impressions of his legal problems: his proposed witnesses were being photographed "and harassed" by the Sheriff's office due to lack of proper identification. "They don't drive," Charlie said. "They don't have licenses, or identification. They live at the side of the road. They don't have an address, like you. The Sheriff calls them 'odd-looking people' but they're my brothers."

Judge Dell asked him if he could read and write, and Charlie replied, "It depends on your level of understanding . . ." He then requested a recording machine "of the kind you speak letters into" to dictate motions for a secretary to type, "because my grammar is poor and my spelling is atrocious."

After hearing the numerous motions, the judge refused most but granted one — a two-week continuance before Manson entered a plea. Judge Dell advised him he was "making a very serious error in choosing to represent himself."

Meanwhile, Susan was appearing in another court on the Hinman murder, and her case was postponed two months.

Told that he, too, would face charges in Hinman's murder, Charlie said excitedly, "See, their finger is at me. They are afraid of me! But I'll tell you this — no matter how scared they get, they aren't going to turn me like those ten psychos upstairs . . . they have this real dumb nigger, and he cleans out the garbage. He is a dummy. A boy. You tell him to clean out the garbage and he picks it up and cleans it out. And you just want to pat him on the head. He is a dummy, and you tell him 'Boy, clean out that garbage.' He was with seven other black friends and the seven others turned state's evidence on him. They are outside and the dummy is in here . . .

149

"The Black Muslims — they know the way, they're ahead of us. Fifty years ahead. They are way ahead of the Black Panthers, dig. They know what's happening. And I turn them on because I'm the only white guy in here that knows about Mohammed. They got things going on in the sewers that you wouldn't believe!"

During a visiting session with Charlie, attorney Reese asked if he needed some cigarettes or toothpaste money, and Charlie answered, "Yeah," to leave three dollars. Manson's mood had changed, Reese observed. He'd shaved off the beard and seemed more "determined — anxious for something." His thoughts grew scattered at moments, only to jump intensely to more personal, "abstract monologues." In the midst of a discussion on material witnesses, Manson "jumped the track and went into a speech," Reese says, "about some doctor or head-shrinker that visited Spahn ranch."

Charlie told the attorney, "This guy helped these little girls get out of jail, there were two or three that he helped. And after he got them out of jail he came up with them to the ranch. He wanted to stay up there and get something from them. He is a fat, sloppy guy who wanted to get some screwing in. And they put him down . . . There are a lot of guys they see these young girls with a little runt like me, and it threatens their masculinity, and they want it back. You go around living with twelve or thirteen young girls and you get a lot of this. There is a buffer line between the love people and the speed freaks, dig. And I stood on the buffer line, in-between. And I saw a lot of violence and I stopped it. These young girls, they come to me and I don't tell them to stay and I don't tell them to go. Their parents didn't want them, they left home. And I show them the hills, and I say the hills are there, dig!"

Then, almost in the same breath, Charlie told Reese, "Suzy Atkins sent me a message. When the time comes she is going to change her story. I'll be getting out of here a lot sooner than most people think, the DA wants to get rid of this case, too much that went on, dig. 'Cause soon the people won't even know what's going on two blocks away. They print in the paper that somebody gets shot by a sawed-off shotgun. And then the police, they find somebody that has the gun, or a gun like it. He is arrested and the DA has the killer. Then a couple of weeks later somebody gets shot with the same kind of gun. Well, the DA doesn't let them print that and tell that to the people because they got this other guy in jail. Now, if this other guy is in jail, then there is no one on the outside that can do that kind of murder. And they don't want to scare the people or let them know what a bad job they are doing — because the people pay the salaries." Attorney Reese said nothing.

"See," Charlie said, "taxes pay the salaries of the guys to keep me in here, dig. They have thirty or forty murders, unsolved that they say I did . . . They are afraid of me. They say he is a psychopathic, a panaman-ic, a panaramanack — ahagathaic —" Charlie wrinkled his face and gar-bled the words — "a terrible terror and they can't let me out — I'm a monster and they are going to believe what they want to and they would be scared to death if I got out . . ."

On another occasion, Charlie explained, "I told the attorney the best way to get to people is through fear. I know the difference. I was in a Rolls Royce driving, smoking a joint, and I got stopped by a bull. He asked for my license, I gave him Wilson's — Dennis Wilson's, and the cop would say, 'Yes, Mr. Wilson, yes, Mr. Wilson, try to slow down a little.' But when you are hitchhiking and a bull stops you, they fear you and they beat on you. I know what it means where the good guys are and where the bad guys are. And the cops are putting fear into these kids, because the cops are the ones that have the fear. Some sixteen or seventeen year old kid is coming home and walking on the street, and the cops get him against the brick wall. 'What are you doing?' and they beat on him, dig, push him and say, 'you got grass, you got this, you got that,' and the kid is probably coming home just from some movie or a friend's house, and the bulls are scaring him. And just when he is most scared and most susceptible to an idea, they push him in the ribs hard and they say 'You got a gun? You gonna kill someone. You got a knife? Who you gonna kill?'

"And if you put a little child in a room, and you tell the child, just don't go through that door, you know when you leave that child is going to go through the door. And that is what is going on with juveniles. You don't know. You don't live on the bottom. But I don't fear that, I know how to put on the face and they are the ones that fear us. It is like in here, they are scared, the bulls. There is a young kid near me and they say he is psy-chopathic, and they have this guy just strapped to his cot. His legs and arms are strapped down and he can't move. And the bulls open up my peekhole and they look in and ask 'How are you?' And I'm sitting there smiling and turn around and growl. Grrrrr! OK, a real mean one, okay.

151

And the bull, he leaves, see, because he knows I'm not afraid of him, and he is the coward, he has the fear. Then he goes next door to the kid, and he doesn't know when I'm listening. And he opens his thing and he says to the kid, that is strapped down, in a rough voice, 'What're you doing?' and the kid answers, 'Nothing.' And the bull says, 'What're you, a wise guy, putting me on?' And threatening to go in there and beat on the kid . . ."

Reese says, "When Charlie stood up he looked very small and very beat, like in ill-health. While simultaneously, during all the talking, he was animated, really alive in his conversation, expression, and his eyes, which have a brilliant twinkle. After spending some time with him he becomes very likable, and an interesting and unusual person to talk to. He can sustain a conversation terribly well, and keep you most interested. I guess he has had practice of the concentrated kind of talking, without the phone ringing while you are talking, or the jumping up and down of some-one to do something else. Visiting hours in jail are precious, and sitting face to face with someone, without anything else, trains you for this kind of ability that Charlie has, to talk and be a forceful storyteller."

But Manson refused to enter a plea and said the judge's entering a plea of innocence for him "leaves a foundation that is very messy. If the public knew how messy, it would have you over here instead of me." He went on to say he'd been so "mired" in legal matters he'd not had sufficient time to prepare for the arraignment. "I can't be expected to plead to those ridiculous charges," he declared.

"While he was acting en pro per," Reese says, "Charlie was so busy visiting with friends and some of the girls from the Family — who took up most of the time — that he admitted to me he hadn't had time to get any work done on the case. As it was, he hadn't even read through the transcripts of the grand jury. He'd joke about it. Actually," Reese says, "his enthusiasm or belief that he'll be released in a short time is so convincing that he even has me wondering a few times."

The motions Manson did prepare and file, in between visits with Family members, were drafted in a legalese almost beyond deciphering. Generally, they attacked various phrases of the proceedings against him. He also informed the judge, "I got a message from Sadie, saying that the district attorney made her say what she said." Manson wanted permission to question Susan, and Judge Dell granted the request, if both she and her attorney agreed.

Two days later, Charlie told Reese that he would be "getting out maybe in thirty days," so he hadn't bothered completing a case. Charlie was grinning. Since he felt he'd be getting out right away, he wanted to know if Reese, also an amateur photographer, would "like to take some movies in the desert," because, Charlie said, there were all kinds of "exciting things" he had done. In the desert they used to build a fire and race the dune buggies around it, and then dance and sing.

"I'm like a child," he told Reese, "playing games . . . I can get from Spahn ranch to Death Valley without using the highway. I have the dune buggies set with a hoist in the front, and hoist one up a ridge, then tie it to a tree, and hoist the others after it. One time the men were after me, and I used a block and hoisted the dune buggie up a tree, and I watched them looking for me — they couldn't find me!" Charlie laughed. He designed dune buggies on the outside, he said. "I had four seats across, and slats that you could put out for sleeping, with the back covered over so you couldn't see the wheels, it was camouflaged."

Reese says, "Charlie was sitting and staring into space for several minutes, and then he said 'I'm mired with all this . . .' Charlie figured it was a conspiracy for both political and financial advantages, and he's planning to file a civil suit for defamation. Charlie says all the others, Katie, Linda, and others are all going to hang together. He said, 'Sadie will be certified insane, so she won't have to testify again. Nobody's going to break. We're all going to stand together.'"

A few days later Susan was in court for the first time since December, and her attorney, Richard Caballero, was granted a trial delay. The lawyer was arranging a meeting between Susan and Manson. He still expected her to testify as the prosecution's key witness, and said the meeting would give him an idea as to how she would react to Manson's cross-examination at the trial. There had been reports that Susan would change attorneys at Manson's request, after their meeting. Caballero said he had heard rumors that Charlie was seeking counsel for all of his co-defendants, but said, "As of now I am her attorney, and I'm busy working in her behalf."

During a hearing, Charlie informed the court he was ready to "be tried immediately."

It was announced the following week that Manson was working on a "legal ploy to unite the accused," with the aid of a Denver attorney ready to enter the case. That lawyer said he was certain Susan would not repeat her testimony at the trial, which meant the grand jury testimony could not be used as trial evidence.

Reese says, "Charlie told me, 'Suzy sent word to me that if I get her a good lawyer, she'll shut up.'"

"Like when they certify Sadie insane," Manson said, and related what he'd learned from his grapevine: "Linda is going to step forward, dig, her attorney's fallen in love with her and he's going to get her off and they'll sail away together in a sailboat. So in order to get her started on their thing, he's already setting it up with Stovitz to get her a deal, giving evidence to the DA. What's going to happen now, they'll make a deal with Linda. But I'm not afraid of it because the truth will come out at the trial."

Reese told him that the truth in courtroom procedure doesn't necessarily come out — one doesn't lead to the other.

"I know that," Charlie said, "But Linda will break down in the trial."

Later, while a meeting was arranged between Manson and Susan, Charlie submitted a petition which he described as "revolutionary" and unorthodox, seeking restoration of certain jail rights. He asked that a commission be appointed to study and recommend procedures to modernize the state's judicial system. Charlie suggested that if the state was not responsive to changes it would become as extinct as "any other cumbersome dinosaur." Judge Keene, who had been assigned the case by Judge Dell, said he would study the brief.

The meeting between Charlie and Susan lasted one hour. They sat face to face, and afterwards, Caballero said Susan was "mulling over" what her future role would be in the prosecution of the case. The attorney said Manson did not request her to withdraw her testimony, but "instead asked her to do what she thought was right." He added: "If Mr. Manson and I can't reconcile those differences and she goes along with him, then I will have no choice but to remove myself as her attorney."

"When you find yourselves," Charlie was to say, "you find that everybody is out for themselves." Yet as the motions continued, Charlie sought to have the group "stand together." If Manson could provide a common legal shelter for himself and co-defendants, one attorney speculated, he might get out from under the murder conspiracy charges against him. Despite contrary legal advice to some of the defendants, it seemed Charlie still ruled the Family. Susan "mulled over" withdrawing the testimony she had offered the grand jury.

At Charlie's bidding, Leslie Van Houten replaced her court-appointed attorney. She also wrote to Tex, then fighting extradition from Texas, asking him to disregard his attorney's advice and come join the Family in Los Angeles.

"Say, Tex," she wrote, "in spite of what anyone may tell you, the family still is. No matter how many miles, institution bars, and confusion may try to separate us, we become closer. One cannot be divided.

"You know the strength of unity. Myself, as well as others, would like very much for you to be with all of us throughout this trial."

As Katie's lawyers also fought extradition from Alabama, Manson wrote to Katie, asking that she join the others in the trial.

The aunt Katie had been staying with at the time of her arrest insisted that the girl "just liked people too much to do anything like this." Katie was "very interested in the Bible. She often talked about it and studied it." Katie's lawyer described her as "a very nervous, frightened and confused young woman." But finally Katie sent a determined note to the district attorney in Mobile, stating she wished to sign extradition papers and return to California immediately.

In court with a wry smile, Charlie told Judge Keene, "I'm going to have to do something about you." He then confided in Reese that he was planning to have Keene removed from the case. "It'll happen," he said.

At 1:46 on the afternoon of March 9, at the County Medical Center, Linda gave birth to a baby boy, under guard. The infant was to be made a temporary ward of the juvenile court. While she recuperated in the hospital, Attorney Daye Shinn met in Judge Keene's chambers with Caballero and the prosecutors. Following the meeting, Shinn announced he had replaced Caballero as Susan's attorney, and said, "She definitely will not testify. There is no chance she will take the stand against Manson and the others."

Meanwhile, Judge Keene had ruled on Charlie's "outlandish" motion, the one Manson considered "revolutionary," and said it proved Manson was incompetent to represent himself. Charlie was visibly shaken in the courtroom. "Fury just poured out of him," one attorney said.

Charlie shouted: "You can't do that! I'm a man! I have a voice! I have a voice!"

His behavior became blatant and odd, and a few days later during a hearing on Susan's substitution of attorneys, Charlie refused to answer Keene's questions on whether he would object to Shinn replacing Caballero. Manson looked about and replied, "Do you dislike me? I think we're all going to need as much help as we can get . . . But there isn't anyone here I don't like."

The judge repeated his question: did he feel there would be a conflict of interests?

"Are you going to shoot me?" Charlie replied, and repeatedly evaded Keene's inquiries. To another question Manson said:

"I think you may be about the same height as me. You seem taller because you're sitting up higher." Then he asked, "Who makes the rules here? Wait . . . Are you going to let them keep Susan locked up?" He smiled, and interrupted again, saying, "All of you can stand up and go someplace."

During a recess, the attorneys were concerned. "What's he doing? Has he gone crazy?"

"I don't know what's the matter with him," said Charles Hollopeter, Manson's newly appointed court attorney.

Charlie muttered irrationally in court and seemed unable to comprehend any of Keene's questions. At one point he threw his glasses along the counsel table to Katie's attorney, saying "You take my glasses and I'll take yours. You look at the judge through mine and I'll look at him through yours, and you'll see him in a different frame than I do." Manson then shook the hand of Hollopeter and announced, "I have no objection" to the appointment of Shinn as Susan's attorney.

Prosecutor Stovitz, who had remained silent during the lengthy byplay, asked the judge for assurance the trial would proceed on March 30. "We want all defendants tried at the same time," he said. "We don't want any musical chairs played."

Hollopeter jumped up and told the judge it was "entirely possible for Manson's case to be severed, and I want the district attorney on notice that I'm not standing by silently to let him run the case."

As the hearing ended and Charlie was being led from the courtroom, he looked up at Judge Keene and said, "I'll tell you this — I've got three hundred gallons of gasoline up in Inyo County."

It was clear the prosecution's current case against Charlie would be destroyed by Susan's refusal to testify at the trial. But a few days later,

Linda and her attorneys met with the prosecutors. The next Sunday she accompanied detectives to the house on Cielo Drive and was in a state of near-hysterics when they left. Then, with representatives from the district attorney's office, she retraced the route she said was taken to the LaBianca home. Her version of the murders, they felt, corroborated the testimony of Susan, even though Linda had remained outside the Tate house.

She could testify that Manson instructed her to dispose of the credit cards he had taken from Mrs. LaBianca, in hopes they would be found, used, and the suspicion diverted. Her lawyer said, "If I agreed to let her testify it would only be on the basis that it would be to her benefit to do so."

The arrangement was made for Linda's immunity, while Charlie unsuccessfully continued his efforts to represent himself. "I don't comprehend that one can represent anyone else," he said. "A man, if he is a man, can only represent himself."

The judge promptly denied the verbal request on that basis, and Manson offered a typed motion specifically requesting that Ronald Hughes be appointed as his attorney, for the sole purpose of "regaining my en pro per status" to act on his own behalf.

Thirty-five-year-old Hughes had passed the Bar examination shortly before, though he had not tried a single case. He had appeared in the courtroom with spectators during most of the pretrial hearings and visited Charlie in jail. He stood up in the courtroom and came forward at Keene's request, when asked if he would be ready for the March 30th trial date. Hughes, a big untidy man with a bushy beard, failed to answer Keene directly. He said he felt he would be "forced to answer directly," and "forced to go along" with the request for continuance.

Keene said, "Mr. Hughes, you're not being forced into anything. I simply want to know if you are going to be ready to go to trial?"

Hughes said he was not. He paced back and forth behind the defense table. "I feel Mr. Manson has been forced all along by you into various positions that are untenable." The lawyer continued to pace nervously while accusing Keene of violating Charlie's constitutional rights on several occasions. He said he also planned to initiate a petition to reinstate Manson's right to act as his own attorney.

At one point, Keene ordered Hughes to "stand still right there so that I can answer you." Keene granted the change of attorneys, and as soon

157

as Hughes was approved, he immediately motioned for withdrawal of the psychiatric examination request made by Manson's earlier court-appointed attorney.

While Hughes began the defense preparation, Charlie formulated the plan as to how his defense would be conducted. Later, he told Reese, "When I go in that courtroom, I'll have all my followers behind me. The jury will be sitting there and when it's time for my opening statement I'll go 'OM,' humming OM, and all those people behind me will pick it up, 'OM,' and it'll fill the room and then all the kids out on the street will rise, *rise!*"

During the time Charlie met with Hughes, he consulted with other attorneys as well. One lawyer said, "He knows how to get to the streets, he believes he can get great support from the kids and people on the street. It's like he's asking for a revolution."

Charlie told Reese, "There's an underground river that runs from Death Valley to New York." Reese says, "Charlie says he can get to Death Valley from County Jail. There's a hole — he has to get into it backwards and he can then go straight to Death Valley where he's got those three hundred gallons of gasoline. He can get there through this hole without being seen at all.

"He says he knows he has the grapevine, like the garbage man. 'You don't even see the garbage man,' Charlie says. Like the prisoners, he knows all kinds of ins and outs and he claims he has direct 'tap lines to the street.' That's where his supporters are. It's in those people, like the garbage man, like the hippies, and what he calls the people in ditches — the garbage people, that he feels he can muster support — and they will be Charlie's chorus . . ."

But the problems Manson had with his attorneys, which would soon include Ronald Hughes, were that his pursuits could not be achieved in a court of law. "There could be no meeting ground," Reese explains. "An ordinary attorney was part of the Establishment. This whole thing — it's Charlie versus the Establishment. It's been going that way for years. This is the finale. This is Charlie's last curtain."

Seventeen

Bobby Beausoleil's second trial began in Keene's courtroom. Marie O'Brien, granted immunity, testified that she and Susan went with Bobby to get money from Hinman, and that during the time they were there Bobby fatally stabbed him.

After the prosecution rested its case, Bobby took the stand. He had not testified in the first trial which resulted in a hung jury. His version matched events already offered the jury, with the exception of who killed Hinman. Manson killed Hinman, Bobby now asserted, after returning to the house with Bruce Davis.

While Bobby's trial was concluding, the grand jury in Judge Dell's court returned three indictments on one count of murder each, naming Manson, Susan, and Bruce Davis — the only one not in custody at the time — as conspirators in Hinman's death.

Then Bobby's jury began deliberations about the same time Manson and Susan were arraigned on the murder. Both appeared unconcerned — bored with the proceedings that could lead them all into California's gas chamber.

Back in his cell, Charlie shrugged off the pressures of what was becoming a legal boxing-in, and on his visit with Reese, he returned to "more personal" issues. He said, "You know, my life really started when I was thirty-three years old — when I got out of prison and in with some hippies, and picked up the father image, I got a family . . . I had someone to protect, people looking up to me. I had everything — I don't blame anyone . . ." He stopped and put his hand against the glass. "My mother," he said wearily, "she was a runaway when she was fifteen years old, and then she got pregnant by a guy and he was only seventeen." He paused for several moments and just stared at the back of his hand. Then he said, "Now all the newspapers and all the magazines they call her a whore, a prostitute, but that's not true. She was what the flower children were, and I was born from love. How can I blame my mother? That's pointless. What would happen is she would just blame her mother and then her mother would blame her own mother . . . People have to blame everybody for themselves. It's a reflection and I don't blame anybody. The truth is what counts. It always comes out."

But what, one wondered, would be Charlie's truth?

On Friday, April 14th, Judge Keene disqualified himself as trial judge. Although he had failed to respond earlier to an affidavit of prejudice by Manson, Keene was obligated to accept the challenge when filed by Hughes as attorney for Manson. Keene said, "It doesn't matter who hears this case, just as long as it's tried."

Objecting to all proceedings and motions for trial delay, Charlie insisted he wanted to go to trial in three days. During the hearing, he slumped with an intense frown.

Judge Dell asked Hughes how soon he would be ready for trial, and Charlie answered with a grunt, "1984."

Then Manson quickly attempted to dismiss Hughes and reinstate his right to represent himself. Dell ruled as quickly in denial. "While Mr. Manson acted as his own attorney," the judge said, "he did such an abominable, dilatory job that he established conclusively his inability to represent himself."

The judge refused to permit any additional arguments by Manson or Hughes about self-representation. When Manson continued to interrupt, the judge threatened to have him gagged. He pointed to a recent U.S. Supreme Court ruling which permitted such an action. Then, in Judge Charles Older's court, the defendants and attorneys were told the trial date would be met. "There's a practical limit as to what the court has to put up with," Older said.

The defendants were returned to their cells, satisfied postponements would be granted. Charlie still believed he'd "outwit" the courts and finally represent himself.

Katie's attorney was set to appeal a denied motion to move the trial, while Leslie was undergoing psychiatric examination. Her lawyer indicated a possible change of plea or an "attempt to prove diminished capacity."

Leslie had seemed despondent after Tex failed to respond to her plea to rejoin the others at the trial.

But even though Tex's uncle was a sheriff, and he had TV in his cell and three meals a day cooked and brought in by his mother — "really special treatment" — Tex was responding to very little.

One friend, Guthrie, says, "I think he just mentally left. . . He was psychologically facing the realization of going back to California, and facing whatever that was, and being bombarded with this 'good Christian boy' in Texas, he came to the realization that here he was — put him in a gas chamber and drop a pellet for doing what he'd done, and I think he could not face what he had done or what was facing him. Just mentally died, or a kind of mental suicide, whichever happened . . . or else just a good act." Yet his lawyer was to continue the extradition fight for more than eight months.

While Watson was still in Texas, Linda remained sequestered from the others, preparing testimony that would sink Charlie, Tex, and the girls, in exchange for her immunity from prosecution.

Daye Shinn had filed a motion to suppress Susan's grand jury testimony, while Bruce Davis, sought in connection with Hinman's murder, was still at large. And while sheriff's deputies continued their search, the jury in Bobby's trial completed its second full day of deliberation without reaching a verdict. Sequestered that night in a hotel, the panel resumed deliberations Saturday morning, April 18th, and that same day they found Bobby guilty of first degree murder.

Attorney Salter said the jurors "believed Marie [O'Brien] and they didn't believe my client." The attorney insisted Marie was protecting Manson because she was in love with him, and because Charlie was the father of her child. He attributed Bobby's guilty verdict to the "Publicity," he said, "which, since December has created an entirely different situation between this trial and the first trial, and . . . an extra witness in this trial — an eyewitness," Marie. Her immunity in the case would continue as long as she sustained cooperation in the future prosecution of Manson, Bruce Davis, Susan and "anyone else involved in Hinman's murder."

Under California law, murder trials are conducted in two stages.

161

The first determines the guilt or innocence, and the second stage is to decide the penalty. Prosecutor Katz, who claimed throughout the trial he would attempt to send Beausoleil to the gas chamber, said the verdict "restores my faith in the jury system."

Three days later, the same jury took less than three hours to return a unanimous death verdict. The first conviction was in, and Bobby would go to the gas chamber.

It became clear to attorney Reese, and to a few others close to Charlie during the long wait to trial, that what they beheld was a rather rarefied example of the "total failure of modern society . . . When I'd look at Charlie," Reese says, "I couldn't help seeing all those years of his life, the brutal and callous indifference of institutions, and that he was beaten on and beaten, really having been molded in the worst juvenile hell-holes we have. Then into one prison after the other.

"He never had a chance. As . . . Susan never had a chance, none of these garbage-eaters, and by the same token Sharon Tate, and Jay Sebring, and the others never had a chance. I don't know. Maybe none of us have a chance, or if we did we sure blew it somewhere along the line."

Finally, in June, 1970, the Tate-LaBianca trial got under way, with Charlie assuming a position of crucifixion, his girls mimicking him, yelling, "Why don't you just kill us now?"

Linda, the state's star witness in exchange for total immunity, did not "crack" as Charlie predicted — though on the days she testified, other family members not in custody carried picket signs reading "Judas Day" and "A Snitch in Nine." Nor would the court even accept the defense motion to have a psychiatrist observe Linda, supposedly unable to determine "fact from fantasy" due to her alleged "three hundred trips on LSD . . . the acid express." Yet as weeks and months passed, almost one hundred witnesses lent piecemeal support to her version of the crimes, along with such prosecution evidence as a rope, a gun, bullets, shell-casings, bloody clothes, fingerprints and dozens of photos — "a panorama of gore," enlarged and in color. And from the start, the prosecution had made it firmly clear that the death penalty would be sought for Manson, Katie, Susan and Leslie.

Clem [Steve Grogan], sought in connection with the LaBianca murder, was to remain in hiding, as did Bruce Davis.

One member of the family died supposedly "playing Russian roulette with a revolver." And there was the question of Shorty Shea —

missing, rumored to have been tortured and then, at Charlie's order, beheaded and buried near the ranch.

One girl in the group, diagnosed by two psychiatrists as in a state of drug-induced schizophrenia, had been committed to Patton State Hospital in San Bernardino.

A friend close to Leslie, seeing her in court late in August, observed, "I could hardly believe it was her. And I talked to her for a moment — she remembered me and was very cheerful about everything, but it wasn't the girl I'd known all those years. It was someone else altogether — not Leslie Van Houten. Something's drastically wrong . . . This girl on trial now . . . She's like a comedienne or mentally unbalanced."

Tex, finally extradited to California, was to lose fifty pounds while "vegetating" in a solitary cell, frightened over his own personal impending doom. He could no longer communicate with others and was unable even to feed himself. All he could manage was a feeble grin. While the others were being tried, he was being force-fed with tubes through the nostrils. Finally, he became so weak that only injections could sustain his life. Described by medical examiners as "catatonic" and "in an acute psychotic state," he was sent to Atascadero State Mental Hospital, where he would either continue to "vegetate" — or recover and stand trial for the murders.

But the "vegetating" part, according to an ex-inmate then at Atascadero, was, like Leslie's "mentally unbalanced" act, a cloak to "get himself declared mentally incompetent — at least at the time of the murders . . . Watson said he had it down pat — go bananas now and eat bananas later. He meant instead of sucking gas. He saw himself getting off scot-free, beating it, in other words, and getting out. He meant out — free. He'd think about name changes, living a different life where he wouldn't be known. Beating it, in other words . . . He once joked about the gun busting when he beat one of them on the head. He said something about his fist being more powerful than the way the gun was made. He said he'd break concrete with his fist . . . But he believed in killing, and killing with a knife was the way to do it. Not kicking in heads, though he'd felt a lot of joy in that, too . . ."

The course of Charlie's conduct in court — including leaping off a table toward the judge, shouting, "In the name of Christian justice someone should cut your head off," threatening to use his three hundred gallons of gasoline "stashed," away, or to escape to his "big hole in the desert," would leave many wondering about the sanity of Manson himself — or of his co-defendants. In a world clearly different from that of the jurors who would sit in judgement on them, the girls would mimic their "master" — repeating meaningless chants over and over, yet professing no meaning to the words — more mumbo jumbo to further establish their "difference."

Still a ninth murder was to be disclosed and more indictments handed down, against Charlie, Bruce Davis and Clem for the torture, beheading and dismemberment of Shorty at the ranch. For almost a year the police and deputies had searched for the body without success, until finally, just before the jury began deliberations on the Tate murders, Chief Deputy District Attorney Joseph Busch decided to prosecute without a corpse. "There is no body recovered in this case, but there is precedent to support a successful prosecution." He said, "We can't excuse murder just because they are clever enough to dispose of the body."

Bruce Davis would make headlines by walking up to the Hall of Justice one day, barefoot, an X on his forehead — copying Manson's symbol of X'ing oneself out of society — with a grin reminiscent of Watson's, and saying, "I've come to get my father out of the tower . . . they want to kill bodies, don't they? I'm here if that's what they're after." Many would wonder about the sanity of Davis, whose manner some felt made him seem even crazier than "Crazy Charlie," as they used to call Manson in prison.

Charlie, who said of the four defense attorneys — "I think I can present a better case than the whole bunch of them" — would never confront the jury with anything but an outburst. There were so many of these that for days on end the defendants were expelled from the courtroom to sit in a locked room listening to testimony over a loudspeaker — if they even bothered to listen. But the defense attorneys would have little more success than Charlie, and in the end they would not call a single witness, and would barely manage to restrain Charlie's girls from acting out their compulsion to confess to the murders — details of which had long since spread around the world.

When asked, "Do you have anything to say?" Charlie said yes, he did. He had a great deal to say. Part spontaneous, part planned as a verbal assault against the entire judicial system and the Establishment in general, Charlie proceeded into a monologue that would run for more than an hour — not including a much called-for recess. Spectators could barely hear him as he began his soliloquy but after several minutes the old scam-man shone through; here was the Charlie the Family knew — the Jesus-God-and-Devil Charlie; the martyr, the guru, the nobody on the street, the king on the mountain . . . He went through almost every change he knew, every "talking blues-song-singer" he was capable of. Trying everyone's patience beyond normal endurance, Charlie seemed to ramble endlessly from the witness stand — as though trying to wedge all he knew into some coherent offering that was, finally, irrelevant and delivered with the jurors absent from the courtroom. Even the prosecution was lost as to what to say in cross-examining the witness.

On days the court convened, Charlie and the girls would be transported from their cells to the courthouse. The trial continued for months, trying the patience and dispositions of many. But for the most part, the defendants, though often disruptive in court, went through it all in good spirits. They were having a good time.

One young girl, Marla Rothasen, in jail three months on a nar-cotics charge, had been Leslie's cellmate during most of the trial, and also got to know Susan, in the same cellblock.

"Right before Christmas," she says, "we had glass balls around the cell where the TV room was. You could volunteer to get up and do paint-ings on the glass balls — Christmas paintings — and Susan Atkins did elves. She did different colors of elves. A black elf, a white elf, a Chinese elf, and trees. She was a real good artist, but I always thought she was eerie. She was more of a loner, you know, she was always by herself. She didn't have as many friends and wasn't as friendly as Leslie, but she smiled a lot. She was toward painting, painting the elves on the wall.

"Leslie and I were the only ones in the cell together when I moved in. It was my first time in jail, and I was quite worried and Leslie really settled me down. She said for me to think of a tree, think of a flower, and she helped me because I was really nervous about the whole situation. She seemed very happy. She changed my whole atmosphere in jail.

"I didn't know at first what she was in for, she just helped me. She was really nice and friendly. After, I asked her what she was in for, and she said 'murder,' and that really blew my mind, but she helped me, she helped a lot. She's very nice. She taught me how to knit, how to crochet, and we used to play cards in the cell . . . lots of people in the cell block were her friends, and she played cards with the people, and she set my hair a couple of times, and made it real curly and natural. She had extra sheets and dresses and she let me use them. She was kind of privileged, you know, which really blew my mind. The guards really treated her better . . . I had a dress that came down to my knees, and was old and baggy. She had two or three dresses, and gave me one that fit me nice, and I really think that she was a nice person. If it wasn't for her when I was moving in — I begged the guards to get me a psychiatrist, because I knew I was going to have a little tiny mirror in the cell and I was going to take the mirror and cut me up because I didn't want to be there, and I wanted a psychiatrist and I couldn't get one because they wouldn't give me one. And if it wasn't for her, you know, I don't know what would have happened."

Leslie and Susan talked through a "kite," Marla says. "You know, they passed little notes. And Leslie had a girl friend — she had been in the same cell with her for a long time, and as soon as they got attached they threw her out. You know, this was Leslie's lover. She really loved the girl. The girl worked at the kitchen for the state, and she was the one that passed the kite, from Susan to Leslie, and one day Manson told them to put an X on their forehead. So they took a pin and they started hitting themselves with little holes until they got an X on their foreheads, and they both looked alike. Leslie's was a real bright red X on her forehead, bleeding and stuff, and I don't know what that signified at first, because she didn't know herself. Manson told her to put an X on her forehead and told Susan to do the same, and so they did."

Over a period of time, Marla "got the feeling Leslie was perfectly happy in jail . . . that it didn't bother her at all. Kinda like this is the way the Establishment wants it and there's nothing they could do so they might as well live with it, and make her surroundings as happy as she can. She had cut out a magazine and there was a picture in it, said something like 'Home Sweet Home' on the wall. It was kinda like a home, you know. She had it all made up. She had her knitting and all her little things in her locker, and it was like this was her home . . . She'd grown accustomed to it.

"The Family philosophy was her main subject, about Charlie, and how much he was like a father to her, in a way, because she never really got on with her father and mother. She was really in love with Charlie — she talked about him like he was God or something like she said, she'd do anything for Charlie . . . She talked a lot about her 'family.' She missed the ranch, and the fun times that they'd had, how they used to sit out on the porch, when Charlie would sing and play guitar. She talked about how pretty it was, and how wonderful Charlie was, and like he made the whole scene come true, and just how much she loved him and respected him . . . but she didn't like Watson very much, because he thought that he could be like Charlie, and he could never be like Charlie, she just didn't care about him as much as Charlie."

Marla explained that "in the cell block there are maybe fifteen cells, and in each cell there's two bunks, and a mattress on the floor, if it gets crowded. In the cell with Leslie and I there was just the two of us. Before I got transferred to Leslie's cell, when I was in with Susan, that was a cell you go into as soon as you get in . . . and then they transfer you. Susan was stationed in that cell and everybody kind of knew it was her, and the major talk in the cell was that — that's the girl that was Charlie Manson's girl, kind of gossip about what she's supposed to have done. And everybody kind of just said 'Hi' to her and everything, but I only stayed in that cell for a few days. When I went down to Leslie's cell, it was more of a friendly thing because they'd all been there for a long time, and they all played cards together, and they talked about very nice things. And the general gossip in the jail was that Leslie — they didn't care if Leslie did it or not. They weren't there to judge her, they were just a friend. People in jail aren't there to judge other people," Marla says. "They don't really care, because they're in there for their own time. They're pretty uptight about their own situation . . . So they were all very friendly, and like I think more than half of them, like myself, didn't think she could possibly do anything like that, because she was just too nice."

It almost seemed Leslie wasn't concerned about the charges against her, Marla says. "She was not really having a ball, but she wasn't depressed about it. She was just herself. She'd smile a lot. She'd laugh a lot. Like I was in jail for something that I knew I was going to get out on. I knew there was nothing they could do to me, it was my first time and it was nothing anything near to murder, but I was scared to death. But Leslie, she'd already been in for over a year, and she wasn't worried about it, she'd grown accustomed to it. She said it was better than living at her parent's house, or something like that . . . She figured it was such a bad trip and such a bad world that, the least you could do is help your brothers and sisters. That was her whole trip — to help everybody else get it together, you know. And at night sometimes, she'd think that I was asleep, and she'd just groan, to herself, and say like, 'what a day,' because she really put a lot of work in the cell block. I can't really say it was happy, but it was the most together cell block. We didn't have anyone screaming or yelling or crying or killing themselves, trying anything foolish like most of the cells do. And I think all that goes on to Leslie's benefit — because she helped everyone."

Leslie's lawyer, Ronald Hughes, who had earlier been fired as Charlie's attorney, had disappeared mysteriously, prolonging the trial and causing the jury to remain sequestered over Christmas. It was 1970 — almost a year and a half after the crimes. Hughes was gone for good, it seemed, and in petulant tantrums in court Leslie would seek to oust her new attorney, following Charlie's lead and demanding with the other co-defendants to represent herself, but to no avail.

With the jury preparing to debate, Charlie would write pompously and in pseudo-biblical terms for an underground publication, his "last will and testament." "God is with me . . . I am but a flute that my father whistles through, and the tune has never been heard on this planet. Your fathers have kept you in darkness . . . I give to man what he deserves . . . himself, and what he has done to others shall be done to him. To live alone forever and ever, no death or relief from his own misery . . . I promised you life forever, there is no death . . ."

Though Charlie promised "life forever," Paul Watkins, whose testimony during the trial prompted the ninth murder charge, says, "It is time we looked at this false prophet. What Charlie sold, in the name of love, was death. In the name of Jesus Christ, he tried to do everything Hitler and Genghis Khan did."

After Charlie's long and often abstract monologues, many would wonder if such a man could really be sane. Before it would end, others would wonder how the court could "judge" Manson, or for that matter, all of the "garbage people." One renowned psychiatrist was to say, "It is inconceivable to me how the courts could try Charles Manson as a rational person. As in the case of the Boston Strangler, this man, Manson, and his cohorts, should be put away and studied — certainly never ever released upon society at large . . . But after all, if Manson isn't sick, who is?"

They had become garbage people and butchered without purpose. They were tried, but long before the verdict came in most could see that the contest was over, that they were going nowhere.

As the trial proceeded through many months, Watson, released from Atascadero State Hospital, was returned to stand trial alone as soon as the jury ruled on Manson and the girls. Held as isolated as possible, Watson was still able to confide in one inmate, "Nothing matters — nothing matters now." Soon after, Watson's attorney would plead him innocent by reason of insanity. But nobody'd finally buy it.

Weeks later, the decomposed body of lawyer Ronald Hughes was found near the Northern California resort where he disappeared.

With more charges yet to come in the Hinman case and the beheading of Shorty at Spahn, Charlie's jury would issue first degree murder verdicts against Susan, Katie, Leslie and their "master."

During the penalty phase of the trial, the girls, seeking vainly to protect Charlie with their lives, said they dreamed up the idea of a "copycat" version of the Hinman murder to make Bobby — in jail — look innocent. Yet it seemed clear to most that Charlie was pulling the strings, even as the girls confessed to what the prosecutor described as a "monstrous, macabre and nightmarish scene of human terror and massacre." He went on to declare that though Watson and the girls were "slavishly" obedient to Manson, still they did not suffer from "diminished capacity." They were, he stated, "suffering from a diminished heart, a diminished soul."

The stabbing? "It was just there to do," Katie said.

She was asked on the witness stand, "Do you have any remorse for these murders you committed?"

She replied, "I don't know what the word means."

"Do you have any sorrow for having murdered these people?"

"No!"

"You feel you did the right thing?"

"It was the right thing, yes," Katie said calmly.

Leslie was asked, "Could you tell us how you feel about it now sitting in the witness box?"

"How I feel? I feel like it happened. I just don't think anymore," she said. "When I leave here, I go in a car and I go to a jail, and I sit in jail and I look at what goes on in the jail. And I come back here and I am in the courtroom. I just don't think about it."

Yet she says her mind is not a blank. "I don't have time to think about what I am doing."

"Do you feel sorrow or shame or a sense of guilt?" she was asked.

"Sorry is only a five-letter word," she replied, and smiled.

One could see that they were going nowhere. There was nowhere to go. As Tex said, "It doesn't matter now." For just as the "Infinite Soul" had been expounded as a dream by Charlie to unite the Family for his own purposes, it nonetheless stemmed from the harsh fortune that had hounded him since the day he was born — finally to come into being as a full-blown "vision" through the dealing out of death — of wanton, mechanical murder.

So the soul had been diminished long before the trip through "the stomach of the monster city," and the taking of lives with no thought, with only one man's malice to go on. It had been enough. No guess work for Charlie. Though there were more trials to come, more murders to wind up, it had ended. After nine months of trial the jurors handed down death in the gas chamber for Charlie and the girls. Yet it was as though the ending meant nothing — as if everything happened according to some blueprint. There had been no surprises. Susan, Leslie, and Katie knew that when they first walked arm in arm to court to account for murder, singing a song that Charlie dreamed up.

Eighteen

The newspaper reporters and television commentators were calling it a "vigil for Manson." The death sentences had been pronounced, and while Charlie and the girls were waiting to die in San Quentin's gas chamber, the other Family members seemed to be sticking to a sort of worship — some kind of support for the "cause."

Throughout history there have been those who believe in their "just cause" for killing. So despite the murders, despite everything, the rest of the family continued in their faith, calm and undisturbed. With shaved heads and X's carved between their eyes in imitation of Charlie, they sat or squatted half-asleep on the Los Angeles Hall of Justice steps. Or, blocking foot traffic, congregated on the corner on Hill and First streets in the heart of the L.A. law buildings.

The girls were Squeaky, Sandra, Skip, Gypsy, the Turtle, Snake, Billie, and others, all waiting for Charlie. Squeaky said, "We sit here every day. We don't have anything else to do, you know." As if in a drug-induced dream, she claimed, "Charlie is with us now, every minute, this moment, in my heart and soul. He's always with us."

There was an almost pious quality about the group as they went about their knitting, singing, speaking softly or whispering in confidential tones. They would wave to the passersby on the street, and even smile at the police.

"The cops, one of 'em brought us an apple pie once," the Turtle recalled. "Some of 'em are just traffic control cops. Like they aren't out to get you, and don't even carry a gun. Lots don't even give tickets. I don't really see any problems . . . We just get stronger and stronger.

"Charlie gives more, he loves more than anyone. He's not a man,

171

really. He is a God." The shining eyes looked away. Her hands were busy with a brocaded vest of incredibly detailed needlework. "We're trying to finish this before Charlie gets out."

Another girl pointed to a vivid cluster of threads "Leslie did that," she said. "We all did. Katie did that part there. All of us. We haven't quite finished it, but we've been working on it almost four years, about twelve of us. There's all our love in it, and there — over — that part, that's the dead part — the part of the killings and the dead. It's a testimonial to our lives . . ." Charlie was still the very core of their lives.

"When he comes out," one said earnestly, "I'll shield him . . . I'll shield him with my body. I may take a bullet, but I'll shield him." She admitted there was nothing they wouldn't do for Charlie. Looking up, she said, "We'd kill every one of you if that's what it takes — if that's how it has to be, and gladly — so gladly."

Snake laughed. "You see, things that goes around comes around the same way. You've decided to kill Charlie — Sadie — the others. So you see, there's twelve of us, and what that means is that there are twelve of us as there were twelve who were standing beside Jesus long before the *Romans* came up to do away with him and nailed him to the cross — which is what you're doing to Charlie. Nailing him to the cross. It is your sins — not his."

They wore cutaway Levi jackets with an embroidered banner across the back: *Devil's Witches - Death Valley*. But they were no longer living in the desert. There was a truck and a van of sorts. They slept wherever they happened to park, and with anyone who happens to join them for the night, or a week — a new recruit in the band of determined worshippers.

"We're here — always — till Charlie comes out," Sandra said. "All the penitentiaries are full of love and soul. The rest — here the people try to make money. They've killed their soul and chosen the dollar, and it's the end. The system judged itself so it's just a matter of time before they all get them and make a revolution."

One girl was clipping newspapers on the Manson case while another jotted notes on paper sacks or shuffled methodically through different colored sheets containing "messages" from Charlie.

Pausing in her work, Squeaky toyed with a pen. "We don't have any parents. Our parents threw us out. We were all thrown out. Everybody's my parent, and they all act and think the same way, and somebody walks down the street and I might just as well say, 'Hi Mom, Hi Dad,' it's all the same."

They agree they would do anything for Charlie, and condemn the Establishment for convicting him. "Right and wrong is what you yourself want to make it," Sandra said. "We killed six people for our brothers, that's where it's at. We did it for love," she said, smiling.

A smiling Snake said, "See, what you have done in that courtroom has been an act of propaganda. You have sentenced people to death for actually giving heart to life. You have taken what is true, and turned it into a lie. That is how you live — how you all live."

The girls squatting on the sidewalk looked at one another and nodded slowly. Each one agreed with the other. There was no mistaking that.

No sooner had society convicted the killers and settled in, sighing that the worst had been done, when the following year the Supreme Court abolished the death penalty. Termed a "permissive delay," the moratorium permanently removed those capital punishment convictions, commuting them to life sentences. All condemned killers would face eligibility for parole. The doors on all death row cells were opened, and the murderers entered the general prison population to await parole hearings.

"We beat the gas!" cheered Bobby on San Quentin's Death Row. "Lone Eagle's gonna fly again!"

Tex Watson's mental dysfunctions improved miraculously with the moratorium. Having hoped at best for some commutation from death to life-imprisonment due to his feigned diminished capacity, Tex would now plan for his potential freedom through manipulating the parole system.

"Sure, there'll be a time before we're eligible for parole, but the point is that we'll *be* eligible. It'll be up to us to show we deserve to be set free — show them that we're different people now."

"You have to beat the opposition," says Susan, "and they're going to put up a real show . . ."

Within a very short time, Susan began concocting the idea of converting to the "born again" Christian movement — "You know, finding God and all that, and being forgiven for what we did," she would say. And Tex, the most brutal and wanton of murderers, was quick to pick up the cue. He could immerse himself in religion as he'd once wallowed in the blood of his victims, and by his "praising the Lord" they'd see he was changed — "a new man." He'd get married — be granted conjugal visits, and he'd spawn children to "show love for the little ones" and speak of the preciousness of life.

Leslie would no longer fret over her pending dose of cyanide, but decided to work on her memoirs. She'd push herself into some alternate school program — outside, the prison, of course, and earn a respectable degree. She'd make herself over from coiffeur to pedicure — show how she *too* could be a respectable member of the society that had condemned her. She'd erase the thrill of murder from her thoughts, though knowing there'd be no changing of that inner impulsive one, the knife-wielding one that Charlie'd sniffed out so successfully. He *knew* she'd kill — knowing she *wanted* to kill, and all he had to do was the put the knife in her hand and deliver her to the nearest victim.

Even Charlie knew — perhaps better than any of them, that all that stuff could be cloaked beneath an adopted respectability. "Ass-kissing the Establishment," he'd say, "like a dog licking the hand of the one that's got the chain and the whip."

"After all," Leslie'd say, "isn't that what it all is anyway? You tuck in that part that's ugly and show them the best face you've got?"

And since Charlie, with a kind of "Jesus Christ-like" refusal to compromise, would soon become the fly in the ointment — "the nigger in the haystack," he'd say, as those Family members convicted of murder turned against him — laying the blame for their actions on Charlie. Hungry for publicity that might dim the horror of her past crimes, Susan would write to the newspapers — condemning Charlie. To the *Los Angeles Times,* she announced, "I can assure you . . . from firsthand experience that his depravity and depth of cruelty make him a truly base human being . . ."

Meanwhile, unlike Susan, Tex, Leslie and the others, Bobby does not shift blame for the killings. In his cell, decorating his torso with neo-Nazi tattoos while espousing his "Aryan Brotherhood philosophy," Bobby recalls his life with the Family, and attempts to assert his own leadership in the events that made history. "The men and women in this family [Manson's], my brothers and sisters," Bobby says, "have followed me through the killings, to the jails, the courts, to prison and to Death Row for the love they have for me . . . But things came down the way they did and I know, somehow, that it's right. I know why we are here . . . We are a family and we, the men, are the white sons of man. Knowing only one, and seeing no one above myself, I say I am the one son of man. But I know my soul and I am many. There are many people in this family. And there are many in this family that don't know they are in this family. And that's why I am here. I am here to show you, and to show all people . . . to testify to what I know as true, and call all those in kind who recognize themselves in me, to give themselves into my family . . .

"We are the outcast of society — rejected by society as not fitting the cookie-cutter. We are the outlaws on the motorcycles, the convicts in prison, the people on the street: the alley people. We are the white faction of the people society has picked out. Society's bad men, that are really the best of men; the freer, the stronger . . .

"Since I was real young I had to scuffle for myself, and this gave me a different understanding of things than most people have. Society didn't like me because my level of understanding clashed with that of the Christian ideology. I have always been the 'bad man' . . . in society's eyes I am the devil and a thief. I take society's daughters into the bushes and make love to them and fuck them. And I don't have any shame — no use for society's kind of morals. And because I am stronger than most men, the young people and the children follow me, and other men like me, and this brings society's house down. And society fears that, so they are afraid of me, and that's why they lock me up in a prison. I show the young people, just as I have learned, that what they are being taught in school, in church, and by their mom and dad is *not true*. That the truth ain't in the church or its teachings. And when they see this, they begin to reject society's values as I have rejected them. They discover that to hold on to those ancient and obsolete values is to live a lie born of madness.

"We are a deadly family — to our enemies that may try to divide, control or destroy us, or any part of our world . . . Every man brings his judgement on himself."

Susan would say she was unable to understand why society does not "forgive" her, since, she says, "God had already forgiven us. Does the American society now place itself above God? Does the public have no mercy in its heart?"

Sean Gotler, a post-Spahn Family member and ex-inmate of Atascadero, found the going tough on the outside. "Because I was still a part of them," he says, "I asked Squeaky if she wanted to go to this place in Salt Lake City and she could have a baby, but she said no, no, she had

to be near Charlie. She belonged to Charlie. She said she and the others —
like Sandra and the others — they'd always belong to Charlie no matter
what, and they had to be close to him. That's why they hung around Daye
Shinn's, and the sidewalk and why she went up to Sacramento for that trip
to get word from Charlie . . ."

Gotler says, "I'm in a position of being able to look back on it
now, and I admit I wouldn't want to know someone like Squeaky and like
Charlie anymore — it's just too much of living in a nightmare and being
at war — being at a war without an end . . ."

Raids, arrests, hold-ups, jail breaks — the Manson Family would
thrive and buck and bulge against the law, but they would not change.
Sandra and Squeaky set up house in an old two-story clapboard house at
1725 P Street in Sacramento, and waged a campaign against the
Establishment. To fully capture the media, Squeaky oiled up a .45 automatic and set out for the Capitol grounds. President Gerald Ford was visiting the California Capitol and as he walked across the grounds, Squeaky
lunged at him with the gun. The hammer was cocked back, but one Secret
Service agent managed to wedge his thumb between the hammer and the
firing pin.

Instantly wrestled into handcuffs, Squeaky was charged with
attempted assassination. She was tried and imprisoned. She would attempt
escapes, managing to draw attention to herself and the "Manson mania" . . .

Sandra, calling herself "Hungry Knife," would be arrested the
following year for threatening government officials and corporate leaders, threatening blood baths by the "International People's Court of
Retribution/Manson." The Nazi swastika appeared everywhere.

Twenty-five years later, Sandra would announce to the press that
the Sharon Tate and the LaBianca murders were justified — "a sort of necessary prelude to social change . . .Those murders were very justified. In
spirit, I'm still at war. That's just as powerful as if I went and put a knife in
some person's stomach in Hollywood."

Manson's fame and wide-spreading "appreciation" is disturbing to
Vincent Bugliosi who prosecuted Charlie and the girls, and who wrote a
best-selling book on the case, which was made into a television movie.
"More than any other crime, the gruesome murders and Manson's power
over his followers have both repelled and captivated the public — world-

wide, now. Over the last twenty-five years, he has come to represent the dark and malignant side of humanity, and for whatever reason, there is a side of human nature that is fascinated with ultimate evil."

Deputy District Attorney Stephen Kay, who helped convict Charlie and the Family, also keeps his own "vigil." He steadfastly opposes the parole of any of the "Manson Family," by reminding members of the State Board of Prison Terms, in graphic detail, of the seven murders that shocked the nation. "Manson and the others are in prison for committing the most brutal murders this nation has ever seen," he says, "for trying to start a race war. These individuals are out to destroy our society, and they are very dangerous. I do not think they should be given another chance to destroy."

None of this impresses Charlie, now a gnarled, ugly little man. "I put Bugliosi on the map," he says, "and he's made more money off me than he'll ever see again . . ."

A recent fellow inmate says, "Charlie would stare at the wall like he was gonna spook or trance the sink, and he'd giggle and laugh to himself, then turn around and look you right in the eyes and still be giggling . . ."

"I'll be out of here," Charlie says with a twisted grin, "one way or another. It's just time. Time. That's all it is, and I have all the time in the world. They can't kill me, you see. They've never been able to kill me. Oh, they try — Bugliosi tried — they *try* to gas me or stick a knife in me and they try to light me on fire, but I'm not gonna die because *they* want me to die. I don't care who shoots who or why they shoot — it's only madmen that adjust to what's going on in your world. I don't care how much money Bugliosi or George Bush makes or if he doesn't make or dies — like President Bill Clinton — personally, I'd like to see them not alive, all of them, and if I had my way I could pull this switch — they'd be dead with a lot of others. I'd kill them right out in the parking lot . . . My message for the future is that my first stop is when I'm out of here in either my body or my head, man, I'm going to Sabzevar, that's right, Sabzevar in Iran, dig. I got people waiting for me to connect to some financial business — I'll get some money for a change instead of everyone making money off me. And then I'm heading to Sri Lanka. There's people there that'll take care of this spirit for a while — feed me special stuff, but no meat — no meat. This is because intuition can be dulled by eating meat. See, I got my own mahatma, dig. He sends me the score, and from Sri Lanka, I'm on my way to New Delhi, and there I am going to *radiate*. Like the sun. Man and sun," he laughs. "It won't matter if I'm seventy-six years old, or if *you* think I'm the walking dead — you think it will matter? I am not the walking dead but walking in the spirits and the minds. What I'm talking about is known and will be *known* when I'm there. New Delhi? Oh, you know who Kali is — Kali's standing right behind me, and so's the octopus — you know what the octopus is? You dig the arms the thing's got? Oh, kill me," Charlie says. "Oh, sure, oh, sure, but you can't kill what is known and what I'm saying, and that is what is going to be said. It is *law* you can't hide from, you can't escape from. What you're going to do is you're going to *see* what I'm saying . . ."

His eyes seem to roll into his head as he bares his teeth and smiles . . .

Also by John Gilmore from Amok Books

SEVERED
The True Story of the Black Dahlia Murder

The grisly 1947 murder of aspiring starlet and nightclub habitué Elizabeth Short, known even before her death as the "Black Dahlia," has over
the decades transmogrified from L.A.'s crime of the century to an almost
mythical symbol of Hollywood Babylon/film noir glamour-cum-sordid-
ness. *Severed*, the first true-crime book published on the strangest of all
"unsolved" murders in the annals of modern crime, offers the docu-
mented solution to the case as endorsed by law enforcement and forensic
science experts.

"The most satisfying and disturbing conclusion to the Black Dahlia case.
After reading *Severed*, I feel like I truly know Elizabeth Short and her
killer." — **David Lynch**

"I love *Severed*. It is the most uncanny evocation of Los Angeles during
and after the war. I've read it about seven times. His portrait of Elizabeth
Short as this strange, unknowable somnambulist sleepwalking through
that unique junction of time and space is permanently haunting."
— **Gary Indiana**

ISBN 1-878923-10-2, (trade paper)
$16.95 US / £12.95 UK
288 pp., illustrated

For individual orders, please contact:

Book Clearing House
Phone: (800) 431-1579
FAX: (914) 835-0398
Email: bookch@aol.com

www.amokbooks.com

Also by John Gilmore from Amok Books

LAID BARE
A Memoir of Wrecked Lives and the
Hollywood Death Trip

Acclaimed as a powerful chronicler of the American Nightmare through his gripping examinations of near-mythic Southern California murders (the Black Dahlia, Tate-LaBianca), author John Gilmore draws upon his own reservoir of personal experiences as he turns his sights on our morbid obsession with Celebrity and the ruinous price it exacts from those who would pursue it. With caustic clarity and 20/20 hindsight, Gilmore unstintingly recounts his relationships with the likes of **James Dean**, **Janis Joplin**, **Dennis Hopper**, **Jack Nicholson**, **Jane Fonda**, **Jean Seberg**, **Lenny Bruce** and many other denizens of the twentieth century's dubious pantheon both on the way up and at the peaks of their notoriety.

"Beautifully written in a style somewhere between Jack Kerouac and Charles Bukowski . . . This is an astonishing book. — *Sight and Sound, U.K.*

ISBN 1-878923-08-0 (trade paper)
$16.95 US / £11.95 UK
250 pp., illustrated

For individual orders, please contact:

Book Clearing House
Phone: (800) 431-1579.
FAX: (914) 835-0398.
Email: bookch@aol.com.

www.amokbooks.com

New from John Gilmore on Amok Audio

LAID BARE CD

Words and Readings by John Gilmore
Music by Skip Heller

The *Laid Bare* CD presents John Gilmore's words and story in his own voice, accompanied by a compelling crime-jazz score. This first Amok CD brings together hard-boiled fiction, soundtrack music, the underside of Hollywood glamour and true-crime literature. The specter of the Black Dahlia, the archetypal doomed would-be starlet, hangs over the proceedings, guiding the young Gilmore through the labyrinthine netherworlds of his fabled birthplace, Hollywood. The tragic 20th-century mythical figures the Black Dahlia, James Dean, Charles Manson, Janis Joplin, Lenny Bruce and Ed Wood, Jr. appear and vanish in recursive spirals, imbuing this audio project with a seductive eeriness.

Composer Skip Heller and his musical collaborators have evoked the tension, dread and transcendent moments of the world Gilmore brings to life—the desperate attempt to embrace the dream. This accomplished CD weaves together passages from three of Gilmore's books, scoring each excerpt with original music.

$16.98
Available October 2000

For individuals orders, please contact:

Book Clearing House
Phone: (800) 431-1579
FAX: (914) 835-0398
Email: bookch@aol.com

www.amokbooks.com